Penguin Education

New Perspectives in Child Development

Edited by Brian Foss

Penguin Modern Psychology
General Editor: Brian Foss

Advisory Board

New Perspectives
in Child Development

Edited by Brian Foss

Penguin Education

Penguin Education
A Division of Penguin Books Ltd,
Harmondsworth, Middlesex, England
Penguin Books Inc, 7110 Ambassador Road,
Baltimore, Md 21207, USA
Penguin Books Australia Ltd,
Ringwood, Victoria, Australia
Penguin Books Canada Ltd,
41 Steelcase Road West,
Markham, Ontario, Canada
Penguin Books (N.Z.) Ltd,
182-190 Wairau Road, Auckland 10, New Zealand

First published 1974
Copyright © Brian Foss and contributors, 1974

Made and printed in Great Britain by
Richard Clay (The Chaucer Press) Ltd,
Bungay, Suffolk
Set in Monotype Times

Contents

Introduction

This book is about the psychological development of infants and young children. It does not attempt to provide a representative survey of the current scene and could hardly begin to do so in this number of pages. Readers who are familiar with a standard reference book such as *Carmichael's Handbook of Child Psychology*, edited by Paul Mussen, will know from the size of its two volumes that there is a very large amount of work being done from a variety of approaches. The upsurge of interest is partly due to an interest in infants and children for their own sake, and because there are new ways of studying children; but it is also due to the fact that the developmental or ontogenetic approach provides a main strategy in human psychology generally. For instance, the new work on the development of vision and hearing has given insights into the mechanisms of adult perception that would never have been gained by studying adults; and the way in which language develops has become a main source of evidence to consider when discussing mechanisms of language and the relation between language and thinking. Nevertheless, anyone with an inquiring mind will find the contemporary work satisfying and stimulating in its own right because of the answers it provides to questions about the basic capacities and functions of infants and children. When does the infant first recognize things? How does it learn? Why does it smile? And anyone who is concerned with rearing children or teaching them will profit from getting new insights into the child's world.

If I were asked to characterize the modern work on child development I would make the following points. As in psychology generally, there is little emphasis on theory; instead there are painstaking investigations of processes like visual recognition, imitation, smiling and so on, with the aim of discovering how such processes work, how they develop, what factors affect them and what the mechanisms underlying them may be. Such work depends heavily on several ingenious techniques which psychologists have developed in the last few years. For instance, it is possible to arrange things so that the way a baby sucks can be made to change what he is given to look at or listen to, so that one can explore what he prefers looking at and listening to, and hence what he can discriminate – long before he is able to speak or even manipulate things.

Then there is an interesting paradox about the psychology of young children. On the one hand, it is clear that a child's world is very different from an adult's and that his thinking is not logical. Piaget claims to have demonstrated this many years ago, a claim which is generally accepted, though with some amendment of details. But on the other hand, it is only now becoming clear that infants 'know' much more about their environment in the first weeks of life than was thought possible. Long before they use language they are able to make quite complicated discriminations, and show elementary learning from the very first days after birth. Another generalization which can be made is that individual differences are found wherever one looks, right from the start. (Anyone who has held newborn babies knows that no two 'feel' the same.) Some of these differences do not stay consistent, but others seem to do so.

It is hoped that this book will show what a variety of perspectives there are in the psychology of child development. The first chapter, by Harry McGurk, is about visual perception. It is a topic which has profited greatly from the invention of new techniques. There are still many people who believe that nothing is really recognized for the first few months of life; but current work suggests that even in the third week, a baby reacts differently to different faces and different voices. It has also been thought that learning would be impossible during early infancy. W. Stuart Millar shows how this is certainly not the case. Whatever the innate equipment of the neonate may be, there is no doubt that it is being modified by the child's immediate environment from the first few days of life. Paradoxically, some of the methods which have turned out to be most useful in studying children were developed by the animal ethologists looking at innate behaviour in animals. As Peter Smith shows in his chapter, the application of ethological methods is a growing enterprise. It is notoriously easy to infer one's own motives and reasoning from children's behaviour. Ethological techniques provide a rigour which helps to offset this. The fourth chapter, by Hildy Ross, is about exploration. Here is a topic which has aroused interest for a variety of reasons – educational, theoretical, evolutionary and practical. On the other hand, the work on attachments, which Carl Corter writes about, has stemmed very much from beliefs about the importance of the child's tie to its mother. Many believe that the success or failure in the development of such a tie is of importance for the later social adjustments of the adolescent and adult. The last chapter, by Richard Cromer, looks at the relevance of child development to the abiding problems of the relation between language and thinking.

When the authors were first approached, I asked them to provide a survey of their particular area, but also to develop in some depth one or two topics within that area which would be of special interest to them. All the authors have done this, and with a variety of interpretations which I had not expected. The reader must therefore expect more individuality than is often found in such collections. It is intended that each chapter should be a balanced whole, and it follows that some topics are dealt with more than once. It is not intended that one viewpoint only should be presented. Indeed, one of the fascinations about work on child development is that it brings together scientists with widely differing perspectives.

B. M. FOSS

Chapter 1
Visual Perception in Young Infants[1]

Harry McGurk

This chapter is concerned with developmental aspects of perception. For the mature adult, environmental information is extracted via a whole range of sensory receptors – visual, tactual, olfactory, somesthetic, kinesthetic and so on – and his percepts represent subtle interactions of information from all these sources. Thus, an apple looks round and red, feels hard and smooth, tastes and smells sweet. A full discussion of perceptual development would require consideration of all these sensory modalities as well as consideration of the social and affective components of perception, and could not be undertaken within the confines of a single chapter. Similarly, a full discussion would require consideration of perceptual development in the entire period between birth and maturity and, again, this is beyond our present scope. Here, therefore, discussion will be largely restricted to the beginning stages of perceptual development, specifically to the development of visual perception during early infancy.

It is appropriate that such discussion should begin with an examination of the visual apparatus with which the infant is endowed at birth. This is the case because the kinds of percepts we can have are limited by the kinds of energy change we can detect, and this, in turn, is restricted by the nature of our sense receptors. For example, human adults cannot perceive ultra-violet light since the visual system is not sensitive to energy transmitted by wavelengths so high on the colour spectrum. Bees, on the other hand, can discriminate light of this colour. We can ask, therefore, to what extent the perceptions of the developing infant are restricted by the nature of his

1. This chapter was written while the author was a Visiting Research Fellow at Educational Testing Service, Princeton, New Jersey. Preparation of the manuscript was supported by grant no. 28105 from the National Science Foundation.

sensory apparatus, to what extent perceptual development is influenced by anatomical and physiological development of the visual system.

The infant's visual system

At birth, the human eye is about half the size and weight of that of the mature adult (Mann, 1964). The infant eye is anatomically identical to the adult eye in that all the parts are there, but the relation of the parts to each other is different from that in adulthood, and not all parts develop at the same rate; for example, at birth the cornea is much closer to its final developmental status than is the iris. The retina – the light sensitive surface at the back of the eye – is fairly well developed at birth. At one time it was thought that the retina of the human newborn was sensitive only to changes in the brightness and intensity of light and not to changes in colour. However, recent anatomical and physiological evidence has demonstrated this view to be mistaken. Horsten and Winkelman (1962, 1964; Winkelman and Horsten, 1962) found that rods and cones were clearly differentiated in the retina of the human foetus from the seventh month of gestation (rods are sufficient for the mediation of brightness differences or for so-called scotopic vision but cones are essential for colour, or so-called photopic vision). Moreover, the same investigators observed that electroretinographic (ERG) recordings from human newborns contained the same photopic and scotopic components as are observed in the ERG records of human adults. This is not to say that no retinal development occurs after birth. For example, the macula, the small yellow area in the centre of the retina which contains the fovea and which, in adults, is the area of clearest vision, is only partially developed at birth. Fovea and macula are structurally differentiated by about four months, but macular development continues into early childhood. However, the systems which mediate brightness and colour vision both appear to be functional at birth.

The optic tract – the bundle of nerve fibres which carry impulses from the retina to the visual centre of the brain – is partially myelinated at birth. In the process of myelinization, a protective sheath grows around the axon of the nerve cell. This sheath serves to insulate the axon from surrounding tissue and enhances its conductivity. In the absence of myelinization, conductivity of the nerve fibres is considerably reduced and electrical activity disperses to surrounding tissue. Myelinization of the optic tract is essential for effective vision, for without the myelin sheath it is probable that the organism may be capable of experiencing only diffuse flashes of light. Compared with adults, however, the myelin sheath around the optic tract of the human newborn is relatively thin. If brief flashes of light are presented to the human eye, changes occur in the pattern of electrical activity, recorded by means of surface electrodes, at the occipital region of the cortex. These changes are called evoked responses. In newborns, the latency between actual presentation of the flash of light, and the occurrence of the evoked response, is longer than is the case with adults (Hrbek and Mares, 1964a, 1964b). Conductivity in the adult optic tract is enhanced by its thicker myelin sheath. Accordingly, information from eye to brain is transmitted relatively more rapidly in adults than in newborns. Myelinization of the infant's visual fibres is almost complete by about four months of age.

It would appear, therefore, that anatomically and physiologically, the visual system of the human infant, although immature, is in a functional state at birth and is capable of responding to stimulation. Thus, a necessary condition for extracting information from the environment is fulfilled. But it is not a sufficient condition. In order for there to be efficient extraction of environmental information, the organism has to be capable of simultaneously orienting both eyes towards the source of stimulation, of focusing upon that source, of resolving the detail of the stimulus, of controlling the amount of light entering his eyes, of making compensatory eye movements for any movement of the stimulus. These are all adjustments which the mature adult achieves spontaneously. It is towards their development in infancy that we now turn.

Ocular control in infancy

It has long been known that from the earliest days of life the human infant is capable of making gross postural movements of the head both to avoid excessively bright visual stimuli and to bring into view light stimuli of lower intensity (Preyer, 1888). Early investigators

(Sherman, Sherman and Flory, 1936) were also able to establish that the pupillary reflex – the mechanism which regulates the amount of light entering the eye under conditions of variable brightness – was functional from shortly after birth and matured rapidly during the first few weeks of life.

Thus, the young infant seems capable of making gross orientations towards a source of visual stimulation and of controlling the amount of light entering his eyes from that source. The question arises, however, as to whether the infant is capable of simultaneously orienting both eyes towards the same stimulus source. Such convergence is necessary if clear vision is to result. Otherwise each eye would obtain different images, a rather confusing state of affairs, to say the least. Moreover, if the stimulus source moves, then, for clear vision to be maintained, both eyes must move together, must move conjugately, to keep the stimulus in view. Hershenson (1965) has demonstrated that convergence occurs from as early as two days in the human infant. He photographed his subject's eyes whenever it was deemed that one eye was directed towards a target stimulus. A record of the corneal reflections of the target was thus obtained and when the reflections from the cornea of the observed eye were compared with those of the unobserved eye, an almost complete overlap was obtained. This could only have occurred if both eyes had converged on the same point. Hershenson, who employed pairs of stationary targets, also observed that the newborn's eyes moved conjugately from one target to another. Evidence for conjugate tracking of a moving target has been reported by Dayton and his colleagues (Dayton and Jones, 1964; Dayton, Jones, Steele and Rose, 1964). Although such tracking was relatively inefficient at birth and involved much back-tracking, there was marked improvement during the first three months of life.

In order to focus upon targets at different distances, the lens of the human eye bends and changes shape, thus accommodating to differences in distance. The development of accommodation of the lens has been investigated by Haynes, White and Held (1965). They employed a technique called dynamic retinoscopy. Under this procedure a sharply focused spot of light is projected into the subject's eye from different distances, through the pupillary opening. Modifications in the reflected image, quantitatively assessed by lenses of known power, are employed as an index of the refractive state of the eye. The principal finding was that at birth the human eye operates much like a fixed-focus camera and no accommodation of the lens occurs to targets presented at different distances. The ideal focal distance for the newborn is around eight inches. Stimuli presented at greater or lesser distances result in blurred retinal images. This state of affairs persists for the first few weeks of life. Thereafter there is a rapid period of development in the accommodative power of the lens and by four months accommodation in the infant is comparable to that in adult subjects.

Two techniques have been employed to study the acuity of the infant's visual system. One of these involves a reflexive response known as optokinetic nystagmus (OKN). If a stimulus of black and white stripes is placed in front of the visual field and the eyes are fixated on the stimulus then, if the stimulus is moved, the eyes deflect in the direction of movement as if in compensation. Such reflexive following is evident from birth onwards. Employing this reflex, infant visual acuity has been studied by Gorman, Cogan and Gellis (1957). Stimuli comprising stripes of various widths are presented to infant subjects and it is noted which elicit OKN and which do not. It is reasoned that striped stimuli which do not elicit OKN cannot be discriminated by the subject. Using this technique, Gorman et al. concluded that newborn infants could discriminate stripes which subtended about thirty-three minutes of visual arc.[2]

Fantz and his colleagues have used a different technique to study visual acuity in infancy (Fantz, 1966; Fantz, Ordy and Udelf, 1962). They objected that reflexive following of a moving pattern, which is under neural control, may yield a misleading picture of infant acuity compared with that when visual exploration is under voluntary control. Accordingly, they presented their subjects with pairs of stimuli one of which was always a plain grey while the other was composed of black and white stripes of equal overall brightness. They had previously observed that infants preferred to look at a patterned stimulus than at a plain one. The stripes, and the spaces between them, varied systematically across stimulus pairs and it was reasoned that as long as the infants could discriminate the stripes

2. For comparison purposes, adults with normal vision can discriminate stripes subtending one minute of visual arc.

from the background, they would look more at the striped (i.e. patterned) stimulus than at the plain grey one. Whenever the stripes become so thin as not to be resolved then, of course, the striped stimulus would be indistinguishable from the grey one and both should be fixated equally. In this way Fantz established that infants of less than one month could resolve stripes $\frac{1}{8}$ inch in thickness at a distance of ten inches. Now, this is equivalent to a visual angle of about forty minutes of arc and thus bears close correspondence to the data reported by Gorman *et al.* Fantz further observed that by two months or so infants could resolve stripes of only twenty minutes of arc and by six months they could discriminate stripes of $\frac{1}{64}$ inch, a visual angle of only ten minutes.

The picture, then, that emerges from our discussion so far is one wherein the young infant is seen to have a visual system which is anatomically and physiologically intact and which, though quite immature by adult standards, fulfils the necessary conditions for the mediation of sensory information. We have seen, too, that the infant, from his earliest days, is able to orient towards a source of visual stimulation, has the necessary muscular control to converge upon a stimulus and to maintain his image of the stimulus even when it is moving, and can do this with both eyes in a coordinated fashion. His accommodative capacity, although initially limited, rapidly improves, as does his ability to resolve increasingly fine detail. In short, from a relatively early stage, the infant is endowed with a visual apparatus which is in good working order and although much development remains to take place, he has the potential to embark on a visual voyage of discovery of the world around him. We turn now to a consideration of what he does with that potential and to a discussion of the nature of the visual world in which the young infant lives.

Perceptual discrimination in infancy

Many of the techniques currently used to investigate the perceptual ability of the human infant have been developed only relatively recently; for example, those employed by Winkelman and Horsten (1962) and by Hershenson (1965) require fairly sophisticated electronic and photographic apparatus not readily available to earlier generations of researchers. Much of what was accepted as fact in an earlier era was based on casual observation and anecdotal report, and such reports tended to stress the immaturity and insensitivity of the infant's visual system. James' (1890) description of the infant's condition as being 'assailed by eyes, ears, nose, skin and entrails at once', feeling it all as 'one great blooming, buzzing confusion' was a persuasive and widely accepted one. The infant was largely regarded as a relatively insensitive organism who had to grow up before he became worthy of serious investigation. A few developmental studies of infant perception were undertaken but such studies were the exception rather than the rule and studies of perceptual development in infancy were relatively few and far between. For example, in a review of *developmental* studies of perception by Wohlwill (1960) covering the period from about 1900 to 1959, fewer than 10 per cent of the 170 or so references cited involved subjects younger than two years.

Since the mid-fifties and early sixties there has been an upsurge in the study of the perceptual world of the infant. For example, an extensive investigation of infant responsiveness to facial and face-like stimuli was carried out by Ahrens (1954). The stimuli which he presented to his subjects included various dot and angle arrangements drawn on round and oval contours, a crossbar on an oval contour, partial and complete drawings of faces, and 3D facial models, as well as actual, live faces. A most interesting finding concerned the amount of facial detail required to elicit smiling from infants at different ages. At six weeks, for example, a crude, two-dot representation of the eyes was most effective; contour was unimportant. Between six weeks and three months, the eye-like pattern was still most effective, but realistic as opposed to schematic representation became important with increasing age. By four months of age, the presence of eyes was still necessary to elicit smiling, but was no longer sufficient; now other facial detail, such as nose and mouth, had to be present, though subjects may not have fixated these directly. At this age also, an actual, live face was most effective in eliciting smiling, followed by a realistic facial drawing, followed, in turn, by a schematic drawing of a face.

Ahrens' work establishes that the eyes are the most salient facial feature for the young infant. Just why this should be the case is not immediately obvious. That the eyes are also a primary focus of attention for older subjects is probably attributable, at least in part, to their mobility. However, Ahrens found that immobile, schematic representations of the eyes were most efficient in eliciting smiling during the beginning months of life. It may be that, as others have suggested, the eyes serve as an innate releasing mechanism (IRM) for the smiling response during early infancy.

Much of the increased interest in the study of infant perception since the mid-fifties is attributable in no small measure to the work of Fantz (1958, 1961). Fantz's procedure was elegantly simple and was one which overcame an earlier reluctance to use infants as experimental subjects due to their limited response repertoire. He was interested in determining the age at which infants first became capable of form and pattern discrimination and reasoned that if a subject looked significantly longer at one than at the other of two forms or patterns, then this could be regarded as evidence that the subject was discriminating between the two stimuli in terms of the dimension in which they differed. Accordingly, he presented his infant subjects, aged between one and fifteen weeks, with pairs of stimuli and recorded how long they spent fixating each member of the pair. The babies lay on their backs within an observation chamber and the stimuli were presented from above. Through a peep-hole in the roof of the chamber the experimenter could observe which stimulus the subject was fixating, such fixation being reflected in an image of the stimulus from off the cornea, above the pupil. By such means Fantz was able to demonstrate that from an early age infants looked longer at circular bull's eyes than at striped squares, more at checkered squares than at plain squares and so on. Thus, he concluded that infants could perceive both form and pattern and that there was an innate preference for complex as opposed to simple stimuli. The procedure employed by Fantz became known as the spontaneous visual preference technique and, as we have already seen, it was later used in a study of infant visual acuity (Fantz, Ordy and Udelf, 1962). The procedure was also employed to demonstrate an early preference for 3D over 2D stimuli of equivalent shape (Fantz, 1961).

One of the more dramatic findings reported by Fantz (1961) concerned what appeared to be an innate preference for facedness in human infants. Subjects between four days and six months were presented with all possible pairs from the following three stimuli:

1 A schematic representation of a human face, with the features drawn in black on a pink background;

2 A form with the same detail as in 1 but with the facial features randomly scrambled;

3 A similar form to the two others but with a solid patch of black at the top equal in area to that occupied by the features in the other two stimuli.

Fantz reported that at all age levels infants looked more at the 'real' face than at the 'scrambled' face and largely ignored the control pattern. Although the differences in preference between the 'real' and 'scrambled' faces were slight, Fantz suggested that the results indicated a primitive, unlearned preference for facedness in human infants. Fantz regarded such preference as an important precursor of later social responsiveness.

Subsequent investigators have not always been able to replicate the results reported by Fantz in his early studies. This is especially true of his finding of a preference for facial stimuli among very young infants. For example, Hershenson (1965) presented newborn infants with all possible pairs of three stimuli, one depicting a female face and the others representing lesser degrees of organization of the same face: a 'distorted' face retained the outline of head and hair but altered the position of other features, and a 'scrambled' face altered the facial contour in addition to scrambling the features. Hershenson reported that the three stimuli did not elicit differential responding. Koopman and Ames (1968) argued that, in the original Fantz (1961) study, infants may have been responding to the symmetry of the realistic face rather than to its facedness *per se*. Accordingly, they presented ten-week-old babies with all possible pairs from a realistic face, an asymmetrical scrambled face, and a scrambled face in which the features, though wrongly located, were symmetrically distributed about the vertical axis. No differences were observed between looking times for the three stimuli. In a further experiment, in which only the realistic and asymmetrically scrambled faces were compared, negative results were again obtained. Wilcox (1969) also found no differences between infant responsiveness to realistic and scrambled facial stimuli in subjects between four and sixteen weeks of age. At sixteen weeks, however, infants manifested a preference for a photograph of a female face over a realistic facial drawing. A well-conducted study by Haaf and Bell (1967) also demonstrated that four-month-old infants show a distinct preference for more face-like over less face-like stimuli. These authors presented their subjects with all possible pairs from four stimuli which were ordered in their degree of facedness. Infants fixated most on the most face-like stimulus, least on the least face-like, with the other two placed intermediate in terms of their facedness. Although earlier, the Haaf and Bell study was methodologically superior to the one by Wilcox in that the former included a control for complexity. In the Wilcox study the more realistic photograph may also have been the more complex stimulus and could have been preferred on this basis (see below).

It is important to note that in the studies by Hershenson (1965), Koopman and Ames (1968) and Wilcox (1969), all of which yielded negative results concerning young infants' preferences for more face-like as opposed to less face-like stimuli, the conclusion to be drawn is *not* that these subjects could not *discriminate* between the various stimuli, but rather that they showed no *preference* for one stimulus over another. This is an important distinction and one which serves to draw attention to a frequently remarked weakness in the spontaneous visual preference procedure employed by Fantz and his colleagues. The spontaneous preference procedure affords data which can be unambiguously interpreted only when significant differences are observed between duration of fixations upon the two stimuli. In the absence of such differences, though the conclusion that the subject has failed to manifest a *preference* for one stimulus over the other may be justified, one is not entitled to conclude that the subject does not *perceive* differences between them. Such differences may be discriminated but the subject not care enough about them to look at one stimulus more than the other. For example, employing the visual preference procedure, Fantz (1958) reported no preference among three-month-old babies for a circle as against a cross, or vice versa. However, Saayman, Ames and Moffett (1964) firstly presented subjects of the same age with a circle (or a cross) for a relatively prolonged familiarization period, before presenting both forms together. It was recorded whether subjects now attended more to the familiar or to the novel stimulus, regardless of its form. Results indicated that three month olds could discriminate circles from crosses, a conclusion which could not be reached on the basis of the Fantz (1958) data. Thus, by itself, the spontaneous visual preference procedure may be a relatively insensitive one for assessing infant capacity to discriminate perceptually between stimuli.

A further problem which confronts the researcher who employs the spontaneous preference procedure is that of controlling adequately for infant position preferences. When exposed to two stimuli, one to the right and one to the left, many infants have a tendency to look more to one side than to the other. It is easy to see how such a tendency, if not controlled for in the experimental design, might have a confounding influence on experimental results. The usual control is to present each pair of stimuli twice and to reverse the relative positions of the two stimuli on each presentation. Duration of fixation to each member of the pair is then summed across the two presentations. Thus, a subject who looked only to the right during both presentations would receive the same score for each number of the pair of stimuli and that is how it should be, for he had shown no stimulus preference, only a position preference. However, Watson (1965) has argued that this procedure may be a counterproductive one. Suppose of two stimuli, A and B, A is likely to be preferred over B by a particular subject and suppose also that, on first exposure, A is presented to the right and B to the left. By scanning back and forth between A and B, the subject learns the location of A and subsequently fixates more upon A. In order to ensure that this is not a case of position preference, we now present the pair again, this time with A to the left and B to the right. Where will our subject look? Watson argues that since A is the preferred stimulus and since A was at the right position on the first exposure, the subject has effectively been reinforced for looking to the right. Thus, when the stimuli are again presented, the subject will continue to look to the right, at least initially. Watson has presented convincing evidence that such conditioning of direction of regard can occur within the relatively brief time spans occupied by the usual spontaneous preference experiment. If such a response does become conditioned then, of course, it will have to extinguish before the subject can change his direction of regard to the left and look again at A; until then, of course, he will be looking at B, the less preferred stimulus. Thus, the effect of controlling for side preference may be to reduce the probability of observing real differences, as indexed by fixation duration, between subjects' preferences for A and B. Despite these acknowledged limitations of the visual preference procedure, it continues to be widely used. Care has to be exercised, therefore, when interpreting the results for such studies, particularly when negative results are reported.

Despite the fact that other investigators have not always been able to replicate findings originally reported by Fantz and despite the methodological weakness inherent in the procedures employed in his early studies, the innovative nature of his work cannot be overstressed. Prior to Fantz, infant perception was a topic of only sporadic interest to psychologists. The enormous upsurge of interest in infant perceptual development that has taken place over the past fifteen years is in no small measure attributable to his pioneering efforts in this field.

The studies which have followed since the early Fantz work fall into two broad categories: those related to what might be called visual *activity* and those related more to perceptual *discrimination*. Perhaps the best known work on infant perceptual activity is that of Salapatek (Salapatek, 1969; Salapetek and Kessen, 1966), who has carried out extensive investigations of newborn and infant scanning of visual stimuli. In an early study, Salapatek and Kessen presented a sample of ten newborn subjects with a black triangle on a white field whilst a control group of ten newborns were shown a homogeneous black visual field. From photographs of eye positions taken at a rate of one per second during each exposure, the investigators were able to reconstruct the scanning pattern of newborns to these kinds of stimuli. Infants exposed to the homogeneous field showed widely dispersed scanning patterns with a marked horizontal component. Infants exposed to the triangle showed much less dispersion of scanning. Instead, most subjects tended to focus on a single feature of the triangle, usually a vertex, and to exercise slight, mainly horizontal, excursions about this point. These findings obtained regardless of the orientation of the triangle, though the preferred vertex varied from subject to subject. Salapatek and Kessen interpreted their data to mean that newborns do not respond to figures as wholes but rather orient towards preferred elements in the visual field. In terms of what mediates newborns' preference for vertices in the present instance, they suggested three alternatives:

1 That newborns respond to transitions in brightness and that orientation towards a vertex is directed by the occurrence of two brightness changes.

2 That newborns have a specific analyser mechanism tuned to angles, analogous to the neurophysiological coding mechanisms for visual stimuli proposed by Hubel and Wiesel (1962).[3]

3 Following Hershenson (1964), Salapatek and Kessen suggested that newborns may respond to an optimal level of brightness which, in the present instance, is to be found only near a vertex.

In a subsequent study Salapatek (1969) reported that between one and two and a half months of age infants showed a shift from fixation of only a limited portion of a visual stimulus towards scanning a more substantial area. Other investigators have shown that changes in visual scanning strategies occur across the whole developmental spectrum. Zaporozhets (1965) reported that three- to four-year-old children spent more time focusing upon the centre as opposed to the contour of a complex form whereas five- and six-year-old children began tracing the outline of the figure. By seven years this pattern of scanning was well established, as if the children were reconstructing or modelling the figure. Older children showed more discrete eye movements than younger children but the actual duration of their fixations was shorter. Across a much wider age span Mackworth and Bruner (1970) observed marked differences in the scanning patterns of six-year-old children compared with young adults. Adult subjects tended to relate important areas of visual displays by long, leaping movements of the eyes whereas children lacked adequate coverage and tended to have many short eye movements about small regions

3. Hubel and Wiesel (1962) have observed that, in the cat's visual cortex, there are individual cells which are maximally responsive to particular aspects of stimulus edges or boundaries. For example, one cell may fire maximally to an edge of a particular shape and minimally to an edge of another shape; another cell may only fire when the edge is at a particular orientation; other cells may only fire when edges move in a particular direction. It has been argued that there are cells in the human visual cortex which function analogously.

of detail, not necessarily the most informative regions. In a study involving children aged six to nine years Nodine and Steuerle (1971) observed a comparable developmental trend. When required to make same–different judgements between briefly exposed pairs of letters, six year olds required more fixations, longer fixation durations and more cross-pair comparisons than older children. Also, six year olds showed less tendency to fixate upon distinctive feature (Gibson, 1969) areas of the letters than did the older children.

What, then, can be concluded on the basis of these visual scanning studies? Clearly, developmental changes occur in the eye-movement strategies which subjects employ when exposed to visual stimuli. It is clear also that such changes are in evidence from infancy, through childhood into adulthood; always, it seems, in the direction of increasing efficiency. In all the data, however, there is no necessary justification for Salapatek and Kessen's view that young infants are capable of responding only to parts of forms rather than to whole forms, on the grounds that their fixations on stimuli tend to be clustered about single units. As Bond (1972) has pointed out, such a view is tenable only if a strict motor copy theory of visual perception is adopted. This position maintains that sufficient information for stimulus recognition is acquired only through active scanning of all its parts (Zaporozhets, 1965). Charlesworth (1968) has argued that there is no necessary reason why an infant has to scan the edges of an object many times in an active fashion before its form will be perceived, and has suggested that such information can be extracted just by 'looking or staring with minimum of eye movement'. Nodine and Simmons (1972) have some relevant data here, albeit concerning older children. They observed that in a paired-comparison discrimination task involving letter-like stimuli, several subjects fixated briefly at a point midway between the two stimuli but were still able to give accurate judgements; such subjects had clearly become proficient in the use of peripheral as opposed to foveal vision. The relative importance of central and peripheral vision during early infancy has never been clearly established. Moreover, it is uncertain whether the response index employed by Salapatek and Kessen reflected central or peripheral perceptual activity. It is known that among newborns a fine beam of light passing through the cornea and the centre of the lens will not strike the fovea, the retinal area of maximum sensitivity. Now, Salapatek and Kessen used corneal reflections as their primary data and employed deviations of images from the centre of the cornea to determine which part of their triangular stimulus was being fixated at a given moment. Exactly what such data mean, therefore, in terms of what was actually being processed by the infants is not at all clear.

Rather than focus upon visual activity as evidenced by scanning patterns, a number of investigators have examined the ways in which infants discriminate and respond to various stimulus dimensions. Doris and Cooper (1966) examined sensitivity to brightness in infants between four and sixty-nine days and observed that discrimination of brightness increased rapidly during the first two months of life. Hershenson (1964) employed a sample of newborn infants to investigate their preferences for different intensities of brightness. He compared fixation preferences to three levels of brightness, 3·56 (dim), 35·6 (medium) and 356 (bright) foot-candles. In a paired-comparisons design, the subjects fixated the medium stimulus more than the other two and fixated the bright stimulus more than the dim one. Hershenson (1964, 1967) makes the important methodological point that before concluding that subjects are responding to a particular stimulus dimension it should be demonstrated that a transitive relationship exists among different values on that dimension, as far as subject responsivity is concerned. Thus, if value A is preferred over value B and B is preferred over C, then A should be preferred over C. If subjects' responses to different dimensional values do not constitute such an ordered set then it cannot be unambiguously concluded that they are responding to the dimension in question. It is clear from Hershenson's data that a transitive relationship was observed among subjects' responses to different levels of brightness and the conclusion is therefore justified that newborns can perceive differences in brightness.

Complexity is another stimulus attribute that has attracted a great deal of attention from psychologists interested in the study of perceptual development. Complexity is one of the many concepts which psychologists have taken over from the common language and attempted to refine for technical usage. Intuitively, we all seem to know what we mean when talking about complexity and we could probably reach a fair level of agreement if asked to classify a group of stimuli into those that were more and those that were less complex. However, we might find it difficult to specify what the criteria were which we employed to determine the complexity level of a particular stimulus, for complexity is not a unitary concept. Similarly, psychologists have experienced great difficulty in agreeing upon an acceptable and viable operational definition of the term. As Schaffer (1971) has pointed out, most definitions have treated complexity in terms of the total quantity of information transmitted by stimuli or 'as the variety or diversity of distinguishable elements contained within the stimulus'. Even so, there have been many diverse definitions; thus Fantz (1966) seemed to equate complexity with the number of stimulus elements, Munsinger and Weir (1967) with the number of turns in the stimulus, McCall and Melson (1970) with the randomness versus the regularity of the stimulus configuration. Not surprisingly a number of conflicting results have been reported on the basis of these differing definitions. One approach which has yielded fairly consistent results has been to equate complexity with the amount of internal contour in a stimulus and to manipulate contour by employing black and white checkerboards of a constant size but of differing densities (2×2 v. 4×4 v. 8×8 checkerboards and so on). This procedure controls for brightness since the black–white ratios are always constant. However, Hershenson (1967) has cautioned that the control for brightness may be vitiated if subjects do not scan the entire stimulus surface (cf. Salapatek and Kessen, 1966).

An initial finding from a study employing the above approach was reported by Berlyne (1958) who reported that infants preferred the most complex stimulus offered. Hershenson (1964), however, reported that newborns showed a distinct preference for a 2×2 as against a 4×4 or a 12×12 checkerboard, that is, they preferred the least complex stimulus. The apparent contradiction between these results was partly resolved by a report by Brennan, Ames and Moore (1966) who found that among infants of three, eight and fourteen weeks, the youngest preferred 2×2 checks, the middle preferred 8×8 checks and the oldest preferred 24×24 checks. Thus, complexity preference was shown to be a function of age. This view was further substantiated by Karmel (1969) who found that between thirteen and twenty weeks there was an inverted U-shaped function between complexity (as indexed by the square root of the amount of contour) and stimulus preference. Moreover, the older infants preferred more complex stimuli so that the peak of the inverted U-curve shifted upwards with increasing age.

Attentional processes in perceptual discrimination

It will have occurred to the reader that a large number of the studies already referred to have regarded differential attention to different stimuli as the primary means of determining whether subjects are capable of discriminating between pairs of stimuli. As we have noted previously, a frequent strategy is to determine whether the subject fixates more upon one member of a stimulus pair than upon another; if the subject does show differential attention in this manner it is reasoned that he has manifested a preference and, *ipso facto*, has discriminated between the stimuli. The role of attention in perceptual discrimination is clearly an important one and it is to a consideration of this topic that we now turn.

Just as Fantz's early experiments provided the impetus for a closer study of infant perception so did they also provide the motivation for a renewed interest in infant attentional processes. He had suggested that infants attend to the more complex of two stimuli. Subsequent investigations directed themselves to the question of what was going on during the attentional process itself. A number of researchers, notably Kagan and Lewis (1965) and their associates, approached this question from the point of view of an oft-noted decline in overt infant attention towards a repeatedly exposed stimulus. In a typical experiment, infant subjects would be presented with the same stimulus over and over again for several trials and attention towards the stimulus would be recorded. Attention was assessed in a number of ways – visual fixation upon the stimulus, changes in heart-rate upon stimulus onset, changes in respiration rate. These measures are usually highly interrelated and in this discussion we will consider only the visual fixation measure. Under the conditions just described it has regularly been observed that the duration of infant fixation on a stimulus declines systematically with each successive presentation. A rather simple and perhaps obvious explanation for such a phenomenon is that the infants' eyes become fatigued and that they therefore look increasingly less at the stimulus as time goes on. However, it is readily demonstrated that such an account is inadequate for, if, after a series of trials with a constant stimulus, a new stimulus of less intensity is now presented, there is almost invariably a recovery of attention to the level observed during initial trials. Such recovery is sufficient to demonstrate that the previously noted decline could not have been due to fatigue.

The procedure just described has come to be known as the violation of expectancy paradigm (Lewis and Goldberg, 1969). The interpretation of results from this procedure that is now widely accepted is based on a theoretical framework whereby, due to repeated exposure of a constant (S_1) stimulus, some central representation or schema of S_1 comes to be established (perhaps through the laying down of a neuronal model, as proposed by Sokolov, 1963). Attentive behaviour (e.g. visual fixation) declines so long as there is a match between external event and internal representation. This is the case so long as S_1 continues to be presented, and the subject thereby develops an expectancy for the appearance of S_1. However, with the introduction of a new stimulus, S_2, the external–internal match no longer obtains; expectancy has been violated and, in order that the resultant discrepancy might be assimilated, there is an increase in attentive behaviour.

The violation of expectancy paradigm, or variations of it, has been widely used to investigate a whole range of problems in the field of infant attentional, perceptual and cognitive development. Thus, Lewis and his colleagues (Lewis, Goldberg and Campbell, 1969) have investigated developmental changes in the efficiency of model acquisition; Caron and Caron (1969) have examined differences in rates of decrement when simple and complex stimuli are repeatedly presented; infant response to novelty has been investigated by this means by Schaffer and Parry (1969). A number of these studies have recently been reviewed by Jeffrey and Cohen (1971).

The application of the violation of expectancy paradigm to studies of perceptual development has been highlighted by Lewis and Goldberg (1969). They argued that the rate of attentional decline during repeated presentations of an S_1 stimulus can be regarded as an index of the subject's ability to assimilate or acquire an internal model or schema of that stimulus. They argued also that the magnitude of attentional recovery upon presentation of S_2 can be regarded as an index of the subject's discrimination between S_1 and S_2. Later, Lewis and Baumel (1970) were able to demonstrate the viability of this approach by showing that, following a series of S_1 trials, differential magnitudes of response recovery were induced by different kinds of stimulus change. It should be noted that this kind of approach to perceptual discrimination moves one away from the traditional stimulus-centered approach, wherein the subject's response is related to variation in some property of the stimulus (e.g. its colour, form, brightness, complexity, etc.) and moves, instead, towards a more subject-centered approach, wherein behaviour is regarded as the product of a relationship between the cognitive structure of the subject, on the one hand, and certain characteristics of the stimulus (e.g. its familiarity or novelty), on the other.

Orientation discrimination in infancy and childhood

We turn now to a more detailed consideration of the application of the above procedure towards the resolution of a perceptual issue which has been of recurrent interest to psychologists for almost a century. The issue in question is the extent to which young subjects are capable of discriminating between stimuli which differ from each other only in orientation and the extent to which such subjects are also able to recognize the identity between stimuli differing only in orientation. The issue has empirical, theoretical and practical interest. Its empirical interest lies in the fact that about half the relevant literature tells us that, at least initially, young children do not discriminate between different orientations of the same stimulus and that they recognize a stimulus equally well in any orientation, whereas the other half tells us that they do so discriminate and that initially children are markedly dependent on the upright orientation for their recognition of stimuli. It would seem worthwhile to resolve this contradiction. The problem has theoretical interest because there are theories of perception (see Fellows, 1968) which impose physiological restrictions on the capacity of human subjects to discriminate orientation, whereas other theories (Ghent, 1961) have built into them the necessity of orientation discrimination. Further, it is important for our understanding of perceptual and cognitive development to know whether the infant lives in a world in which objects are recognized regardless of orientation, or one in which such recognition is orientation-specific; clearly, the latter is a less stable, more complex world than the former. Finally, the problem has practical importance because of the well-known difficulty which many young children have, when they come to learn to read, of discriminating between letters which differ from each other only in orientation (d, p, q, b; n, u; m, w). It would seem important to establish what the nature of this difficulty is.

A few years ago the present author undertook a research programme into the nature of orientation discrimination in infants and young children. Up to that point, despite its developmental relevance, there had been only two previous studies involving infant subjects, and they had produced conflicting results. Ling (1941) had concluded that infants of six months were insensitive to orientation differences in their perception of form, while Watson (1966) reported that, between thirteen and fourteen weeks, young infants could discriminate between upright and ninety- or 180-degree orientations of the human face; neither younger nor older infants in the Watson study appeared capable of this discrimination. Both studies suffered from considerable methodological weakness (see McGurk, 1970). In a preliminary study, McGurk exposed a small group of infants of between six and twenty-six weeks to three different experimental procedures to assess their discrimination of orientation. Two-dimensional abstract shapes and three-dimensional, life-like models of the human face were employed as stimuli. The Fantz spontaneous preference procedure was employed in one experiment; two otherwise identical stimuli were simultaneously presented, one in the upright, the other at a 180-degree orientation, and duration of infant fixation on each orientation was recorded. A second experiment involved the violation of expectancy paradigm outlined above. One stimulus, either in the upright or the inverted orientation, was presented for a series of twenty-second trials separated by ten-second intervals. Thereafter the stimulus was rotated through 180 degrees and presented for a further twenty seconds. Infant fixation on the stimulus was recorded during each trial. The third experiment involved a modification of the violation of expectancy design, one previously employed by Saayman, Ames and Moffett (1964). Here, a pair of identical stimuli, in the same orientation, was presented for a continuous familiarization period. Thereafter, the orientation of one member of the pair was modified by 180 degrees and the pair again presented. Throughout the procedure, infant fixation on each member of the pair was recorded.

Under the Fantz procedure few infants at any age level appeared to discriminate between different orientations of either the facial or the abstract stimuli. By contrast, such discrimination was apparent under the two experimental procedures which had incorporated a familiarization phase. Although both these procedures yielded comparable results, the clearest results were obtained under the standard violation of expectancy procedure. Here, infants at all age levels showed a systematic decline in attention during those trials when the stimulus, either facial or abstract, was presented at a constant orientation. When, on the final trial, the orientation was modified, infants at all age levels showed a significant recovery of attention, thus signifying that they had perceived that a change in the stimulus had occurred. Once more, this was true for both realistic and abstract stimuli.

Data from these experiments, then, served two purposes. Firstly, they served to underline the inadequacies of the spontaneous preference procedure discussed earlier; clearly, failure to manifest an attentional preference for one of two stimuli cannot be construed as a failure to perceive differences between them. Secondly, and more importantly, the data strongly suggested that infants between six and twenty-six weeks could perceptually discriminate between different orientations of the same stimulus. The question could therefore be raised whether young infants were also capable of recognizing the identity between different orientations of the same stimulus. That is, do young infants recognize a stimulus as the *same* stimulus when it appears in different orientations, or is it the case that, for them, identity is dependent upon orientation, so that change of orientation is equivalent to change of identity?

In designing an experiment that would provide a meaningful answer to this question, a more elaborate model of the violation of expectancy paradigm was developed. In the standard paradigm, as we have seen, a constant stimulus is repeatedly presented and attentional decline over successive presentations is regarded as evidence that the subject is developing an expectancy for the appearance of the stimulus. Let us, for present purposes, call this the Constant condition. Now, suppose instead of always presenting the same stimulus, we present a completely new stimulus on each trial, what then should we expect? Well, since no expectancy can develop concerning a stimulus the identity of which is always changing (except, perhaps, an expectancy for change itself), we would expect little attentional decline to occur, such decline having previously been regarded as an index that an expectancy *is* developing. It was decided to include such a changing condition in the new experiment; let us call it the Identity condition. There are, of course, alternatives between presenting exactly the same stimulus on every trial and presenting a quite new stimulus each time. For example, one could always present the same form but, instead of presenting it at the same orientation, its orientation could be varied from one trial to another. Such a condition was also incorporated in the new experiment and it was, in fact, the critical one; let us call it the Orientation condition.

Now, what should be the attentional pattern under the Orientation condition as compared with that under Constant or Identity conditions? Clearly, much depends upon how orientation change is perceived by the subjects under study. Subjects who discriminate orientation but who do not conserve identity through change in orientation, who do not recognize a stimulus as the *same* stimulus when it appears in different orientations, should behave in the same way under the Orientation condition as under the Identity condition; that is, they should show little attentional decrement. On the other hand, subjects who, though capable of discriminating orientation, none the less recognize the identity of a stimulus regardless of its orientation, should show a pattern of responding under the Orientation condition more similar to that under the Constant condition than that under the Identity condition; i.e. such subjects should show some degree of attentional decline across successive trials.

Such modifications of the violation of expectancy paradigm had never previously been employed with infants and it therefore seemed advisable to attempt to validate the model on a criterion group of subjects about whom independent evidence was available concerning their discriminations of orientation. As was earlier observed, there is considerable confusion in the literature concerning the role which orientation plays in young children's perception. Several studies seem to demonstrate that below the age of about six years young children are relatively insensitive to orientation differences (e.g. Davidson, 1934; Rice, 1930) whereas other investigators (e.g. Ghent, 1961; Podell, 1966) report that such children discriminate between different orientations of the same stimulus with relative ease. McGurk (1972a) was able to demonstrate that the important variable in such studies was the extent to which experimental conditions elicit attention to orientation as a discriminative cue. He argued that young children *were* capable of discriminating orientation but that this was a stimulus dimension of relatively low salience, attracting little attention, especially when other stimulus dimensions were also subject to variation. An experiment was therefore conducted involving a sample of children between three and five years old. Under one condition, subjects were presented with pairs of otherwise identical figures, both realistic and abstract, one member of which was upright, the others inverted or at ninety degrees. They were simply asked to point to the one which was upside-down or wrong. The results were clear-cut; without exception the disoriented form of the realistic figure was correctly identified whether that form was inverted or at ninety degrees. Similar results were obtained for the abstract figure. Thus, these children had no difficulty in discriminating between stimuli differing in orientation alone.

Under a second condition, subjects were required to judge among a selection of variants in terms of their similarity to a standard figure. Realistic and abstract stimuli were again employed. All variants had the same form as the standard and one was, in fact, identical to it in every detail. Two variants differed from the standard in orientation, one by ninety, the other by 180 degrees; another was half the size of the standard and one was a different colour from the standard; finally, one variant was half the size, a different colour and also differed from the standard in orientation. A paired-comparisons design was employed: with the standard always present, all possible pairs of variants were presented and for each pair subjects were asked to say which member was more like the standard. Again the results were fairly clear-cut and were identical for abstract and realistic figures. Generally speaking, though there were some age differences in this respect, subjects judged the identical variant, and the two variants which differed from the standard in orientation, all to be equally similar to the standard; the variant which differed in size and the one which differed in colour were judged next in similarity to the standard whilst the variant which differed in size, colour and orientation was judged least similar of all. Note that it was clearly established earlier that all these subjects could perceive differences between different orientations of the same figure, yet here was a failure to discriminate between different orientations in terms of similarity to a standard figure. Instead, they responded to stimuli as equivalent over a range of orientation differences; that is, they recognized a stimulus as the same when it appeared in different orientations. Such subjects, therefore, would provide an ideal criterion group on which to test the validity of the modified violation of expectancy model outlined above.

The three conditions of the modified violation of expectancy experiment were accordingly run with a sample of three- to five-year-old children drawn from the same subject pool as those who participated in the study just described. Subjects sat within a three-sided surround and stimuli were rear-projected onto a screen located in the centre of the front panel. For the Constant condition, the upright orientation of a schematic face was repeatedly presented. Under the Orientation condition, the same face was again repeatedly presented but now it appeared in a different orientation on each trial. Finally, under the Identity condition, different schematic faces were presented on each trial. Two episodes of such familiarization trials were run for all subjects, after each of which a different violation trial occurred. These were arbitrarily called *identity change* and *orientation change*. The rationale for their inclusion will become clear as we proceed. During each trial, subjects' visual fixations on stimuli were recorded.

Under the Constant condition, subjects showed a marked decline in attention towards the stimulus over successive trials. Under the Identity condition, there was hardly any attentional decline. Under the Orientation condition, responses were more similar to those under the Constant condition than those under the Identity condition, and there was once more a marked decline in attention towards the stimulus from trial to trial. These were exactly the results that were predicted for the subjects under study so that, thus far, the experimental model had been validated. Further confirmation for its validity came from subjects' responses during the two violation trials. On one of these, the identity change trial, subjects under all conditions were presented with an upright facial stimulus to which they had not been previously exposed; on the other violation trial, the orientation change trial, all subjects were exposed to the facial stimulus presented during the familiarization trials under Constant and Orientation conditions, except that the face was now presented upside-down, i.e. at an orientation not previously encountered.

Subjects exposed to the Constant condition had presumably acquired an expectancy for a constant face at a constant orientation. Both the identity change and the orientation change stimuli, therefore, represented violations of that expectancy and should have resulted in a recovery from the previously observed attentional decline. This was indeed the case; both violation stimuli elicited a marked recovery of attention. Subjects exposed to the 'Orientation' condition could only have developed an expectancy for the identity of the facial stimulus, but not for its orientation since this was subject to continual change. Thus, only the identity change stimulus should have elicited recovery. Again, this expectation was fulfilled: when the orientation change stimulus was presented, which merely represented further variation on a dimension which had also varied during familiarization, what was observed was a continuation of the attentional decline noted during familiarization trials. There was no evidence of any expectancy having developed, as indexed by attentional decline, on the part of subjects exposed to the Identity condition; thus none of the violation stimuli were expected to elicit response recovery. Again, results were more or less as expected, although the orientation change stimulus did elicit a slight increase in attention over that shown on the final familiarization trial. These various results are depicted in Figure 1.

The results from the experiments just described were regarded as validating the revised violation of expectancy model elaborated earlier. Subjects who were known to be capable both of discriminating between different orientations of the same form and of recognizing the identity between different orientations of the same form manifested such capacities under conditions where direction and duration of ocular regard were the only response measures employed. It was clear, therefore, that the method was a suitable

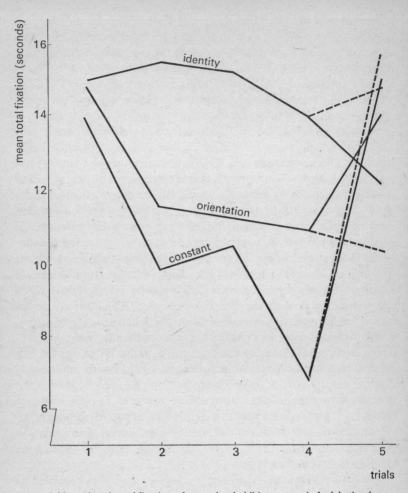

Figure 1 Mean duration of fixation of pre-school children towards facial stimulus under different familiarization (trials 1 to 4) and violation (trial 5) conditions. Solid line depicts response to change of stimulus identity at trial 5 and broken line depicts response to change of orientation

one for use with infant subjects and it was decided to employ it in a renewed investigation of the role of stimulus orientation in infant perception during the first year of life.

One hundred and forty-four infants participated in the new study

(McGurk, 1972b). They were from four age groups, three, six, nine and twelve months, and within each age group equal numbers of subjects were assigned to the Constant, Orientation and Identity conditions of the experiment. The stimuli used in the main part of the experiment are presented in Figure 2. Each subject experienced two familiarization episodes, each followed by a different violation episode. These two familiarization–violation sequences were separated by a series of filler trials during which all subjects experienced the same conditions. During filler trials, a schematic representation of the human face was presented for four trials in the upright orientation; on a fifth trial, the same face was again presented but now at an orientation of 180 degrees. The purpose of the filler trials was to permit recovery of any general habituation which may have occurred to the stimulus materials employed in the main part of the experiment.

A rear-screen projection method was again employed; infants sat on their mothers' knees within the U-shaped surround, facing the screen. All trials were of twenty-second duration with a ten-second

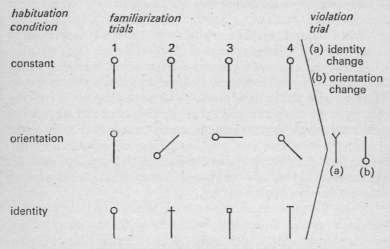

Figure 2 Examples of figures employed as stimuli with infant subjects during familiarization and violation trials. All subjects experienced the same stimulus at trial 1, but under Orientation and Identity conditions, the sequence of presentation of stimuli exposed during trials 2, 3 and 4 was varied randomly. The sequence of presentation of violation stimuli was counter-balanced across subjects. Adapted from McGurk (1972b)

interval between each trial. Duration of infant fixation on stimuli was recorded for each trial.

The results from the main part of the experiment are presented graphically in Figure 3. From Figure 3, it is apparent that three-month-old subjects behaved differently from infants in the other three age groups. Three month olds showed no habituation of attention towards stimuli under any of the experimental conditions and maintained a high level of fixation across all trials. On the other hand, the fixation responses of six-, nine- and twelve-month-old infants discriminated between conditions during the familiarization trials and during the violation trials. Under the Constant condition these subjects showed a consistent pattern of attentional decrement during familiarization trials. Moreover, on the violation trials, change of orientation and change of identity both elicited significant recovery of attention. Thus, under present conditions, subjects of six months and older are clearly capable of discriminating between different orientations of the same form. Under the Orientation condition, subjects older than six months again showed consistent decrement of attending responses during familiarization trials. Their response during violation trials was a function of the kind of stimulus change involved therein; change in orientation merely resulted in continuation of the response decrement pattern observed during familiarization trials, though there were minor age differences in this respect; on the other hand change in identity resulted in significant response recovery. These subjects, therefore, appeared to be responding to the constant identity of the stimulus during familiarization trials and only change in identity was capable of eliciting increased attention. Finally, under the Identity condition, there was no evidence of response decrement on the part of any group during familiarization trials. Consequently, neither change in identity nor change in orientation elicited response recovery during violation trials.

During the filler trials subjects of six months and older showed consistent attentional decrement when a facial stimulus was repeatedly presented in an upright orientation. When the orientation of the face was subsequently modified, these subjects showed a marked recovery of response. These results are illustrated in Figure 4.

To summarize, in terms of the experimental paradigm on which the present study was based, only infants of six months and older can be

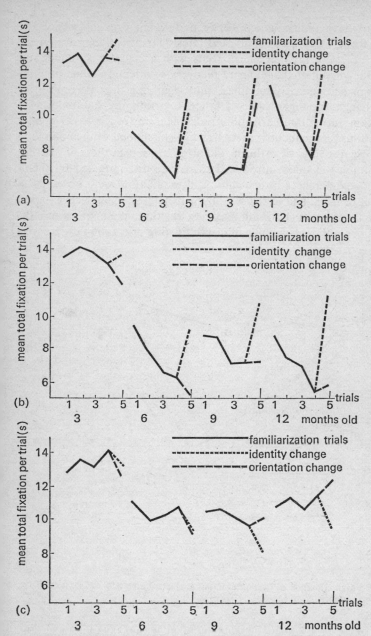

Figure 3 Duration of fixation of infant subjects under (a) Constant condition, (b) Orientation condition and (c) Identity condition. Adapted from McGurk (1972b)

said to have discriminated between different orientations of the same form. Only they manifested consistent attentional decrement over successive familiarization trials with a constant stimulus and only they manifested significant recovery of attention when orientation was subsequently modified, thus signifying their perception of the change. Younger subjects failed to show any habituation of attention during familiarization trials under any of the experimental conditions; consequently, there was little likelihood of their showing response recovery *per se* during violation trials, regardless of whether the stimulus changes introduced then were discriminated by them. Such age differences in orientation discrimination were observed in respect of facial and abstract stimuli. Results from subjects exposed to the Orientation condition make it clear that infants of six months and older, although capable of discriminating orientation differences,

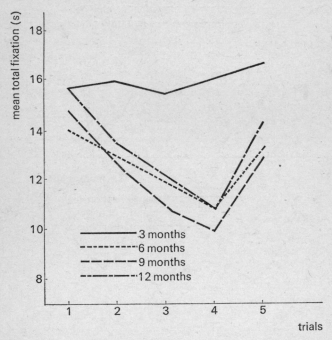

Figure 4 Mean duration of fixation of infant subjects during filler trials with facial stimulus. Adapted from McGurk (1972b)

none the less recognized the identity between different orientations of the same form. If subjects who were familiarized under the Orientation condition had been unable to recognize the similarity between the figure presented on successive trials, that is, if for these subjects orientation change had been equivalent to identity change, then they would have been expected to show a response pattern more similar to that shown by their counterparts exposed to the Identity condition. Subjects exposed to the latter showed little or no evidence of systematic response decrement.

The failure of the three month olds to show either attentional decrement or attentional recovery under any of the experimental conditions makes it impossible to draw any firm conclusions concerning such young subjects' discrimination of orientation. They may or may not perceive differences between different orientations of the same form, may or may not recognize the same form in different orientations. However, unlike that of infants in an earlier study (McGurk, 1970), the attentional behaviour of subjects younger than six months in the present study was insensitive to the experimental conditions manipulated. Accordingly, the data are inconclusive concerning the role of orientation in form perception by such young infants.

It is not obvious why three-month-old subjects in the earlier study should have shown attentional decrement to repeated presentation of a constant stimulus followed by attentional recovery on a change of orientation, while their counterparts in the present study failed to do so. However, one major difference between the two sets of experimental conditions may be of relevance. In the earlier study, infants sat within an observation chamber, all surfaces of which were more or less equally illuminated. In the later study, testing took place in a darkened room and illumination emanated from the screen on which stimuli were rear-projected. It may be that under conditions where there are marked differences between the brightness of a stimulus source and its surround, and where light emanates from a point source, the probability is maximized that 'stimulus-locking' or 'obligatory attention' will be observed in very young infants, and the probability correspondingly reduced that habituation of attention will occur. Under less extreme conditions, that is under conditions where the contrast between the brightness of a stimulus and its surround is reduced, habituation of attention in young infants may be more likely to occur.

Actually, there is considerable confusion in the literature over whether infants as young as three months show habituation of attention when repeatedly exposed to a constant stimulus. Positive findings have been reported by Caron and Caron (1969), McGurk (1970) and Friedman (1971); on the other hand, negative results have been reported by Fantz (1964) and Lewis, Goldberg and Campbell (1969). These studies, however, differed from each other on a number of parameters – nature of stimuli and method of presentation, number and duration of presentations, and duration of intervals between presentations. There is a clear need, therefore, for systematic examination of the various parameters that might influence infant responding in the situation under consideration. In this way, it may become possible to specify the conditions under which very young infants may and may not be expected to show habituation of attention.

Due to the inconclusiveness of results from three-month-old subjects, present findings are less precise than one might have wished concerning the age at which orientation discrimination first occurs. Similarly, the issue remains unresolved of whether there is a stage in infancy at which orientation is of prime salience, so that the identity of a form in different orientations is not recognized; or a stage at which infants are incapable of discriminating between different orientations of the same form. What appears more likely, however, is that from an early stage in development, infants are *potentially* capable of discriminating orientation – that is, they have a visual apparatus that registers orientational differences (possibly in a manner similar to that described by Hubel and Wiesel, 1962) – and that under certain conditions the young infant attends to orientation and discriminates between stimuli on this basis, from at least as early as six months and probably earlier. It is also clear, however, that under other circumstances, orientation remains relatively unattended to and the infant attends more to the identity between different orientations of the same form. Such a strategy has ecological validity and is in the cognitive service of the infant, for it enables him to conserve invariance under conditions of perceptual change, thus ensuring a primitive kind of object constancy. Because of its adaptiveness, this may indeed become the dominant mode of responding and may lead to confusion of orientations at later stages of development. What has been demonstrated by the series of experiments reported above is that whenever such confusion arises, it cannot be attributed to any inherent difficulty in discriminating orientation, such as the neurophysiological limitations on orientation discrimination proposed by Fellows (1968). From an early stage in development, the human organism is capable of detecting orientation differences. Whether or not different stimulus orientations will be responded to discriminatively in a given situation will depend upon the extent to which conditions elicit attention to similarities or to differences between stimuli.

Vision and other sensory modalities

Outside of the controlled conditions of the laboratory, it is rare that the perception of even an isolated event is the result of the operation of a single sensory system. In the perceptual world of the adult, there is a subtle and intimate relationship between the various sensory systems. It is this interrelationship that ensures the richness of perceptual experience. It is remarkable, therefore, that although there have been extensive studies of intersensory integration in young children (e.g. Birch and Lefford, 1967; Rudel and Teuber, 1964), there have been few studies of infant perceptual development involving stimulation to more than one sensory modality. To be sure, a wide range of modalities have been independently studied, including olfactory and auditory (Bridger, 1961; Engen and Lipsitt, 1965) as well as visual. In addition, some investigators have compared infants' responsiveness to stimulation to one modality with their responsiveness to stimulation to another. For example, both Melson and McCall (1970) and Lewis and Groch (1971) have compared infant responsiveness to auditory and visual stimuli. The former reported that, among five-month-old girls, attention to auditory stimuli could be predicted from the looking pattern displayed by subjects when they were previously presented with a set of visual stimuli; the latter observed that attentional responses of three-month-old females discriminated more clearly between auditory and visual stimuli than did the responses of three-month-old males.

Only a few investigators have attempted to study the degree to which infants coordinate simultaneous stimulation to different sensory modalities, when such stimulation emanates from a single source. The results of the few studies which have been carried out tend to be controversial. Piaget (1952), on the basis of detailed observation of his own three children, argued that coordination between vision and hearing was not achieved until three months of age. By this age, his children appeared to search visually for the face of a speaker once having heard his voice, and they appeared also to search for the source of a familiar sound, say the noise of a rattle, once having heard the sound itself. With respect to the schemata which thus develop, Piaget comments, '. . . the human face is one entity with regard to looking, listening, etc., and once he has acquired, in this case and some other privileged examples (rattles, etc.), coordination between hearing and sight, the child will search systematically and everywhere for correlations between sounds and visual images' (p. 87). It is Piaget's contention that prior to the achievement of such coordination, the infant does not attempt to *look* at *what* he hears, but merely tries to see *while* he hears. The infant is visually excited by the sound, but does not necessarily know that the sound is a property of a particular visible object.

In Piaget's observations, the visual and auditory components of stimulation always occupied the same spatial location. In a recent study, Aronson and Rosenbloom (1971) created a spatial discrepancy between the mother's face and the sound of her voice, and observed how infants of thirty to fifty days reacted. They argued that if the infants coordinated sight and sound by perceiving both modalities within a common audio-visual space, then they should experience the discrepancy between the mother's face and her voice as confusing and distressing. Infant and mother were located in separate rooms, but faced each other through a glass screen. The mother communicated with the infant over two loudspeakers, one of which was located at the baby's right, the other at his left. The baby sat midway between the speakers and it was assumed that when the speakers were in balance, the infant would experience the mother's voice as coming from straight ahead. With one speaker completely dominant, however, the voice would appear to emanate from ninety degrees to the infant's right or left. Mothers were instructed to speak normally to the infants. The straight ahead condition was always presented first, followed by an episode when the voice was presented from the right or left. The mother faced the infant and spoke continuously during both conditions.

Aronson and Rosenbloom report that the infants appeared relaxed during the straight-ahead condition but became visibly distressed when the mother's voice was dislocated. The distress reaction included thrashing of the arms, legs and torso, facial grimacing and mouthing of the tongue. The authors report that the infants could be readily calmed by turning them away from the mother's sight. The distress reaction, however, became immediately evident again if the infant was turned back to face the mother, even if the straight-ahead condition was resumed. It was thus concluded that infants as young as thirty days had learned that speaker and voice emanate from a single spatial unit. Such a conclusion, if justified, places the achievement of audio-visual coordination at a much earlier age than was suggested by Piaget (1952).

McGurk and Lewis (1972) have attempted to replicate the Aronson and Rosenbloom finding. In their experiment, however, no assumptions were made about infant stereophonic perception. Instead, three speakers were employed, one straight ahead of the infant, one three feet to his left and the other three feet to his right. Moreover, each subject experienced four episodes in immediate succession. During episode 1, the mother's voice relayed over the centre speaker as a counterpart to Aronson and Rosenbloom's straight-ahead condition. During episodes 2 and 3 the mother's voice was relayed over right and left speakers successively; half the subjects heard the left speaker first and the others began with the right. Finally, during episode 4, the mother's voice was again relayed over the centre speaker. Each episode was of thirty seconds' duration. Three groups of infants, aged one, four and seven months, were tested. In other respects, the conditions and procedures were similar to those of Aronson and Rosenbloom.

Little reaction was observed on the part of the one month olds who participated in the McGurk and Lewis study, regardless of the direction from which the mother's voice came. At four months, about half the subjects looked from time to time towards the direction from which the voice came, whenever it was dislocated from the frontal position, and at seven months this behaviour was observed in the majority of subjects. At both ages, however, infants spent the major portion of the time during each episode focused upon the mother's face. At no age level was there evidence of the widespread distress reported by Aronson and Rosenbloom, a finding which suggests that this distress may have been an artefact of the experimental conditions employed by them.

Infants in the McGurk and Lewis study showed no upset following sight–sound separation. Accordingly, Aronson and Rosenbloom's contention that such separation is experienced as disruptive must be viewed with caution. Clearly, further investigation is necessary in order to reveal the basis upon which coordination between sight and sound develops during the infancy period.

Bower (1971) has investigated the extent to which visual experience with an object gives rise to expectancies concerning the object's tactual qualities. Employing subjects of only a few days of age, he presented them with realistic and illusory objects. The illusory objects were presented by means of an optical apparatus which created a stimulus with the visual properties of a 3D solid, but which was, in effect, merely a bounded volume of air, having no solidity whatever. The newborn subjects were supported in a semi-upright position, with hands and arms free to move. Their reaction was observed when their hands reached the space occupied by the objects. According to Bower, all his subjects touched and grasped the real objects quite happily. However, whenever their hands reached the intangible object's location, the infants become distressed. Bower argues that this finding represents evidence that, even in early infancy, visual input from an object gives rise to an expectancy for tactual input. He argues also that, in view of the early age of his subjects, this intermodal transfer must be an inborn property of the nervous system.

It may surprise some readers to learn that visually guided reaching and grasping can be observed in newborn subjects. Traditionally, such behaviour is not thought of as developing until around six months or so. Whilst Bower acknowledges that newborn infants do not reach for objects in the same way that older infants do (for example, newborns may reach out and grasp at empty air), he believes that the reaching behaviour he observed was intentional. It has also been argued, however, that he may only have observed excited thrashing and fortuitous touching (Lipsitt and Eimas, 1972). Still, it is the difference in the affective response to the real and illusory objects, consequent upon the infant's hand reaching their location, that represents the intriguing aspects of Bower's report. The phenomenon is clearly worthy of further investigation.

Future research in infant perception

Due to limitations of space and to the inevitable operation of the author's bias for particular problems of perceptual development, much that might have been written about other areas of infant perception has had to be omitted. Thus, a whole range of problems concerned with the development of depth and space perception, with the perception of movement, with the development of the perceptual constancies and with the development of the perceptual illusions has been left unconsidered. The interested reader is referred to Gibson's (1969) excellent book for a discussion of these and related topics.

A great leap forward in our understanding of the processes of perceptual development was made when psychologists chose to disregard the traditional views of the infant as a passive, relatively insensitive organism, and instead accepted the challenge of designing experiments which, whilst recognizing the infant's limited response repertoire, none the less would provide information about the kind of perceptual world within which the infant lived. Some of the knowledge that has been gained in this pursuit has been outlined above. Whilst there are still many gaps to be filled and whilst many empirical issues remain to be settled, it appears from our present knowledge that the young infant lives in a visual world not essentially different from the one we experience as adults, in terms of the visual information available to him (Bond, 1972). However, as already noted, little is understood of how the infant integrates and coordinates visually received information with information which he receives via other sensory modalities. This would appear to represent a research area ripe for further investigation. Coordination between the visual and the auditory modes during the infancy period deserves particular attention, firstly because the auditory system, like the visual system, appears to be functional more or less from birth onwards (Bartoshuk, 1964), and secondly, because many significant objects in the young infant's environment have distinctive auditory and visual features. The latter is especially the case with social objects. For example, the extent to which the infant is able to integrate simultaneous stimulation to these different modalities, in order to arrive at a single, composite percept or schema, will have important consequences for the development of person perception.

The kind of *cognitive* world the infant is able to construct on the basis of the *visual* information available to him is also becoming of increasing interest to students of perceptual development. Recent studies by Nelson (1971) and Bower (1971) illustrate how visual behaviour can be used as an index of cognitive status. For example, by observing young infants' visual tracking of stimuli as they describe realistic and impossible trajectories, Bower has concluded that for infants under sixteen weeks or so, an object may exist at a given location or may move continuously but the same object cannot move from stationary place to stationary place. For older infants an object can move from stationary place to stationary place, even to invisible termini. According to Bower, the younger infants respond not to objects but to places and to movements. 'In contrast, older infants have learned to define an object as something that can go from place to place. . . . They identify an object by its features rather than by its place or movement' (Bower, 1971).

It is in areas such as these – perception in the service of cognition, and intersensory coordination – that future studies of perceptual development appear to offer their most exciting prospects.

References

AHRENS, R. (1954), 'Beitrage zur Entwicklung des Physiognomie und Mimikerkennes', *Zeitschrift fur experementelle und angewandte Psychologie*, vol. 2, pp. 412–544, 599–633.

ARONSON, E., and ROSENBLOOM, S. (1971), 'Space perception in early infancy: perception within a common auditory-visual space', *Science*, vol. 172, pp. 1161–3.

BARTOSHUK, A. K. (1964), 'Human neonatal cardiac responses to sound: a power function', *Psychonom. Sci.*, vol. 1, pp. 151–2.

BERLYNE, D. E. (1958), 'The influence of the albedo and complexity of stimuli on visual fixation in the human infants', *Brit. J. Psychol.*, vol. 49, pp. 315–18.

BIRCH, H. G., and LEFFORD, A. (1967), 'Visual differentiation, intersensory integration, and voluntary motor control', *Mongr. Soc. Res. Child Devel.*, vol. 32, no. 2.

BOND, E. K. (1972), 'Perception of form by the human infant', *Psychol. Bull.*, vol. 77, pp. 225–45.

BOWER, T. G. R. (1971), 'The object in the world of the infant', *Sci. Amer.*, vol. 225, pp. 30–38.

BRENNAN, W. M., AMES, E. W., and MOORE, R. W. (1966), 'Age differences in infants' attention to patterns of different complexities', *Science*, vol. 151, pp. 354–5.

BRIDGER, W. H. (1961), 'Sensory habituation and discrimination in the human neonate', *Amer. J. Psychiat.*, vol. 117, pp. 991–6.

CARON, R. F., and CARON, A. J. (1969), 'Degree of stimulus complexity and habituation of visual fixation in infants', *Psychonom. Sci.*, vol. 14, pp. 78–9.

CHARLESWORTH, W. R. (1968), 'Cognition in infancy: where do we stand in the mid-sixties?', *Merrill-Palmer Q. Behav. Devel.*, vol. 14, pp. 25–46.

DAVIDSON, H. P. (1934), 'A study of reversals in young children', *J. genet. Psychol.*, vol. 45, pp. 452–65.

DAYTON, A. O. Jr, and JONES, M. H. (1964), 'Analysis of characteristics of fixation reflexes in infants by use of direct current electro-oculography', *Neurology*, vol. 14, pp. 1152–6.

DAYTON, A. O. Jr, JONES, M. H., STEELE, B., and ROSE, M. (1964), 'Developmental study of coordinated eye movements in the human infant: II. An electro-oculographic study of the fixation reflex in the newborn', *Arch. Ophth.*, vol. 71, pp. 871–5.

DORIS, J., and COOPER, L. (1966), 'Brightness discrimination in infancy', *J. exp. child Psychol.*, vol. 3, pp. 31–9.

ENGEN, T., and LIPSITT, L. P. (1965), 'Decrement and recovery of responses to olfactory stimuli in the human neonate', *J. comp. physiol. Psychol.*, vol. 59, pp. 312–16.

FANTZ, R. L. (1958), 'Pattern vision in young infants', *Psychol. Res.*, vol. 8, pp. 43–7.

FANTZ, R. L. (1961), 'The origin of form perception', *Sci. Amer.*, vol. 204, pp. 66–72.

FANTZ, R. L. (1964), 'Visual experience in infants: decreased attention to familiar patterns relative to novel ones', *Science*, vol. 146, pp. 668–70.

FANTZ, R. L. (1966), 'Pattern discrimination and selective attention as determinants of perceptual development from birth', in A. H. Kidd and J. L. Rivoire (eds.), *Perceptual Development in Children*, International Universities Press.

FANTZ, R. L., ORDY, J. M., and UDELF, M. S. (1962), 'Maturation of pattern vision in infants during the first six months', *J. comp. physiol. Psychol.*, vol. 55, pp. 907–17.

FELLOWS, B. J. (1968), *The Discrimination Process and Development*, Pergamon.

FRIEDMAN, S. (1971), 'Newborn visual response to repeated exposure of "novel" targets', Paper presented at meeting of Eastern Psychological Association, New York City.

GHENT, L. (1961), 'Form and its orientation: a child's -eye view', *Amer. J. Psychol.*, vol. 74, pp. 177–90.

GIBSON, E. J. (1969), *Principles of Perceptual Learning and Development*, Appleton-Century-Crofts.

GORMAN, J. J., COGAN, D. A., and GELLIS, S. S. (1957), 'An apparatus for grading the visual acuity of infants on the basis of optokinetic nystagmus', *Pediatrics*, vol. 19, pp. 1088–92.

HAAF, R. A., and BELL, R. Q. (1967), 'A facial dimension in visual discrimination by human infants', *Child Devel.*, vol. 38, pp. 893–9.

HAYNES, H., WHITE, B. L., and HELD, R. (1965), 'Visual accommodation in human infants', *Science*, vol. 148, pp. 528–30.

HERSHENSON, M. (1964), 'Visual discrimination in the human newborn', *J. comp. physiol. Psychol.*, vol. 58, pp. 270–76.

HERSHENSON, M. (1965), 'Visual discrimination in the human newborn', *Dissert. Abstr.*, vol. 26, p. 1793.

HERSHENSON, M. (1967), 'Development of the perception of form', *Psychol. Bull.*, vol. 67, pp. 326–36.

HORSTEN, G. P. M., and WINKELMAN, J. E. (1962), 'Electrical activity of the retina in relation to histological differentiation in infants born prematurely and at full term', *Vision Res.*, vol. 2, pp. 269–76.

HORSTEN, G. P. M., and WINKELMAN, J. E. (1964), 'Electroretinographic critical fusion frequency of the retina in relation to the histological development in man and animals', *Documenta Ophth.*, vol. 18, pp. 515–21.

HRBEK, A., and MARES, P. (1964a), 'Critical evoked responses to visual stimulation in full-term and premature newborns', *EEG clin. Neurophysiol.*, vol. 16, pp. 575–81.

HRBEK, A., and MARES, P. (1964b), 'The development of electrophysiological reactivity of CNS in children', *Activ. Nerv. Sup.*, vol. 6, pp. 92–3.

HUBEL, D. H., and WIESEL, T. N. (1962), 'Receptive fields, binocular interaction and functional architecture in the cat's visual cortex', *J. Physiol.*, vol. 160, pp. 106–54.

JAMES, W. (1890), *Principles of Psychology*, Holt.

JEFFREY, W. E., and COHEN, L. B. (1971), 'Habituation in the human infant', in H. Reese (ed.), *Advances in Child Development and Behavior*, vol. 6, Academic Press.

KAGAN, J., and LEWIS, M. (1965), 'Studies of attention in the human infant', *Merrill-Palmer Q. Behav. Devel.*, vol. 11, pp. 95–127.

KARMEL, B. Z. (1969), 'The effects of age, complexity and amount of contour on pattern preferences in human infants', *J. exp. child Psychol.*, vol. 7, pp. 339–54.

KOOPMAN, P. R., and AMES, E. W. (1968), 'Infants' preferences for facial arrangements: a failure to replicate', *Child Devel.*, vol. 39, pp. 481–7.

LEWIS, M. (1969), 'Infants' responses to facial stimuli during the first year of life', *Devel. Psychol.*, vol. 1, pp. 75–85.

LEWIS, M., and BAUMEL, M. H. (1970), 'A study in the ordering of attention', *Percept. mot. Skills*, vol. 31, pp. 979–90.

LEWIS, M., and GOLDBERG, S. (1969), 'The acquisition and violation of expectancy: an experimental paradigm', *J. exp. child Psychol.*, vol. 7, pp. 70–80.

LEWIS, M., and GROCH, A. (1971), 'Cardiac response to visual and auditory stimulation in the first two years of life', Paper presented at the Society for Psychophysiological Research meeting, St Louis, Missouri.

LEWIS, M., GOLDBERG, S., and CAMPBELL, H. (1969), 'A developmental study of information processing within the first three years of life: response decrement to a redundant signal', *Mongr. Soc. Res. Child Devel.*, vol. 34, no. 9.

LING, B. C. (1941), 'Form discrimination as a learning cue in infants', *Comp. Psychol. Mongr.*, vol. 17, no. 86.

LIPSITT, L. P., and EIMAS, P. D. (1972), 'Developmental psychology', *Ann. Rev. Psychol.*, vol. 23, pp. 1–50.

MCCALL, R. B., and MELSON, W. H. (1970), 'Complexity, contour and area as determinants of attention in infants', *Devel. Psychol.*, vol. 3, pp. 343–9.

MCGURK, H. (1970), 'The role of object orientation in infant perception', *J. exp. child Psychol.*, vol. 9, pp. 363–73.

MCGURK, H. (1972a), 'The salience of orientation in young children's perception of form', *Child Devel.*, vol. 43, pp. 1047–52.

MCGURK, H. (1972b), 'Infant discrimination of orientation', *J. exp. child Psychol.*, vol. 14, pp. 151–64.

MCGURK, H., and LEWIS, M. (1972), 'Audio-visual coordination in early infancy', unpublished research bulletin, Educational Testing Service, Princeton, New Jersey.

MACKWORTH, N. H., and BRUNER, J. S. (1970), 'How adults and children search and recognize pictures', *Human Devel.*, vol. 13, pp. 149–77.

MANN, I. (1964), *The Development of the Human Eye*, British Medical Association.

MELSON, W. H., and MCCALL, R. B. (1970), 'Attentional responses of five-month girls to discrepant auditory stimuli', *Child Devel.*, vol. 41, pp. 1159–71.

MUNSINGER, H., and WEIR, M. W. (1967), 'Infants' and young children's preferences for complexity', *J. exp. child Psychol.*, vol. 5, pp. 69–73.

NELSON, K. E. (1971), 'Accommodation of visual tracking patterns in human infants to object movement patterns', *J. exp. child Psychol.*, vol. 12, pp. 182–96.

NODINE, C. F., and SIMMONS, F. G. (1972), 'Development of cognitive strategies for processing distinctive features of letter-like stimuli', Paper presented at meeting of Eastern Psychological Association, Boston, Mass.

NODINE, C. F., and STEUERLE, N. F. (1971), 'Development of perceptual-cognitive strategies for differentiating graphemes', Paper presented at meeting of Eastern Psychological Association, New York.

PIAGET, J. (1952), *The Origins of Intelligence in Children*, International Universities Press.

PODELL, J. E. (1966), 'Ontogeny of the locus and orientation of the perceiver', *Child Devel.*, vol. 37, pp. 993–7.

PREYER, W. (1888), *The Mind of the Child: I. The Senses and the Will*, Appleton.

RICE, C. (1930), 'The orientation of plane figures as a factor in their perception by children', *Child Devel.*, vol. 1, pp. 111–14.

RUDEL, R. G., and TEUBER, H. L. (1964), 'Cross-modal transfer of shape discrimination by children', *Neuropsychologia*, vol. 2, pp. 1–8.

SAAYMAN, G., AMES, E. W., and MOFFETT, A. (1964), 'Response to novelty as an indicator of visual discrimination in the human infant', *J. exp. child Psychol.*, vol. 1, pp. 189–98.

SALAPATEK, P. (1969), 'The visual investigation of geometric pattern by one- and two-month-old infants', Paper presented at meeting of the American Association for the Advancement of Science, Boston, Mass.

SALAPATEK, P., and KESSEN, W. (1966), 'Visual scanning of triangles by the human newborn', *J. exp. child Psychol.*, vol. 3, pp. 155–67.

SCHAFFER, H. R. (1971), *The Growth of Sociability*, Penguin.

SCHAFFER, H. R., and PARRY, M. H. (1969), 'Perceptual-motor behaviour in infancy as a function of age and stimulus familiarity', *Brit. J. Psychol.*, vol. 60, pp. 1–9.

SHERMAN, M., SHERMAN, I., and FLORY, C. D. (1936), 'Infant behavior', *Comp. Psychol. Mongr.*, vol. 12, no. 91.

SOKOLOV, Y. N. (1963), *Perception and the Conditioned Reflex*, Macmillan Co.

WATSON, J. S. (1965), 'Evidence of discriminative operant learning within 30 seconds by infants 7–26 weeks of age', Paper presented at meeting of Society for Research in Child Development, Minneapolis, Minn.

WATSON, J. S. (1966), 'Perception of object orientation in infants', *Merrill-Palmer Q. Behav. Devel.*, vol. 12, pp. 73–94.

WILCOX, B. M. (1969), 'Visual preferences of human infants for representations of the human face', *J. exp. child Psychol.*, vol. 7, pp. 10–20.

WINKELMAN, J. E., and HORSTEN, G. P. M. (1962), 'The ERG of premature and full-term infants during their first days of life', *Ophthalmologica*, vol. 143, pp. 92–101.

WOHLWILL, J. C. (1960), 'Developmental studies of perception', *Psychol. Bull.*, vol. 57, pp. 249–88.

ZAPOROZHETS, A. V. (1965), 'The development of perception in the pre-school child', *Mongr. Soc. Res. Child Devel.*, vol. 30, pp. 82–101.

Chapter 2
Conditioning and Learning in Early Infancy

W. Stuart Millar

Introduction

Writing in the early seventies on the topic of conditioning in the human infant, it is difficult to imagine that psychologists were ever disinclined to consider the infant capable of learning or conditioning. After all, earlier theorists such as Freud (1905), Piaget (1953) and Watson (1924) have all emphasized infancy as a highly formative period in the life span; a period encompassing dramatic organismic change in terms of neuromuscular, perceptual, intellectual and social status. Paradoxically, however, it is only since the late 1950s that psychologists have, in fact, generally been inclined to consider the human infant capable of learning. Moreover, as recently as 1965, the question as it applied to the neonate or newborn was still largely an open one (Bijou and Baer, 1965). Indeed, the quite dramatic upsurge of infant research during the last decade really stands witness to the reaction against the earlier conception of the human infant as essentially a passive, neuromuscularly incompetent and in many respects an insensate organism.

Lipsitt (1966) points out that one of the major effects of the genetic-maturational bias prevalent between 1920 and 1950 was the distinct tendency to inhibit and certainly undervalue the investigation of experiential factors in behavioural change, especially in early infancy. Coupled with this maturational bias was the related emphasis on the limited response potentialities of the infant, a marked orientation towards developing infant maturity measuring instruments and an overstressing of data suggestive of an extremely limited capacity for learning in the infant (Gesell, 1954; Morgan and Morgan, 1944). In consequence there was considerable inertia with regard to the investigation of conditioning processes in young infants, and this applied in particular to the use of operant or instrumental conditioning tactics. Not surprisingly the infant operant literature was negligible prior to the mid-1950s. However, the early trend-setting studies of Brackbill (1958) and Rheingold, Gewirtz and Ross (1959) provided the necessary impetus for a radical reorientation of infant learning research which took place in the 1960s.

Definition of learning

In the broadest sense, *conditioning* or *learning* subsumes behavioural effects which can be attributed to environmental interaction, which involve *associative processes* and which exclude effects deriving solely from genetic, maturational and physiologically produced changes in behaviour. Thus, behavioural change attributable to fatigue, sensory adaptation and drugs would not be considered as learning. Conventionally, learning has been quite specifically defined within the classical or respondent and the operant or instrumental conditioning paradigms. In the classical situation, the acquisition of associative behaviour or conditioning is achieved through the *paired presentation* of stimuli: the unconditioned stimulus (UCS) which normally elicits the unconditioned response (UCR) together with the neutral or conditional stimulus (CS).

After repeated contiguous pairings of the CS and UCS, the previously neutral and ineffective CS will, in the absence of the UCS, elicit a conditioned response (CR), more or less similar to the response elicited by the UCS. In the case of operant or instrumental conditioning, the occurrence of a response, referred to as the *operant*, results in reinforcement. Initially the operant response has a relatively low rate of occurrence and this is usually determined during a baseline period when no reinforcement is available. But, with successive reinforcements of the response, operant responding becomes more frequent. Thus operant conditioning involves changes in the frequency of emission of some operant as a function of the rewarding or punishing consequences of the response. In this case, the associative connection is between the operant response and the reinforcing consequence of the behaviour. Conditioning effects within both the classical and operant paradigms are characterized by increased frequency or strength of the response in the course of conditioning. Recently, however, there has been some broadening of these operational criteria to include habituation phenomena which, on the contrary, involve decreases in response frequency or response strength, but which nevertheless fit the broad definition of learning (Lewis, Goldberg and Campbell, 1969; Thompson and Spencer, 1966). The present chapter is, for the most part, concerned with the conventional conditioning paradigms.

Classical conditioning

In spite of the earlier undermining theoretical influences, there have been many attempts to demonstrate classical conditioning in the human infant. Probably the most documented of these early studies was the investigation by Dorothy Marquis (1931) in which she purported to classically condition sucking responses to the sound of a buzzer (CS) within ten days of post-natal life. Infants were bottle-fed six times a day with a buzzer accompanying the feeding. On test instances, when the buzzer was sounded immediately preceding the normal feeding time, conditioned sucking was observed in seven of the eight infants. Similar anticipatory non-nutritive sucking was not observed in a control group of infants. In another early study Wenger (1936) established classically conditioned eyelid closure in three infants by the fifth day of life. In this case, the unconditioned stimulus, a flash of light, was paired with tactual vibration of the foot. Conditioning commenced on the second day of life and by the ninth day the experimental infants showed eyelid closure to tactile stimulation in 58 per cent to 74 per cent of the presentations of the CS. For control infants, tactile stimulation elicited eyelid closure on 29 per cent of the presentations. A subsequent study by Marquis (1941), in which she manipulated the feeding schedules of a group of sixteen neonates, provided evidence for temporal conditioning in the neonate.

However, these studies have been criticized mainly on the grounds that they failed to incorporate adequate controls for pseudo-conditioning or sensitization effects (Bijou and Baer, 1965; Lipsitt, 1963). Pseudo-conditioning or sensitization is said to occur when a conditioning-like effect is obtained despite the fact that the UCS and CS have not previously been paired. In this respect such effects are not true conditioning. A more recent study by Lipsitt and Kaye (1964) has highlighted the importance of taking precautionary measures to control for this effect. These investigators demonstrated successful conditioning of sucking to a low frequency tone of fifteen seconds duration in three- to four-day-old neonates. In order to control for sensitization or pseudo-conditioning, both the experimental and control groups were presented with identical amounts of stimulation, but in different CS–UCS temporal sequences. For experimental infants a non-nutritive nipple was inserted for fourteen seconds in the infant's mouth, one second after the onset of the fifteen-second CS tone. For control infants, the nipple was inserted for the same duration, but approximately thirty seconds after the offset of the tone, i.e. the CS and UCS were not contiguous. As expected, the experimental group showed conditioned responding to the CS on test trials. However, the pseudo-conditioning group also revealed a reliable increase in responsiveness to the CS, although this was reliably less than that observed in the conditioning group. Effectively, then, the pseudo-conditioning procedure also resulted in increased responsiveness to the CS despite the absence of temporal contiguity between sucking and the tone. This finding suggests, in fact, that the procedure adopted had only limited success in controlling for pseudo-conditioning. Moreover, the qualified success of this investigation of classical appetitional conditioning necessarily casts some doubt on the purported success of the earlier studies which did not systematically or adequately control for pseudo-conditioning effects and suggests that these studies be re-examined to determine the extent to which genuine conditioning or learning was demonstrated.

However, despite these reported successful demonstrations, it is generally recognized that classical conditioning is not obtained with any facility in neonates and older infants (Kessen, 1963; Lipsitt, 1963). For instance, Wickens and Wickens (1940), in a study of newborns, paired a buzzer (CS) with electro-tactual shock (UCS) which when applied to the foot produces withdrawal. An experimental group received thirty-six paired trials over a period of three days. On test trials presentation of the buzzer alone showed conditoned foot withdrawal. In a second group, designed specifically to control for pseudo-conditioning effects, the twelve infants received thirty-six trials of electro-tactual shock applied to the foot but in the absence of the buzzer. On test trials when the buzzer was presented alone, the investigators unexpectedly found that these control infants also elicited foot withdrawal to the buzzer, despite the fact that for this group the buzzer and shock had never been paired. Thus, in terms of the performance of both experimental and control groups on the test trials, the pairing of the buzzer with the shock for experimental infants really proved redundant. Alternatively, it has been argued that effectively Wickens and Wickens may have simply conditioned the infants to the sudden onset of stimulation which would certainly account for the increased responsiveness of the control group.

More recent attempts to condition an auditory CS to foot withdrawal, although involving greater sophistication in terms of instrumentation, have enjoyed no more success than the early study by Wickens and Wickens (Crowell, cited in Bijou and Baer, 1965; Gullickson, cited in Bijou and Baer, 1965; Marum, cited in Lipsitt, 1963). A further study involving aversive responding (Lipsitt and Kaye, in Lipsitt, 1963) paired an auditory stimulus (CS) with the nasal presentation of acetic acid vapour, to which the unconditioned response is withdrawal or increased bodily activity. Nevertheless, despite refinements of technique, classical aversive conditioning eluded these investigators.

While this consistent failure to demonstrate conditioned aversion might indicate something specifically attributable to the use of aversive stimulation (Lipsitt, 1963), other studies employing non-aversive stimuli, which have been equally unsuccessful, suggest otherwise. For instance Usol'tsev and Terekova (1958) unsuccessfully attempted to condition the eyeblink response to change in skin temperature in one- to four-month-old infants. In another study, Rendle-Short (1961) was unable to establish conditioned eyeblink responding in infants under six months of age, but was successful with infants over six months of age. However, in this study there were only twenty trials in which an air puff (UCS) was paired with the sight of the apparatus (CS) and thus the age effect which was observed is more likely to suggest that more than twenty trials are necessary for younger infants, than that they cannot be conditioned (Lipsitt, 1963). The extensive work on individual and age differences in conditionability carried out by Papoušek (1967) would certainly suggest this to be a more adequate explanation of this failure to condition. Less easily explained, however, is the Soviet neonatal conditioning research literature, for in spite of Lipsitt and Kaye's (1964) successful conditioning of three- to four-day-old neonates, Soviet psychologists have seldom reported the successful application of Pavlovian conditioning with infants under eight or nine days of age (Bystroletova, 1954, cited in Fitzgerald and Porges, 1971).[1] Even in those cases where conditioning has been successful, most procedures have required weeks or even months to establish stable conditioned responding.

The paradox of the neonate

Admittedly the unsuccessful attempts to classically condition infants are not entirely restricted to the neonatal period; however, the difficulties encountered by investigators during this period have provided a focus for speculation. Quite simply, investigators have been hard pressed to reconcile the paradoxical difficulty in establishing classical conditioning in neonates with data demonstrating unequivocally the infant's competence and adaptiveness at birth.[2] The neonate's difficulty, moreover, would not seem to derive simply from a failure to detect stimuli in his environment. Sameroff (1971)

1. Early investigators reported indeterminate results for foetal conditioning (Sontag and Wallace, 1934), although Spelt (1948), using a loud sound as the UCS and tactile vibration applied to the maternal abdomen, reported conditioned foetal movement in six-and-a-half- to eight-and-a-half-month-old foetuses. Extinction, spontaneous recovery and retention effects were also reported.
2. The *habitation* phenomenon, in which the organism shows progressively decreased responsiveness on repeated exposure to a redundant stimulus, has been documented for certain responses in the newborn (Disher, 1934; Engen, Lipsitt and Kaye, 1963). But note that Lewis, Goldberg and Campbell (1969) report the failure to obtain habituation to a redundant visual stimulus in infants under about three months of age. Other investigators, notably Hutt *et al.* (1968), argue against habituation in the neonate and propose instead that the behavioural effects which have been observed are directly attributable to changes in arousal state of the organism.

Theoretically, this response-decrement or extinction-like process has been viewed not as a simple decrease in the operating efficiency of receptor–effector systems, i.e. a peripheral effect, but rather has been attributed to changes deriving from central information processing, specifically to the development of a cognitive *model* or *schema* corresponding to the stimulus input (Lewis, Goldberg and Campbell, 1969; Sokolov, 1963).

has recently reviewed a large number of studies of infant reactivity to stimulation which demonstrate that the infant's problem lies elsewhere than at the receptor level. It may be, however, that while the neonate is certainly capable of sensory discrimination of a remarkably high order, he is not yet capable of associative coding of stimuli (Kessen, 1963). Certainly, from this viewpoint, data on the progressive myelination of the central nervous system and developmental changes in the EEG activity of the brain would lend support to the view that neurologically speaking the neonate is immature. From yet another vantage point, Sokolov (1963) has argued that adequate orienting behaviour is prerequisite to successful conditioning in the infant. It is suggested that the orienting response is as yet incomplete in the neonate and that, instead, stimulation generally elicits a defensive-type response, even to stimuli which are non-traumatic. If this argument holds, then successful conditioning would not be expected to occur until the orienting response was sufficiently differentiated. A further related point is that, within the classical paradigm, a previously *neutral* stimulus (CS) is associated with an unrelated UCS. However for the neonate, the neutral stimulus is very likely to be a novel stimulus, with the implication that it would elicit a defensive-type reaction as opposed to an orienting response. What may be of even greater importance from a cognitive point of view is that for the newborn, only the UCS component will already be part of an established (built-in) schema, whereas it is highly likely that there will be no pre-existing schema corresponding to the CS component. According to this cognitive approach, classical conditioning will be unsuccessful if the infant cannot coordinate independent schemata and/or if a pre-existing schema corresponding to the CS is not present (Sameroff, 1971).

Interaction of stimulus and response

These attempts to account for the failure to classically condition are for the most part highly speculative; less so however is the important research undertaken during the last decade by Brackbill and her associates. These investigators have sought to examine the nature of the relationship between the CS and the response components in the classical conditioning paradigm. In this respect their research goes beyond straightforward demonstration of conditioning phenomena and represents an attempt to understand conditioning processes in early infancy. Their research has been stimulated primarily by the Soviet literature on the role and nature of the CS. Soviet physiologists contend that the CS and not the UCS is the critical component in the classical paradigm. That is, they take the view that the CS alone determines the course of conditioning quite independent of the nature of the response or the reinforcement. Soviet physiologists further contend that, ontogenetically speaking, there is a fixed developmental sequence in terms of which sensory modalities of conditioned stimuli become effective for conditioning purposes during the first twelve months or so. Kasatkin (1948) has ordered the sensory modalities in terms of their first becoming effective for conditioning as follows: vestibular, auditory, tactile-kinesthetic, olfactory, gustatory and visual. While Brackbill and her associates confirm the Soviet position that the CS is important, their data make the far more interesting point that it is the interaction between the CS and the response which is critical for conditionability.

On the basis of a long series of investigations, Brackbill *et al.* conclude that one of the greatest constraints on early classical conditioning is whether the CS and the response are neurologically *compatible*. The source of innervation of the response system appears to be critical for successful conditioning, and for theoretical and practical considerations Brackbill and Fitzgerald (1969) have distinguished between *somatically* mediated and *autonomically* mediated responses. This dichotomy, based on response innervation, seems to provide the best fit for their data as follows. For instance, conditional sucking (somatic response) has been successfully demonstrated in one-month-old infants to tactual and to auditory conditional stimuli, but not to a temporal conditioned stimulus (Abrahamson, Brackbill, Carpenter and Fitzgerald, 1970).[3] Similarly, conditional eyeblinking (somatic response) has been established to auditory and tactile conditioned stimuli, but not to a temporal CS (Fitzgerald and Brackbill, 1968).

3. In temporal conditioning, the UCS is presented repeatedly at fixed time intervals. Temporal conditioning occurs when, on test trials, the UCS is omitted, but on the timing out of the fixed interval some semblance of the habitual response to the UCS is elicited. That is, the fixed intertrial interval has effectively served as the CS for the conditioned response.

By contrast, autonomically innervated pupillary dilation and constriction responses have been successfully conditioned to a temporal CS in infants as young as twenty-six days (Brackbill, Lintz and Fitzgerald, 1968; Fitzgerald, 1968).

These autonomically regulated responses could not, however, be conditioned to either auditory or tactile CSs. Effectively, then, these investigators were unable to cross-condition across somatically and autonomically regulated response systems. The findings of other investigators fit this dichotomy: conditional ipsilateral head-rotation (a musculo-skeletal somatic response) has been obtained with auditory CSs (Papoušek, 1967), and conditional Babkin[4] responding (a somatically regulated response) has been obtained to both tactile-kinesthetic and auditory CSs (Connolly and Stratton, 1969; Kaye, 1965). Similarly, Lipsitt and Ambrose (1967) reported temporal conditioning of autonomically regulated cardiac rate in neonates. But, in the case of these responses no attempt appears to have been made to cross-condition. However, not all the data conveniently fit Brackbill *et al.*'s dichotomy. For instance, Lipsitt and Ambrose also reported temporal conditioning (thirty-second intertrial interval) of somatically regulated body activity in neonates. Theoretically, according to Brackbill *et al.*'s dichotomy, this should not have been possible. On the same point, Abrahamson *et al.* (1970) and Brackbill, Lintz and Fitzgerald (1968), during unsuccessful attempts to temporally condition eyeblinking and sucking responses (somatically mediated), have reported incidentally a temporal effect in the form of increased excitability during test trials. Moreover, there is the suggestion that temporal CSs of relatively long duration (three to four hours) may, in fact, be effective with somatically regulated gross motor activity (Marquis, 1941). Obviously, as Brackbill, Lintz and Fitzgerald (1968) admit, other autonomic and somatic responses require to be examined in this light. Nevertheless, while the model will undoubtedly require qualification in the light of future research, it provides the basis for a rationale for developmental studies in classical conditioning. If generally borne out, this research marks a tremendous advance towards the understanding of the young

4. *The Babkin reflex*, elicited by pressing the palms of the newborn's hands, has three components as follows: mouth opening, head-turning towards the midline and often the raising of the head to the midline.

infant's level of functioning, particularly as such findings may closely relate to differential rates of cerebral integration and organization within the early months. At last, sixty-seven years since the earliest documented investigations of classical conditioning with infants (Bogen, 1907, and Krasnogorskii, 1907, cited in Fitzgerald and Porges, 1971), investigators are possibly on the threshold of gaining substantial headway in making sense of and conceptualizing the implications of the diverse findings from developmental studies of classical conditioning.

The mixed model: combined classical and operant tactics

A series of successful studies has been carried out by Papousek (1967) in which he has employed a head-turning response. Papoušek's research represents an interesting departure from the pure classical paradigm, since his modified procedure incorporates both classical and operant conditioning components. Typically the CS is a bell or a buzzer, with milk as the UCS being delivered from a feeding bottle upon ipsilateral head-turning. In the main the procedure fits the classical model since the infant is administered reinforcement on every trial whether or not he responds voluntarily. It is operant in nature firstly, in so far as the reinforcement is contingent upon the infant making a criterion head-turn, and secondly, since the time it takes the infant to make the head-turn after the onset of the buzzer (i.e. the response latency) effectively determines the interval between the CS and UCS. Papoušek (1967) obtained stable conditioned head-rotation (thirty degrees) responding at four to six weeks of age, discrimination between two stimuli at three months and reversal of this discrimination at four months. In both this and subsequent work, conditioning was demonstrated to be more rapid with increasing age and also to be positively related to the amount of conditioning which the infant had previously experienced. Siqueland and Lipsitt (1966), in a series of experiments adopting Papousek's mixed procedure, selectively strengthened tactually elicited head-turning responses (i.e. conditioned rooting behaviour to a buzzer CS). In one experiment a buzzer was paired with stroking of the infant's cheek, thereby eliciting ipsilateral head-turning which was contingently reinforced with a solution of dextrose. Ipsilateral head-turns to tactual stimulation of the cheek occur on about 30 per cent of occasions. Siqueland and Lipsitt's procedure increased this rate of head-turning to 80 per cent. Control infants who were not contingently reinforced were matched on the amount of nutrient, but this was delivered eight to ten seconds after offset of auditory and tactual stimulation. Under these circumstances no increase in the rate of head-turning occurred. Aside from demonstrating the mixed paradigm, this study also demonstrated the relative efficacy of the operant paradigm compared to the classical paradigm. Despite the pairing of the auditory and tactual stimulation, there was no evidence that the auditory CS elicited anticipatory head-turning, i.e. there was no classical conditioning to the buzzer, although only twenty trials were employed. Operant responding was, however, established in the course of the twenty trials.

This incidental finding by Siqueland and Lipsitt really highlights the view that Pavlovian tactics may be inappropriate and that in order to demonstrate early learning, investigators should resort to instrumental or operant techniques, that is, to make some reinforcing event contingent upon response emission (Kessen, 1963). Admittedly this is an extreme position and possibly the more realistic question would be 'To what types of environmental contingencies will the human infant respond more readily?' In operational terms which paradigm, classical, operant or otherwise, will be more or less effective in revealing learned changes in behaviour?

Operant conditioning

It has taken developmental psychologists some time to realize the potential of the operant paradigm in infant learning research. Brackbill's (1958) successful demonstration of social conditioning of the smiling response in four-month-old infants, followed by Rheingold, Gewirtz and Ross's (1959) operant conditioning of vocalization in three-and-a-half-month-old infants, marked the breakthrough of the operant paradigm in infancy research. In the Brackbill study, the effect of regular and intermittent social reinforcement on operant smiling was compared for a group of eight three-and-a-half- to four-and-a-half-month-old infants. Operant level of smiling (i.e. rate of smiling prior to the introduction of reinforcement) was established during a preceding baseline period. During the conditioning phase, the infant's smiling was contingently reinforced regularly or intermittently by a complex sequence of social acts (reciprocal smiling by the experimenter, soft speech, being picked up and patted, all of which took forty-five seconds to administer). During an extinction phase the experimenter simply stood motionless and expressionless at a distance from the infant as in the baseline period. Overall the procedure involved two or three sessions ranging from ten to sixty minutes spread over eight to sixteen days. Reliable increases in smiling occurred during conditioning, followed by decreased responding in the extinction phase. Moreover, a partial reinforcement effect emerged, with the intermittently reinforced group taking reliably longer to extinguish than the regularly reinforced group. Employing a similar procedure, Rheingold, Gewirtz and Ross found that this global social-vocal and tactile reinforcement contingent upon an infant's vocalizations increased the rate of vocalizations. Extinction procedures effectively diminished the response.

Both these studies have been criticized for not incorporating procedures to control for potential eliciting and arousal effects of the reinforcing stimulation, i.e. the very presence of a vocalizing adult may have served as an arouser or releaser of infant vocal behaviour. A further study by Weisberg (1963) replicated Rheingold, Gewirtz and Ross's study and incorporated non-contingent stimulation controls. Infants in a control group were presented with the same amount of stimulation as the experimental subjects. But, in the case of the control subjects, this stimulation was not related to their operant vocalizations, i.e. stimulation was non-contingent. Weisberg was thus able to separate out the eliciting effects of the reinforcement from the reinforcement effect itself, i.e. distinguish between *stimulus* and *operant* control of behaviour. In addition, this study evaluated the effect of social versus non-social reinforcement upon infant vocalization. The inclusion of non-contingent presentation of stimulation to a control group represented an important methodological innovation in infant operant research. More recently Routh (1969) and Todd and Palmer (1968) have again confirmed the social conditioning of vocal behaviour in infants. Todd and Palmer employed tape-recorded voices (adult absent) and non-taped voices (adult present) to demonstrate that human presence is not a necessary factor for infant vocal conditioning, but that it serves to enhance the reinforcing effectiveness of the human voice. Routh's study demonstrated conditioned differentiation of vocal responses in infants aged between two and two and a half months. In one group, all consonant sounding vocalizations were contingently socially reinforced, while in a second group all vowel sounds were reinforced. In a third group all vocalizations were reinforced. During the conditioning phase there was increased production of vocal responses generally including both 'consonants' and 'vowels' relative to vocal responsiveness during baseline. But, despite this general increase in vocal responsiveness, infants increased their production of the selectively reinforced class of vocal responses more than their production of the non-reinforced response class.

One of the enduring problems in infant operant research concerns the particular response class employed. Neuromuscular development greatly restricts the range of operants available and represents an overriding consideration especially if age comparisons in conditionability are being sought. It has been suggested that the 'delicacy' or 'maturity' of the response is a critical factor for successful conditioning (Watson, 1965). Watson points to the fact that two of the early studies which conspicuously failed to obtain conditioning employed 'gross motor' responses (Friedlander, 1961; Smith, Zwerg and Smith, 1963). Friedlander's study required the infant to reach and pull on a cord in order to produce contingent perceptual feedback. No increase in frequency of responding was observed during conditioning; however, this cord-pulling technique has since been successfully employed in a series of experiments with four- to eight-month-old infants (Millar, 1970). The studies of Smith, Zwerg and Smith probably represent the most discrepant failure to obtain operant conditioning in infants under twelve months. These investigators were concerned to investigate the infant's behavioural regulation of the stimulus properties of the environment. In one particular study, the infant was placed in a slowly rotating playpen and in order to maintain perceptual contact with a televised picture of the mother, a stranger or an imageless stimulus, he had to make gross transport movements in order to compensate for the rotation of the pen. On the basis of these data, Smith, Zwerg and Smith arrived at the somewhat discrepant conclusion that not until after twenty-two months did decisive changes take place in the infant's capacity for exercising control over the perceived visual environment. It appears, however, that this failure was largely attributable to the over elaborate experimental procedures and possibly to the remoteness of the contingency events rather than to the gross nature of the response systems used (Millar and Schaffer, 1973). However, despite the success with 'delicate' responses such as vocalizing and smiling and the early difficulties with 'gross' responses, it now appears that the 'delicacy' of the response is not the important consideration here. Successful conditioning with head-turning, a gross musculo-skeletal response even in neonates, largely discounts the 'delicacy' issue *per se*, and suggests rather that *response maturity* may be an important factor in early conditioning.

The importance of stimulus and response variables is probably accentuated in infancy research. Seligman (1971) has recently pointed out that a fundamental premise of *general process learning theory*, that all events are equally associable as espoused by Pavlov (1927) and Skinner (1938), is undoubtedly false. Instead Seligman conceptualizes a continuum of *preparedness*, such that an organism is prepared to associate certain stimulus–response contingencies, *unprepared* for some and *contraprepared* for others. The degree to which an organism is prepared to associate a particular set of contingent events is definable operationally in terms of the amount of input, e.g. number of learning trials required to achieve a given criterion of acquisition. For the most part, investigations of infant operant learning have examined arbitrarily related contingencies as opposed to natural contingencies in the infant's environment. There have, however, been notable exceptions. For example, the successful demonstrations of operant conditioning of head-turning (Siqueland, 1964; Siqueland and Lipsitt, 1966), even in neonates (Siqueland, 1968), may in part be attributable to the relative *preparedness* of the response complex employed in these studies, and the organism's relative *preparedness to associate* the stimulus and response components in the learning situation. The procedure adopted by Siqueland and Lipsitt (1966) involved three light strokes of the experimenter's finger moving vertically on the infant's left cheek starting from the corner of the mouth. This effectively elicits ipsilateral head-rotation (rooting reflex) on about 30 per cent of occasions. Reinforcement consisted of the administration of dextrose solution contingent upon criterion head-turns. In this situation the contingencies are far from arbitrary. In fact, they have unquestionable functional or ethological significance (Lipsitt, 1970).

Moreover, in terms of *preparedness*, conditioning procedures would be expected to be more successful where the procedure entails what for the infant is an already integrated pattern of responding, e.g. tactual stimulation of the face → head-turning → nutritive reinforcement. In these circumstances the infant's congenital response repertoire renders him more prepared or susceptible to environmental pressures with consequent response modification, than if more arbitrary contingencies had been employed.[5] In a further study, Siqueland (1968) took advantage of the functional significance of head-turning and demonstrated operant conditioning of ipsilateral head-turning using presentation of a non-nutritive nipple as reinforcement in neonates with a median age of eighty hours. On this occasion tactual stimulation of the face was omitted and the response was treated as a free-operant. However, the head-turning response has also been successfully employed in situations which have not involved sucking or food ingestion. Caron (1967) and Levison and Levison (1967) successfully conditioned operant head-turning to visual reinforcement in three- to three-and-a-half-month-old infants.

The sucking response provides another example of a deeply ingrained response system of critical ethological significance which has been successfully employed in operant research with infants. Sucking behaviour has been observed as early as the third postconceptual month and is thus likely to be relatively differentiated and mature at birth, although often some initial priming is required before it will run-off. Frequently observed non-nutritive sucking, i.e. sucking in the absence of food ingestion or associated food ingestion stimuli, provides an illustration of a highly prepared response system. It is not surprising, then, that sucking has been successfully employed as an operant across a range of nutritive and non-nutritive situations (Lipsitt, Kaye and Bosack, 1966; Sameroff, 1968; Siqueland and DeLucia, 1969). Lipsitt, Kaye and Bosack (1966) used a non-optimizing (a poor eliciter of sucking) intra-oral stimulus (quarter-

5. Foetal head-movements have been observed by the third gestational month and are fully functional at birth (Minkowski, 1928, as cited in Papoušek, 1967).

inch laboratory rubber tubing) and demonstrated that an initially low level of sucking on this non-optimal stimulus could in fact be reliably enhanced by the delivery of dextrose solution contingent upon sucking. A control group of infants which received the same amount of dextrose solution, but non-contingent upon the occurrence of sucking, revealed no significant change in their sucking behaviour. In a more sophisticated investigation, Sameroff (1968) demonstrated systematic changes in various parameters of the sucking response. An initial study capitalized upon the observation that the infant can obtain nutrient from a nipple by either of two responses: an *expression* component whereby the infant squeezes the nipple between his tongue and palate and a *suction* component which operates by the infant producing negative pressure in the mouth cavity thereby causing the flow of nutrient from the nipple into the mouth. By differentially reinforcing either the expression or suction component, Sameroff demonstrated that neonates of two to five days of age could in fact modify their sucking behaviour in order to maximize pay-off. That is, it was possible to strengthen selectively each sucking component by contingent reinforcement. Similarly, in a second study, when either high or low expression amplitude was required in order to obtain nutrient reinforcement, the infants altered their sucking performance accordingly. However, the findings from the Sameroff studies and the earlier study by Lipsitt, Kaye and Bosack are in certain respects problematic. Sameroff, partly on the grounds that the performance changes did not persist from the first to the second session, attributed the experimental effects largely to *adaptation* as opposed to learned behaviour changes. For the most part, Sameroff's conclusions are in line with the point made somewhat earlier by Kessen (1963) that it may well be inappropriate to consider all behaviour modification to be functionally related to reinforcement contingencies and that short-term behavioural phenomena, such as those obtained by Lipsitt, Kaye and Bosack, and Sameroff, might be more appropriately labelled *adaptation*.

The sucking response (non-nutritive) has also been employed as an operant outside the food ingestion situation. In an ingeniously devised study, Siqueland and DeLucia (1969) demonstrated operant conditioning of high amplitude sucking using conjugate visual feedback in four- and twelve-month-old infants. Conjugate reinforcement is a relatively recent operant technique in which there is a direct relationship between response rate and the magnitude and intensity of the reinforcement delivered. In one study, three groups of four-monthers were used providing baseline data, experimental and control data respectively. The experimental group (SR) was reinforced for criterion amplitude sucks with contingent presentation of projected visual stimuli. For the control group (SW) the emission of criterion amplitude sucks produced contingent discrete withdrawal of the visual feedback and moreover, each criterion suck delayed the discrete onset of the visual stimulation for five seconds. Coloured slides of geometric patterns, cartoon figures and human faces were used. While no differences were observed among the three groups during a baseline period, reliable differences in sucking behaviour occurred during the conditioning phase. The SR group revealed reliable acquisition and extinction effects. By contrast, no reliable changes occurred in the SW group. Thus, it can be seen from the Lipsitt, Kaye and Bosack, and the Siqueland and DeLucia studies that sucking behaviour can be modified apparently no less effectively in both nutritive and non-nutritive settings in accordance with environmental contingencies.

It would appear, therefore, that the sucking response can be employed as an operant across a range of situations in which the response is not necessarily functional in terms of food ingestion. This demonstrates quite clearly the infant's preparedness to associate this response system beyond the constraints of the feeding situation. While purely speculative, this would seem to suggest that the young infant's preparedness to associate (Seligman, 1971) certain stimulus response elements is more so dependent upon the preparedness of the response system than upon whether reinforcement is appropriate to the function of the response. Thus, except where the response is obviously irrelevant or incompatible to the demands of the situation, the organism's preparedness to associate certain stimulus–response elements may largely be reducible to the preparedness of the response system. Other things being equal, functionally or ethologically significant responses would be most readily associated with a wide range of stimuli (reinforcers) which are not incompatible with the response.

Investigating the acquisition process

From this review of the infant operant literature, it is apparent that most investigations can be described and classified as essentially demonstrative. By employing a range of responses, a diversity of reinforcing events and various age groups, investigators have made quite determined efforts, which for the most part have been successful, to demonstrate behavioural effects within the operant paradigm. But despite considerable success in demonstrating operant conditioning, even at the neonatal level, little attention has been directed specifically to the study of the actual acquisition process. Little in the way of definitive data exists on the critical parameters of learning in the infant. Demonstrating the infant's capacity to learn does not of itself identify the functional processes. As Horowitz has succinctly put it: 'It is not sufficient to demonstrate only that the infant is conditionable. This important step has been taken' (Horowitz, 1969, p. 90). What are the situational requirements necessary for the infant to conserve the response-feedback contingency in the operant paradigm? What processes determine how or when an event will be effective as a reinforcer? What are the defining *spatio-temporal* parameters for infant learning? Quite obviously, until considerably more is known about these process variables, the wide-ranging demonstrations of infant learning are of extremely limited value to an understanding of infant development.

Watson (1966) has speculatively proposed a computer-type analogy in an attempt to examine the operant acquisition process. Watson's core thesis proposes that the acquisition of operant behaviour necessitates a functional awareness of the response-feedback contingency. In terms of the computer analogy, the infant achieves this awareness through a hypothetical process of *contingency analysis*, defined as the infant's tendency to scan his memory records for the response output and stimulus input and to isolate the response which immediately preceded the occurrence of the reinforcing event. The model presumes that the infant is pre-programmed to analyse and remember sequential relationships between events. The model focuses attention on the elapsed time interval between one occurrence of the response-feedback contingency and the next emitted response. Watson argues that the infant's restricted memory span at this age constitutes an absolute overriding factor, i.e. unless the infant responds again within this critical time period he will be oblivious to the contingency. Basically, Watson is arguing that in infant learning 'the law of effect is dependent on the infant's memory span for contingency experiences' (Watson, 1967, p. 56). In a subsequent paper, Watson (1967) presented a retrospective analysis of data from two earlier studies which affords some supportive evidence for his model. These data broadly indicated that for infants of about three months of age the extent of their memory span for contingencies in an operant conditioning situation was of the order of five seconds. At most, however, in view of the *post hoc* nature of the analysis, these data can only be considered suggestive. The real contribution lies in the heuristic value of the model, for it represents a speculative initiative in attempting to go beyond the mere demonstration of conditioning phenomena to determine information-processing parameters of early learning.

Spatio-temporal parameters of early learning

Recently a series of investigations has been undertaken to examine the infant's capacity to integrate response and feedback components in an operant situation (Millar, 1970; Millar and Schaffer, 1972). Specifically these investigators were concerned with the spatio-temporal parameters in operant response acquisition in early infancy. In an initial experiment (Millar, 1970) employing a hand-pulling response and discrete audio-visual perceptual reinforcement, it was demonstrated that four- to eight-month-old infants could rapidly discriminate response-contingent from response non-contingent stimulation. When the feedback was programmed to be contingent upon cord-pulling, infants demonstrated reliable increases in responding, with the older infants (six to eight months) making more rapid and more marked gains than the younger infants (four to five months). By contrast, performance under non-contingent stimulation did not differ from an absolute control group which received no experimental stimulation throughout the seven-minute procedure. In a subsequent series of experiments with six- to eight-month-old infants, delayed reinforcement procedures were introduced. These experiments differed from Watson's interest in that, whereas he was concerned with the interval between one reinforced response and the next emitted response, the investigation by Millar examined the interval between response emission and the occurrence of reinforcement. Operationally these experiments were designed to reveal the point at which the infant could no longer discriminate between delayed reinforcement and non-contingent stimulation, i.e. the experimental procedures really attempted to determine the infant's span for contingency integration. One-, two- and three-second delay intervals were used. Infants were unable to discriminate reliably between response-contingent feedback when it was delayed by as little as three seconds and non-contingent stimulation. Reliable acquisition occurred under one-second and two-second delayed feedback, although performance under these conditions was significantly inferior to acquisition under immediate reinforcement (see Figure 1). The consistent effect of the three-second delay to disrupt acquisition completely is confirmed by the recent findings of Ramey and Ourth (1971) from a study of delayed reinforcement of vocalization rates in three-, six- and nine-month-old infants. Characteristic acquisition and extinction effects were demonstrated under a zero delay condition. However, performance levels under three-second and six-second delayed reinforcement did not differ from baseline performance. It has thus been possible to determine the average *span of integration* for three- to nine-month-old infants. The development of this *gap-bridging* behaviour, i.e. the extent to which it increases with age, is clearly of paramount importance for an understanding of the extent to which the infant is aware of his instrumental behaviour.

Millar and Schaffer (1972), capitalizing upon the infant's capacity to differentiate contingent from non-contingent stimulation, employed this paradigm to investigate the influence of spatially displaced feedback on the operant conditioning performance of six-, nine- and twelve-month-old infants. Infants sat facing a table-top on which were located three aluminium canisters, each incorporating a miniature loudspeaker and coloured lights. One of these canisters, the manipulandum, was fixed to the table-top directly in front of the infant and within easy touching distance. The manipulandum also provided audio-visual feedback for the 0° displacement condition; in this case there was no spatial separation of feedback from the response location. The two additional canisters were placed at a distance of fourteen inches from the infant and offset at 5° and 60° from his visual

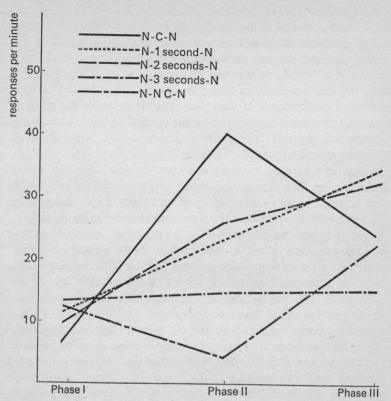

Figure 1 Mean number of responses for baseline (Phase 1) and Phases II and III. C represents a period of contingent feedback; 1 second, 2 seconds and 3 seconds represent periods of delayed feedback; and N C represents a period of matched non-contingent stimulation. Adapted from Millar (1970)

centre line, either to his left or right side. The dependent variable was frequency of discrete manipulative responding per sixty-second interval. A seven-minute procedure comprising a one-minute baseline period, during which operant level was determined, was followed immediately by two successive three-minute periods (Phases II and III). During Phase II, feedback was delivered at either the 0°, 5° or 60° position, contingent or non-contingent upon the infant touching the manipulandum (0° canister). Feedback involved a one-second pulse of audio-visual stimulation. The auditory component further ensured that infants oriented towards the source of the feedback. Phase III comprised a standard extinction period in that no feedback was administered to any of the conditions. Periods of contingent stimulation involved stimulus feedback contingent upon touching the manipulandum, whereas non-contingent stimulation involved presentation of a matched amount of stimulation on a predetermined random time schedule, in order to control for potential eliciting effects of the feedback. It was thus possible to assess the effect of spatially contiguous stimulation on the operant response acquisition.

Figure 2 presents curves for each age group across *baseline*, *conditioning* and *extinction* phases for contingent and non-contingent presentation of feedback stimuli at each of the three degrees of spatial displacement. Exposure to contingent feedback resulted in a highly significant increase in responding when feedback was delivered at $0°$, $5°$ and $60°$ locations for the nine- and twelve-month-old infants. Exposure to non-contingent stimulation produced reliable decrement of responsiveness. However, the six-month-old infants revealed a somewhat different acquisition pattern. Reliable increased responding occurred when contingent feedback was delivered at $0°$ and $5°$ displacements, but not at the $60°$ displacement. The six-month-old group's performance under $60°$ displaced feedback did not differ from their performance under the $60°$ non-contingent stimulation. While these findings are obviously limited to the range of displacements employed, they do show that spatial discontiguity *per se* need not be disruptive to learning. In the $5°$ condition, despite the distance separating the manipulandum and feedback, even the youngest infants found the task of integrating the response and feedback components to be no more difficult than in the $0°$ condition where the feedback emanated from the manipulandum itself. Moreover, they appeared to do so as effectively as the two older groups. The question to be asked was why the $60°$ displacement caused the six-month-old infants, in particular, such difficulty? In terms of sheer distance the $60°$ canister was no further away from the infant than the $5°$ canister. But, what did differentiate the $5°$ from the $60°$ condition was the relative visual accessibility of these two canisters. In the $5°$ condition, manipulandum and feedback source were sufficiently close within the infant's visual field to permit almost simultaneous attention to be paid to them, and under these conditions the task of relating the two stimuli made no greater demands on the infant's capacity to integrate

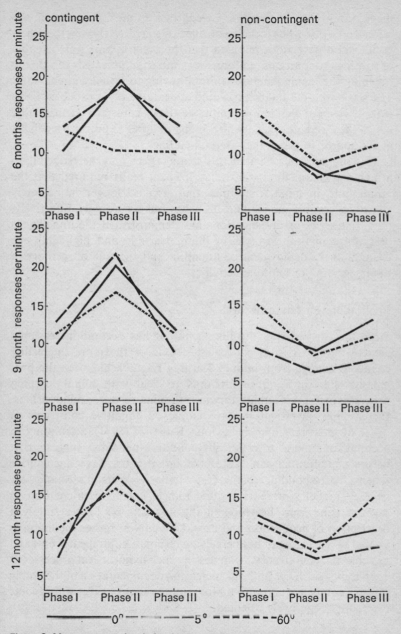

Figure 2 Mean response levels for three age groups across Phases I, II and III under contingent and non-contingent stimulation presented at 0°, 5° and 60° spatial displacement. Adapted from Millar and Schaffer (1973).

them than in the 0° condition. By contrast, in the 60° condition, the infant could not, while focusing on one canister, directly view the other. Incidental observations revealed that the older infants were capable of fixating the source of reinforcement and simultaneously repeatedly touching the manipulandum without having to visually attend to it. The six-month-old infants, it would appear, were not capable of this feat. They were unable to manipulate the 0° canister systematically, which they were not visually inspecting, in order to produce feedback at the source to which they were attending.

This suggests, in fact, that this spatial effect may be reducible to a memory factor, for the 60° displacement really required that the infant hold in mind a stimulus that was no longer immediately visually accessible and regulate his behaviour accordingly. Effectively, then, this series of investigations has demonstrated the importance of spatio-temporal variables in infant learning and highlights age changes in the deployment of attention and the role of memory in the integration of multiple activities.

Implications for future research

Since the early sixties, the human infant has become increasingly accredited with cognitive capacities. One of the more interesting trends to emerge from infancy learning research has been the progressive shift away from attempts to deal with infant learning processes in terms of straightforward stimulus–response relationships. Increasingly, investigators have employed cognitive constructs in order to interpret infant behaviour. Sameroff (1971), attempting to account for failures to classically condition neonates, suggests that before conditioning can 'take' the infant must have a cognitive schema corresponding to the CS. Similarly, Watson's *contingency analysis* model represents a quite radical cognitive orientation to operant behaviour. Learning in the infant is no longer simply a description of acquisition and extinction curves, rather the infant is viewed as perceiving or not perceiving response-contingent events and as achieving contingency awareness by such hypothetical processes as *contingency analysis*. With the increasing documentation of the young infant's competence, future infant research looks as if it will become even more cognitively oriented.

One of the more important issues to emerge from this review relates to Seligman's conceptualization of a dimension of preparedness to associate contingencies. Implicit in this idea is that instinctual responding and learning are really continuous, merely representing two points on a dimension. Recent findings suggest that such a conceptualization may be particularly relevant to the investigation of early learning in both the classical and operant conditioning paradigms. The principle of equivalence of associability, that is, that all events are equally associable, can hardly be said to fit the recent classical conditioning findings with young infants. Brackbill *et al.*'s failure to demonstrate cross-conditioning across somatically and autonomically regulated response systems represents the most telling evidence against this premise. Even in the operant context, investigators are becoming increasingly conscious of the importance of taking into account the ethological or functional significance of the response system for the organism. The implication being that those responses which are most deeply ingrained in the behavioural repertoire and which presumably have the greatest functional relevance for the organism will more readily be susceptible to environmental pressures and modification. Moreover, as the reviewed data demonstrate, these responses can be modified beyond the actual situation in which the response is *functional*. Thus parameters of the sucking response can be modified in both nutrient (functional) and non-nutrient (non-functional) reinforcing situations. Ease of establishing operant acquisition may well depend importantly upon the ontogenetic precocity of the response system employed. While largely speculative, it seems that the organism's preparedness to associate may in large part be dependent upon the preparedness of the response system in question, with the most prepared responses being modifiable over a wide range of reinforcing situations and less prepared responses being associable over a more limited range. However, certain insurmountable difficulties may be inherent in this situation, given, as appears to be the case, that ontogenetic precocity directly relates to the unconditioned occurrence of the response, e.g. sucking. Thus, by capitalizing upon the precocity of the congenital response repertoire, one may simply be moving towards the *instinctive responding* end of Seligman's dimension of *preparedness*.

So far the learning studies which have been examined have exclusively been concerned with the classical and operant conditioning paradigms. However, as previously noted, habituation phenomena, despite the fact that they involve decreased responsiveness, nevertheless broadly fit the general definition of learning (Lewis, Goldberg and Campbell, 1969; Thompson and Spencer, 1966). From a cognitive point of view, habituation is considered to indicate the retention of information about stimulation (Sokolov, 1963). In this respect it may represent the simplest and possibly earliest form of learning. The problem is now one of relating these diverse manifestations of *learned* behavioural change. Basically, this really raises the issue of a *taxonomy of learning tasks*. Do these several paradigms tap some general organismic capacity to modify behaviour, i.e. a *plasticity factor*; or do they represent quite specific and possibly unrelated capacities? The position is far from clear at the present time. The findings to date unequivocally demonstrate the relative facility with which operant conditioning can be established in the neonate when compared with the classical conditioning data. This finding by itself makes for obvious theoretical difficulties. Even in the case of habituation phenomena, some investigators have questioned whether habituation is possible in the neonate (Hutt *et al.*, 1968), although other investigators purport to have demonstrated clear-cut instances of the phenomenon (Engen, Lipsitt and Kaye, 1963; Friedman, Nagy and Carpenter, 1971) using visual and olfactory stimuli. Moreover, the extent to which the habituation phenomenon itself represents a unitary behavioural function which cuts across response modalities is far from clear-cut. For instance, are fast and slow habituators to visual stimuli respectively fast and slow habituators to stimuli presented in other modalities? Moreover, there are some incidental indications that there may be differential rates of habituation across different input modalities (Millar, 1970).

This issue of a taxonomy of learning tasks assumes even greater significance when it is considered in the context of individual differences in acquisition performance across classical, operant and habituation paradigms. Given that habituation, classical and operant conditioning represent instances of *learned* behaviour, to what extent is there individual consistency in performance? Lewis, Goldberg and Campbell (1969) have suggested that decremental rate in the habituation paradigm, in which a redundant stimulus is repeatedly presented, may provide a sensitive index of cognitive or information-processing efficiency. Furthermore, these investigators have demonstrated that habituation performance is related to and predictive of performance on cognitive tasks. In a study of infants aged forty-four months, it was found that response decrement was predictive of performance on concept formation and discrimination learning tasks. Moreover, it was observed for the same infants that response decrement as measured at twelve months of age was significantly correlated with Stanford-Binet IQ scores at forty-four months of age. In all cases, the greater the response decrement, the superior the performance on these cognitive tasks. To what extent is habituation predictive, if at all, of conditionability in the operant and classical paradigms? Is the infant who shows rapid response acquisition within operant situations likely to condition relatively more easily under classical circumstances? What range of stability exists over the early years in the young child's learning potential? What factors may facilitate or, probably more important, what factors may retard learning in the infant? These questions all point to highly researchable areas. For instance, Lewis and Goldberg (1969) have proposed that exposing an infant to a wide range of response-contingent events may produce a *generalized expectancy* in the child, such that the infant believes that his behaviour will be effective. In this context it is interesting to note that Lewis and Goldberg further found that in the case of three-month-old infants, the more contingent stimulation which the mother provided for the infant, the greater was the infant's response decrement to a repeated visual stimulus. Quite clearly the suggested interrelationships here are highly complex and developmental psychologists have really only just begun to delineate these.

Quite stable individual differences across a range of behaviours, e.g. sucking, general activity and reactivity, have been observed within the first days of life (Bell, 1960; Kessen, Williams and Williams, 1961). The question arises as to whether these apparently inherent differences relate in any systematic fashion to the infant's capacity to learn or condition. Papoušek's (1967) work has already provided some promising data on the stability of conditioning over the first six months. To what extent, however, does this relative stability extend into early childhood and even later? Specifically within the operant situation, there are usually quite marked individual differences in operant or baseline levels of responding. At the one extreme, some infants have quite low operant levels, while at the other extreme, some infants' operant levels are characterized by fast latency responding. To what extent do these variations represent consistent differences in response style or tempo for the infant, and more important, to what extent do these differences relate to conditionability? Provisional data suggest that these differences may be less critical than might otherwise be expected. In fact, in an analysis of operant acquisition data in which infants were dichotomized into high and low responders in terms of their baseline performance, it was found that operant level was not predictive of subsequent acquisition (Millar, unpublished findings). Rather, what may appear to be critical to successful operant acquisition, is the patterning of responses and this really refers back to Watson's *contingency awareness* model in which he emphasized the critical nature of the inter-response interval for learning to be possible.

Greater concern for individual differences, their antecedents, their consequences for conditionability and their correlates with other learning phenomena may well provide a fruitful avenue to the investigation of learning processes in the infant.

References

ABRAHAMSON, D., BRACKBILL, Y., CARPENTER, Y., and FITZGERALD, H. E. (1970), 'Interaction of stimulus and response in infant conditioning', *Psychosom. Med.*, vol. 32, pp. 319–25.

BARTOSHUK, A. K. (1962), 'Human neonatal cardiac acceleration to sound: habituation and dishabituation', *Percept. mot. Skills*, vol. 15, pp. 15–27.

BELL, R. Q. (1960), 'Relations between behaviour manifestations in the human neonate', *Child Devel.*, vol. 31, pp. 463–77.

BIJOU, S. W., and BAER, D. M. (1965), *Child Development: II. Universal Stage of Infancy*, Appleton-Century-Crofts.

BRACKBILL, Y. (1958), 'Extinction of the smiling response in infants as a function of reinforcement schedule', *Child Devel.*, vol. 29, pp. 115–24.

BRACKBILL, Y., and FITZGERALD, H. E. (1969), 'Development of the sensory analysers during infancy', in L. P. Lipsitt and H. W. Reese (eds.), *Advances in Child Development and Behavior*, vol. 4, Academic Press.

BRACKBILL, Y., FITZGERALD, H. E., and LINTZ, L. M. (1967), 'A developmental study of classical conditioning', *Mongr. Soc. Res. Child Devel.*, vol. 38, no. 8.

BRACKBILL, Y., LINTZ, L. M., and FITZGERALD, H. E. (1968), 'Differences in the autonomic and somatic conditioning of infants', *Psychosom. Med.*, vol. 30, pp. 193–201.

CARON, R. F. (1967), 'Visual reinforcement of head-turning in young infants', *J. exp. child Psychol.*, vol. 5, pp. 489–511.

CONNOLLY, K., and STRATTON, P. (1969), 'An exploration of some parameters affecting classical conditioning in the neonate', *Child Devel.*, vol. 40, pp. 431–41.

DISHER, D. R. (1934), 'The reactions of newborn infants to chemical stimuli administered nasally', *Ohio State Univ. Study*, no. 12, pp. 1–52, Ohio State University Press.

ENGEN, T., LIPSITT, L. P., and KAYE, H. (1963), 'Olfactory responses and adaptation in the human neonate', *J. comp. physiol. Psychol.*, vol. 56, pp. 73–7.

FITZGERALD, H. E. (1968), 'Autonomic pupillary reflex activity during early infancy and its relation to social and nonsocial visual stimulus', *J. exp. child Psychol.*, vol. 6, pp. 470–82.

FITZGERALD, H. E., and BRACKBILL, Y. (1968), 'Interstimulus interval in classical pupillary conditioning', *Psychol. Rep.*, vol. 23, pp. 369–70.

FITZGERALD, H. E., and PORGES, S. W. (1971), 'A decade of infant conditioning and learning research', *Merrill-Palmer Q. Behav. Devel.*, vol. 17, pp. 71–117.

FITZGERALD, H. E., LINTZ, L. M., BRACKBILL, Y., and ADAMS, G. (1967), 'Time perception and conditioning of an autonomic response in young infants', *Percept. mot. Skills*, vol. 24, pp. 479–86.

FREUD, S. (1905), 'Three contributions to a theory of sex', in A. A. Brill (trans. and ed.), *The Basic Writings of Sigmund Freud*, Modern Library, 1938.

FRIEDLANDER, B. Z. (1961), 'Automated measurement of differential operant performance in human infants', *Amer. Psychol.*, vol. 16, p. 350 (abstract).

FRIEDMAN, S., NAGY, A. N., and CARPENTER, G. C. (1971), 'Newborn attention: differential decrement to visual stimuli', *J. exp. child. Psychol.*, vol. 10, pp. 44–51.

GESELL, A. (1954), 'The ontogenesis of infant behavior', in L. Carmichael (ed.), *Manual of Child Psychology*, Wiley.

HOROWITZ, F. D. (1969), 'Learning, developmental research and individual differences', in L. P. Lipsitt and H. W. Reese (eds.), *Advances in Child Development and Behavior*, vol. 4, Academic Press.

HUTT, C., VON BERNUTH, H., LENARD, H. G., HUTT, S. J., and PRECHTL, H. F. R. (1968), 'Habituation in relation to state in the human neonate', *Nature*, vol. 220, pp. 618–20.

KASATKIN, N. I. (1948), *Early Conditioned Reflexes in the Ontogenesis of Man*, Mediz, Moscow (in Russian).

KAYE, H. (1965), 'The conditioned Babkin reflex in human newborns', *Psychonom. Sci.*, vol. 2, pp. 287–8.

KESSEN, W. (1963), 'Research in the psychological development of infants: an overview', *Merrill-Palmer Q. Behav. Devel.*, vol. 9, pp. 83–94.

KESSEN, W., WILLIAMS, E. J., and WILLIAMS, J. P. (1961), 'Selection and test of response measures in the study of the human newborn', *Child Devel.*, vol. 32, pp. 7–24.

LEVISON, C. A., and LEVISON, P. K. (1967), 'Operant conditioning of head-turning for visual reinforcement in three-month infants', *Psychonom. Sci.*, vol. 8, pp. 529-30.

LEWIS, M., and GOLDBERG, S. (1969), 'Perceptual-cognitive development in infancy: a generalized expectancy model as a function of the mother–infant interaction', *Merrill-Palmer Q. Behav. Devel.*, vol. 15, pp. 81-100.

LEWIS, M., GOLDBERG, S., and CAMPBELL, H. (1969), 'A developmental study of information processing within the first three years of life: response decrement to a redundant signal', *Mongr. Soc. Res. Child Devel.*, vol. 34, no. 9.

LIPSITT, L. P. (1963), 'Learning in the first year of life', in L. P. Lipsitt and C. C. Spiker (eds.), *Advances in Child Development and Behavior*, vol. 1, Academic Press.

LIPSITT, L. P. (1966), 'Learning processes of human newborns', *Merrill-Palmer Q. Behav. Devel.*, vol. 12, pp. 45-71.

LIPSITT, L. P. (1970), 'Developmental psychology', in A. Gilgen (ed.), *Contemporary Scientific Psychology*, Academic Press.

LIPSITT, L. P., and AMBROSE, J. A. (1967), 'A preliminary report of temporal conditioning to three types of neonatal stimulation', Paper presented at the meeting of the Society for Research in Child Development, New York, March.

LIPSITT, L. P., and KAYE, H. (1964), 'Conditioned sucking in the human newborn', *Psychonom. Sci.*, vol. 1, pp. 29-30.

LIPSITT, L. P., KAYE, H., and BOSACK, T. (1966), 'Enhancement of neonatal sucking through reinforcement', *J. exp. child Psychol.*, vol. 4, pp. 163-8.

MARQUIS, D. P. (1931), 'Can conditioned responses be established in the newborn infant?', *J. genet. Psychol.*, vol. 39, pp. 479-92.

MARQUIS, D. P. (1941), 'Learning in the neonate: the modification of behavior under three feeding schedules', *J. exp. Psychol.*, vol. 29, pp. 263-83.

MILLAR, W. S. (1970), 'Operant conditioning in early infancy', unpublished doctoral thesis, University of Strathclyde.

MILLAR, W. S., and SCHAFFER, H. R. (1972), 'The influence of spatially displaced feedback on infant operant conditioning', *J. exp. child Psychol.*, vol. 14, pp. 442-53.

MORGAN, J. J. B., and MORGAN, S. S. (1944), 'Infant learning as a developmental index', *J. genet. Psychol.*, vol. 65, pp. 281-9.

PAPOUŠEK, H. (1967), 'Experimental studies of appetitional behavior in human newborns and infants', in H. W. Stevenson, E. H. Hess and H. L. Rheingold (eds.), *Early Behavior: Comparative and Developmental Approaches*, Wiley.

PAVLOV, I. P. (1927), *Conditioned Reflexes*, Dover.

PEIPER, A. (1925), 'Sinnesempfindungen des Kindes vor seiner Geburt', *Monatsschrift für Kinderheilkunde*, vol. 29, pp. 236-41, as reported by LIPSITT (1963).

PIAGET, J. (1953), *The Origin of Intelligence in the Child*, Routledge & Kegan Paul.

RAMEY, C. T., and OURTH, L. L. (1971), 'Delayed reinforcement of vocalization rates of infants', *Child Devel.*, vol. 42, pp. 291-7.

RENDLE-SHORT, J. (1961), 'The puff test: an attempt to assess the intelligence of young children by use of a conditioned reflex', *Arch. Dis. Childhood*, vol. 36, pp. 50–57.

RHEINGOLD, H. L., GEWIRTZ, J. L., and ROSS, H. W. (1959), 'Social conditioning of vocalizations in the infant', *J. comp. physiol. Psychol.*, vol. 52, pp. 68–73.

ROUTH, D. K. (1969), 'Conditioning of vocal response differentiation in infants', *Devel. Psychol.*, vol. 1, pp. 219–26.

SAMEROFF, A. J. (1968), 'The components of sucking in the human newborn', *J. exp. child Psychol.*, vol. 6, pp. 607–23.

SAMEROFF, A. J. (1971), 'Can conditioned responses be established in the newborn infant?', *Devel. Psychol.*, vol. 5, pp. 1–12.

SELIGMAN, M. E. P. (1971), 'On the generality of the laws of learning', *Psychol. Rev.*, vol. 77, pp. 406–18.

SIQUELAND, E. R. (1964), 'Operant conditioning of head-turning in four-month infants', *Psychonom. Sci.*, vol. 1, pp. 223–4.

SIQUELAND, E. R. (1968), 'Reinforcement patterns and extinction in human newborns', *J. exp. child Psychol.*, vol. 6, pp. 431–42.

SIQUELAND, E. R., and DeLUCIA, C. A. (1969), 'Visual reinforcement of non-nutritive sucking in human infants', *Science*, vol. 165, pp. 1144–6.

SIQUELAND, E. R., and LIPSITT, L. P. (1966), 'Conditioned head-turning in human newborns', *J. exp. child Psychol.*, vol. 3, pp. 356–76.

SKINNER, B. F. (1938), *The Behavior of Organisms*, Appleton-Century-Crofts.

SMITH, K. U., ZWERG, C., and SMITH, N. J. (1963), 'Sensory-feedback analysis of infant control of the behavioral environment', *Percept. mot. Skills*, vol. 16, pp. 725–32.

SOKOLOV, Y. N. (1963), *Perception and the Conditioned Reflex*, Macmillan Co.

SONTAG, W. W., and WALLACE, R. F. (1934), 'A study of fetal activity: a preliminary report of the Fels Fund', *Amer. J. Dis. Children*, vol. 48, pp. 1050–57.

SPELT, D. K. (1948), 'The conditioning of the human fetus in utero', *J. exp. Psychol.*, vol. 38, pp. 375–6.

THOMPSON, R. F., and SPENCER, W. A. (1966), 'Habituation: a model phenomenon for the study of neuronal substrates of behavior', *Psychol. Rev.*, vol. 173, pp. 16–43.

TODD, G., and PALMER, B. (1968), 'Social reinforcement of infant babbling', *Child Devel.*, vol. 39, pp. 591–6.

USOL'TSEV, A. N., and TEREKOVA, N. T. (1958), 'Functional peculiarities of the skin temperature analysers in children during the first six months of life', *Pavlovian J. higher nerv. Activ.*, vol. 8, pp. 174–84.

WATSON, J. B. (1924), *Behaviorism*, Norton.

WATSON, J. S. (1965), 'Evidence of discriminative operant learning within thirty seconds by infants seven to twenty-six weeks of age', Paper presented at the Society for Research in Child Development, Minneapolis, March.

WATSON, J. S. (1966), 'The development and generalization of contingency analysis in early infancy: some hypotheses', *Merrill-Palmer Q. Behav. Devel.*, vol. 12, pp. 123–35.

W. Stuart Millar 83

WATSON, J. S. (1967), 'Memory and contingency analysis in infant development', *Merrill-Palmer Q. Behav. Devel.*, vol. 13, pp. 55–76.

WEISBERG, P. (1963), 'Social and non-social conditioning of infant vocalizations', *Child Devel.*, vol. 34, pp. 377–88.

WENGER, M. A. (1936), 'An investigation of conditioned responses in human infants', in M. A. Wenger, J. M. Smith, C. Hazard and O. C. Irwing (eds.), *Studies in Infant Behavior III*, University of Iowa Study in Child Welfare, vol. 12, no. 1, pp. 7–90.

WICKENS, D. D., and WICKENS, C. A. (1940), 'A study of conditioning in the neonate', *J. exp. Psychol.*, vol. 26, pp. 94–102.

Chapter 3
Ethological Methods
Peter K. Smith

Since the 1940s, 'ethology' has been used to describe the naturalistic observation and study of animal behaviour. A classic example is the work of Konrad Lorenz, whose observations of typical behaviour patterns in birds and fishes is familiar to many people through *King Solomon's Ring* (1952), as well as in more specialist publications. Lorenz – described as the 'founder of modern ethology' by Tinbergen (1963) – was in fact developing a tradition going back to Darwin. Darwin's theory of evolution, and his pioneering work in comparative psychology, *The Expression of the Emotions in Man and Animals* (1872), provided a stimulus for zoologists to observe and describe the behaviour of an animal species – just as previously they had observed and described its anatomy, for example – and to speculate on how such behaviours had evolved, and evolved differently in different species. This approach was pursued by zoologists such as Otto Heinroth in Germany, C. O. Whitman in the USA and Julian Huxley in England, at the turn of the century. By the late 1930s Lorenz had put the subject on a more systematic footing, and Lorenzian ethology, followed and developed by Tinbergen at Oxford and Thorpe at Cambridge, dominated the pre-war and early post-war work in Germany and England.

The ethologists put much emphasis on the observation and description of how an animal behaved in its natural habitat, and spent much time out in the field or in the forest observing them. They also had available an evolutionary perspective from which to appreciate *why* the animal behaved this way (i.e. what its survival value was), and why different but related species might have developed somewhat different behaviours in the different environments which they might inhabit. Lorenz (1941), for example, described the patterns of behaviour in a number of species of ducks and geese, and discussed how the variations in these patterns might have come about through natural selection. Tinbergen (1951) described the complex sequence of courtship and mating behaviour of the three-spined stickleback. He also succeeded in showing the function of less obvious components of the behaviour. The increasingly red colour of the red underparts of the male serves as a stimulus to attract the female; it also functions to prevent mating with the similar, black-coloured, ten-spined stickleback (reproductive isolation). After the eggs are laid, the fanning movements of the male, directing a current of water over the eggs with strong fin and tail movements, function to ventilate the eggs which require oxygen from the water. Experimental variation of the oxygen content of the water produced compensatory changes in fanning rate.

A recent and authoritative account of the history and present status of animal ethology is given by Tinbergen (1969). This kind of approach was very different from that common in animal psychology at the time, although both shared the same field of study – animal behaviour. Much work on animal psychology followed the behaviourist tradition so powerful in the USA during this period, and examined rather few species of animals (mostly rats and pigeons) in closely defined experimental situations (maze learning, Skinner box). A great deal of this work now seems rather sterile, in the absence of the more basic knowledge which the ethologists were obtaining; this is not to say that detailed experimental studies are not worthwhile, but rather that they are likely to be premature before the range of behaviours which a species shows and their function and survival value, are known to some extent.

The merging of ethology and comparative psychology

The explanatory framework of Lorenzian ethology relied heavily on concepts of pre-programmed or genetically determined aspects of behaviour typical to a species – fixed action patterns, innate releasing mechanisms, sign stimuli. Behaviour was considered as being energized by a small number of drives, and a 'hydraulic' model of motivation was used to explain 'displacement activities' and 'vacuum activities' (Lorenz, 1950). Most of these concepts have since been shown to be oversimplified even in the case of birds and fishes (on which most of the earlier ethological studies were made), and much more so for higher mammalian species (Hinde, 1959; Lehrman, 1953). Over the past two decades ethologists have been putting more emphasis on the effects of learning and environmental stimulation. At the same time, animal psychologists have been concerning themselves with a wider range of behaviours (such as maternal behaviour, play and exploration) and of species, and have become more sophisticated in considering how some behaviours may be readily changed by learning experiences (environmentally labile), whereas other behaviours of a species are more resistant to change (environmentally stable). Harlow's work on the development of maternal and play behaviours in rhesus monkeys is a good example of this. As a result, the earlier distinction between ethology and animal psychology is no longer very clear; although ethologists have retained a tradition of observational work, much research has moved on to relevant experimental investigations of particular aspects of behaviour. This trend is evident in journals such as *Behaviour* (first published 1948) and *Animal Behaviour* (first published 1953, but called *British Journal of Animal Behaviour* up to 1957), and in textbooks such as Hinde's *Animal Behaviour: A Synthesis of Ethology and Comparative Psychology* (1966).

Recent developments in ethology/comparative psychology

Besides the merging of ethology and comparative psychology, two other developments have become apparent in the last ten to fifteen years. One of these is the rapid (in fact exponential) growth of primate studies. Much information is now being gathered on the behaviour and group composition of monkeys and apes in their natural surroundings, of which Jane van Lawick-Goodall's observations on chimpanzees are only one example (1968). Such studies are supplemented by others on primates in captive but semi-natural surroundings, and in laboratory situations. Two specialist journals – *Primates* and *Folia Primatologica* – have been in publication since 1957 and 1963 respectively.

More recently still the most advanced and complex primate – man – is beginning to be tackled from an ethological viewpoint. The earlier ethologists often speculated on the relevance of animal studies to human behaviour, and psychoanalysts such as John Bowlby were influenced by the ideas of Lorenzian ethology as long ago as 1958 (Bowlby, 1958). It is perhaps only in the last five years, however, that there has been a substantive amount of work on human behaviour by a variety of workers appreciative of the benefits of a sophisticated ethological approach, evident in a number of articles, and in books such as those by Blurton Jones (1972a), Bowlby (1969), Eibl-Eibesfeldt (1970), Hutt and Hutt (1970a, 1970b) and McGrew (1972a). It is this area of 'human ethology' which has been presented and speculated on in a number of popular and semi-popular publications such as those of Ardrey (1961, 1967, 1970), Eibl-Eibesfeldt (1971), Hass (1970), Lorenz (1966), Morris (1967, 1969, 1971) and Tiger and Fox (1972). However, while one should not decry attempts to make the esoteric available to a wide audience, it should be made clear that 'human ethology' itself is still in its infancy. Many of the implications or conclusions in these popular works – for example on the 'innateness' of aggression, or on imprinting and homosexuality – rely mainly on analogy with some animal species, and are much more speculative than they are made out to be. Although much of the excitement of 'human ethology' is that it seems to hold promise of giving more insight into these and other important human problems, it will hopefully be apparent after reading this chapter that the major research tasks have only begun to be tackled.

To date, the major amount of research in the area of human ethology has been done on children. This is probably because children are often together in groups to be observed, often do not mind or do not notice that they are being observed, and in the early years do not 'fake' behaviours or become so devious in their motivations as adults. In general – and apart from looking at the significance of relatively stereotyped facial expressions and gestures – researchers in this area seem to have considered it most profitable to look first at the relatively less complex young of the species rather than at the adult. It is probable that, for example, aggressive and defensive behaviours (agonistic behaviours) may be relatively invariant in form at the age of three years, but that in adulthood the circumstances and expression of such behaviours will vary widely between different individuals and different cultures. Thus an answer to the sort of questions ethologists ask (what behaviours are specific to the species? how did these behaviours evolve in this and related species?) may well require an unusual degree of emphasis on the young of a species in which so much of behaviour is environmentally labile. (However, adult human behaviour is far from infinitely labile, and it may well be very important to know the more environmentally stable basis – the modified ground-plan of mammalian/primate behaviour – on which it is based, to arrive at many important and sensible conclusions in adult human psychology.)

It is the present state of 'child ethology' which will be discussed in the remaining sections of this chapter. Before this, however, the second main recent development in ethology must be mentioned. This is the widening of the scope of ethology to include what Crook (1970) calls 'social ethology' (Crook and Goss-Custard, 1972). Basically this is looking at group organizations and behaviours in much the same way that the ethologists traditionally looked at individual behaviours – seeing how they vary with the animal's environment (socio-ecology), what the survival value is in terms of population dynamics and mortality (socio-demography), how group behaviours are learned and cultural changes produced in the individual (social systems research). This is especially important in primates, where cultural differences between populations of a species living in different environments may be appreciable. It has been possible to discuss how differences in aspects of social organization (such as sex ratio, mother–infant relations, dominance relations) vary both within and between primate species such as baboons, in relation to ecological aspects (such as food availability and presence of predators).

A number of authors – for example Chance and Jolly (1970), Fox (1967), Reynolds (1968) and Tiger (1969) – have extended the data on primate social behaviour to consider the probable effects of environmental pressures on aspects of social structure in primitive man. It is also possible to see how human social organization varies across existing cultures – the traditional concern of social anthropology. Such knowledge can give greater insight into the survival value and environmental lability of, for example, the nature of mother–infant attachment, the development of sex differences, the forms of agonistic behaviour – all important issues in child psychology.

Thus, at present, research relevant to human ethology is scattered through journals on a variety of subject matters – psychology, zoology, sociology, human biology, physical anthropology and social anthropology at least. In so far as human ethology may be considered a coherent field of study then, different from human psychology, it is a growth area at the mutual boundaries of the above disciplines, with especial emphasis on observation of behaviour in natural surroundings, description of a wide range of behaviours in basic terms, and a wide (evolutionary) perspective on the development and function of these behaviours. This provides a 'new perspective' to child psychology.

Characteristics of an ethological approach to child behaviour

In considering what an ethological approach has to offer to the study of children's behaviour, then, it is important to realize that it is not so much an alternative to traditional child psychology as a widening of perspective of the area of study. Thus it would be futile to attempt to define 'child ethology'. However, the characteristics of ethology discussed above are those one would expect to find in ethological approaches to children's behaviour; in discussing their relevance below, it will be clear that there are differences from the traditional methods of child psychology. To what extent experimental child psychology suffers from the lack of an ethological perspective, and also to what extent an ethological approach can hope to be useful in areas such as language and thinking, are matters of contention. I will comment on the latter at the end of the chapter.

Observation of behaviour in natural surroundings

For the animal ethologist this has meant a period of watching an animal species, in order to get an understanding of the range of behaviours that are shown by different individuals, and the context in which they occur. By 'natural surroundings' is meant an approximation to the kind of environment in which the animal species has evolved, and to which its behavioural inclinations and capacities are adapted – what Bowlby (1969) calls the 'environment of evolutionary adaptedness'. If you observe chimpanzees in a cage in the zoo you will not observe them nest-building in trees, fishing for termites with roughly fashioned twigs, or hunting small mammals; instead you may observe stereotyped rocking, hair-pulling, and so on. If you wanted to understand a complex machine, you would want to see it working first before taking it apart and seeing what went wrong; similarly, the ethologist would say, we should see how an animal's behaviour functions within a natural environment (the only kind of environment likely to elicit a full range of adaptive behaviours) before applying experimental constraints or placing the animal in a grossly maladaptive environment. Premature use of the latter – for example operant conditioning of a pecking response in pigeons – may not tell us much about the quite different kinds of 'learning' pigeons show in, for instance, courtship or maternal behaviour; whereas experiment subsequent to observation can tell us a lot, for example experiments showing exactly what kinds of stimulus bring about the observed begging behaviour in the young herring gull chick (Tinbergen, 1951).

In the case of human children one is immediately faced with the question – what is a 'natural environment'? Is such a concept applicable? Even in primate species such as baboons, different populations may be adapted in different environments (such as forest or more open savannah). In man, cultural variations in behaviour patterns are much greater. Nevertheless there is probably a limited range of environments within which any primate, including man, can be said to be effectively adapted. From present behaviour patterns such as within-species aggression, population instability and resource exploitation, it does not appear that agricultural-industrial society at present is such an environment. Apart from the last 10,000 years or so, *homo sapiens* has evolved as a hunter-gatherer species; it is this period of about two million years that saw the change from *australopithecus* to *homo sapiens*, with corresponding deep-seated genetic changes in behavioural potentialities and proclivities. Such changes were brought about by natural selection pressures on individual and group behaviour, involving a complex interaction between (genetic) potentialities and (culturally) learned expression (Connolly, 1971). Although such pressures would have continued into the agriculturalist-industrialist phase of human history, this period was probably too short for many deep-seated (genetic) changes to have occurred, as opposed to less deep-seated (cultural) changes.

Thus man's environment of evolutionary adaptedness would seem to approximate to that which we may suppose characteristic of hunter-gatherers: mobile or semi-mobile groups of some twenty to a hundred individuals of all ages and sexes relatively open in character; semi-skilled use of a wide range of tools; subsisting on hunting, fishing and gathering activities, with some sexual division of labour; and practising food sharing; and in particular children would be (a) carried about and suckled (over a long weaning period) by the mother, (b) be in contact with a large number of other adults, and children of various ages, and (c) expected to acquire adult technology and language (Lee and DeVore, 1968). While in an industrial society we cannot hope to observe children in the kind of ecological and cultural environment characteristic of hunter-gatherers, it is worth bearing this in mind in considering the survival value of certain child behaviours (such as attachment behaviour – Bowlby, 1969), and in the biological naturalness of environments such as the home of a nuclear family, or a play group, where observational studies are usually carried out.

Description of a wide range of behaviours in basic terms

Rather than assume that he understands the significance of all the behaviours he may observe, the animal ethologist first describes them in mainly physical terms, i.e. the facial expressions, vocalizations, bodily postures and limb movements involved; by seeing which behaviours occur together, in what situations they occur, and what similar behaviours occur in related species, he then tries to reach conclusions as to their present function and evolutionary significance (survival value). Traditionally he is interested in 'species-specific' behaviours – those characteristic of most/all healthy members of a species (rather than of a few individuals), and different in varying degrees from corresponding behaviours in related species; these 'define' the species in behavioural terms, just as 'species-specific' physical characteristics define it in physical terms. In both cases it is species-specific characteristics that are useful in making generalizations about function and survival value (e.g. Lorenz's geese and Darwin's finches).

Again there are some objections to applying this approach to human children and adults. Firstly, haven't we as individuals observed sufficient human behaviour to make detailed observational studies superfluous? Secondly, can we realistically describe 'species-specific' behaviours in humans?

The answer to the first point is that 'common-sense' experience of behaviour does not give us sufficiently detailed knowledge; instead it will be based on terms such as 'anger', 'attachment', 'play', 'smiles', etc. Ainsworth (1964), for example, has described some thirteen patterns of mother–infant attachment behaviours – such as 'lifting arms in greeting' and 'approach through locomotion' – patterns which may share a common function but which typically appear at different ages, often do not occur together, and cannot usefully be lumped together as 'attachment' (except using the latter purely as a catalogue term to indicate an area of study). Grant (1969) has described eight kinds of smile; here the physical appearance of the behaviours are, at a very superficial level, similar; but the motivations are different – the 'upper smile' being used in greeting situations for example, the 'broad smile' in active physical play, the 'oblong smile' when some agonism is present (see Figures 1 to 4). It is detailed descriptions like these, also necessary if useful cross-cultural (or cross-species) comparisons are to be made, that were lacking in most earlier observational work in child psychology (Smith and Connolly, 1972).

It is already established that the behaviours mentioned above are present in several different cultures; other behaviours, such as infant babbling and many neonatal reflexes, are doubtless species-specific. The number of individual human behaviours which are environmentally stable enough to be unambiguously called species-specific may not be very large beyond the neonate stage; but although cultural variation is considerable, there is growing evidence that many kinds of human behaviour – such as non-verbal communication (e.g. gestures, facial expressions), social development (characteristic behaviours in attachment, exploration, play and aggression), and social organization (e.g. all-male groups, incest taboos) – have culture-invariant aspects or bases upon which cultural variations are imposed (Blurton Jones, 1972a; Hinde, 1972; Izard, 1971; Tiger and Fox, 1966). This is exactly analogous to human language, where the actual words spoken vary between cultures, but there is evidence for the existence of linguistic universals (such as basic grammatical structure,

Figure 1 Play face

Figure 2 Upper smile

Figure 3 Simple smile

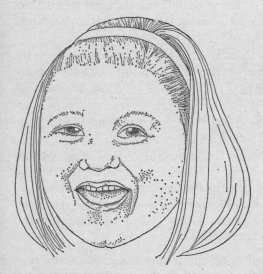

Figure 4 Broad smile

range of phonemes used) in the structure of all human languages, which are species-specific in the true sense of the word. Thus the use of the term species-specific in the human case seems realistic if we look at the universal aspects or 'deep structure' of behaviour, describe the cultural variations, and try and explain why these have occurred (i.e. what human adaptive potentialities are involved). It is then apparent that social ethology and cross-cultural studies have much to contribute to the possibilities of an ethological approach to child/human behaviour.

Wide (evolutionary) perspective on development and function

Ethologists have always emphasized that there are a number of ways in which we gain further insight into why an animal behaves in a certain way; in other words, if we ask 'why does an animal behave like this?' we can have various kinds of answers. Basically the answers can be either immediate or historical, and individual or species-relevant.

For example, if we ask why a young child shows a typical pattern of sleeping and waking, we have these possible kinds of answers:

1 Immediate individual – due to complex biochemical interactions occurring between midbrain and cortex, the organism is in a particular sleep state;

2 Historical individual – these kinds of interaction occur because the central nervous system has developed in a certain way since conception, with mutual influences of embryological processes, and environmental pressures (e.g. to sleep at certain times);

3 Immediate species – the function of sleep is (perhaps) to facilitate bodily and brain growth processes;

4 Historical species – this particular method of facilitating growth, and the relative amount and proportion of different (REM and NREM) sleep states, is (potentially) explicable as an evolutionary adaption made by a species with very great cortical learning capacity, on the basic sleep/activity regulating system of warm-blooded animals (Jouvet, 1967; Oswald, 1969).

Answers of types 1 and 2, dealing with causes or mechanisms of behaviour, are traditional in psychology. Answers of types 3 and 4, relating to function or survival value, have until recently been less common. There is of course another type of answer, much used in traditional psychology, namely, that of verbal report or introspective data (which for obvious reasons was not available to animal ethologists). In our example above, verbal reports or introspections as to when and why people sleep ('usually eight hours a night', 'when I'm tired') would obviously not be very useful in answering what might be considered the important questions. While I do not wish to launch into an extended discussion of the merits and demerits of observed behaviour as opposed to reported or described behaviour, it is I imagine clear that in many areas of human behaviour besides the sleep example quoted above, observational/descriptive research will be indispensable in helping to answer basic questions of the kinds outlined above.

Subsequent to observation/description, many kinds of more experimental investigation will be necessary. These investigations might involve manipulation of broad environmental characteristics, rigid control of stimulus input, investigation of individual differences (and age and sex differences) and physiological investigations. However, the point should be emphasized that, to be most useful, such studies should postdate observation and description of behaviour and preferably some preliminary structural analysis. Research into individual differences in sleep requirements would hardly be worthwhile if we had not previously observed and classified the different kinds of sleep states. Another example is language development in children; earlier work showing that four year olds had a so-much larger vocabulary of nouns and verbs than three year olds, or longer sentence length (McCarthy, 1954), is rather irrelevant to the current kinds of research interests in which, for example, development of primitive syntactic structures is being considered, on the basis of analyses prior to and concurrent with the research (McNeill, 1970). An ethologist would take a similar view with regard to areas such as socialization, aggression and attachment, for example. Observation and basic description are needed in order to free oneself of narrow culture-bound or discipline-bound assumptions, or use of global categories; on the other hand, some structural analysis of the observational data will greatly facilitate the ease with which subsequent comparative studies and experimental studies can be carried out.

These three defining characteristics of an ethological approach are not independent but interrelated. Before discussing in more detail recent research on children to which these characteristics apply, I will give an example – of a particular kind of behaviour – to show this interrelatedness.

Rough-and-tumble play: a paradigm for the ethological approach

The first description in any detail of the rough-and-tumble play of young children was published by Blurton Jones (1967). Prior to this, this quite prominent kind of behaviour had been virtually ignored in literature on child behaviour and development (Smith and Connolly, 1972). Blurton Jones noted his observations of this and other behaviours during the course of watching preschool children in a nursery school; an example of the use of direct observation without preconceptions as to what behaviours should be recorded (or at least less narrow preconceptions – Blurton Jones was aware of descriptions of rough-and-tumble play in rhesus monkeys).

Rough-and-tumble play in children can take a variety of forms and a comprehensive description is still not available. Apart from a recent study on Bushmen children, the only systematic studies have been made on English preschool children, in nurseries or play groups. These latter do not provide information on rough-and-tumble play between preschool and older children (or adults), which undoubtedly occurs and might have been prevalent in hunter-gatherer groups of children. The following description refers to three and four year olds in England.

This kind of behaviour takes its name from a cluster of behaviours involving wrestling and tumbling about, rolling over, an open-handed arm beat at another child (usually without contact), rapidly jumping up and down with legs together and arms flapping up and down, and open-mouthed or broad smile often with squealing or chuckling (see Figures 5 to 8). However, there are other clusters of behaviours which seem to be partially associated with these (i.e. may precede or follow them) and which are usually considered as rough-and-tumble play. One is chasing and fleeing – one child running around chasing another, who often glances back; both children often laughing or squealing; sometimes the fleeing child turns round and becomes the

Figure 5 Standing grapple

Figure 6 Kneeling grapple

chaser. A variant of this is group running – here anything from two to six or eight children may run around, usually in a circle, often fairly equally spaced and often laughing; reversals seem to be rather rare here (see Figure 9). Other children may be attracted to join in the running, meanwhile some in the running may drop out, but the activity may continue for some minutes.

More complex forms of rough-and-tumble play (i.e. which seem to occur with older and more socially experienced children) involve objects. In a playgroup at Sheffield, I have several times observed a 'group chair push', where the group running pattern is adapted, each child pushing a chair around in front of him (a very noisy experience!). Shooting games may develop from the basic patterns (wrestling, chasing, running), involving a wooden block, drumstick, or in the absence of these, fingers, as an imaginary gun; 'banging' or 'shooting' play noises are made and the arm holding the object is extended at another child, sometimes slightly upward (a similar position to the open-handed arm beat – sometimes beating movements occur with

Figure 7 Tumble

the shooting). Chasing games may be done on tricycles, with perhaps several children on tricycles pursuing each other or another child who is crawling or rolling on the floor pretending to be a wild animal or monster. A variant of this I have observed involves a number of children crawling on all fours, making animal noises and 'walking on' wooden blocks held in their hands. With these later forms imaginative role-playing is often involved, such as cowboys and indians, hunting an animal, pretending to be a monster.

These forms of 'play-fighting' or 'play-hunting' are sometimes confused by nursery or playgroup staff with actual aggressive behaviour – especially the more basic behaviours of wrestling, chasing, beating. However, motivational analysis shows it to be fairly clearly distinct. This can be shown using the three methods traditionally used by ethologists (Tinbergen, 1959) – seeing which behaviours are associated together in time (temporal analysis); seeing in what context the behaviours occur; what the result is (situation analysis); and comparing the behaviours to those which occur in other contexts and other species (form analysis).

Figure 8 Roll over

Blurton Jones (1972a) used principal component analysis on data recording which behaviours occurred together in five-minute periods, in nursery-school children in London. He obtained a component linking together open-mouthed smile, run, jumps, hit at (or open beat) and wrestle. This was quite distinct from another component of aggressive behaviours such as pinch, bite, kick, slap, punch, throw, grab. Smith (1973) used hierarchical cluster analysis on data recording occurrence of behaviours together in half-minute periods, in day-nursery children in Sheffield. He obtained two related clusters of behaviours; one of laugh, smile, run, and chase/flee; another of wrestle/tumble, crawl, lie, play noise. These two clusters were also loosely associated with other behaviours such as climbing, sliding, swinging, jumping or hopping. All these behaviours linked to form one hierarchical cluster, distinct from other clusters of aggressive behaviours, isolate behaviours, and stationary object-oriented play.

The situations in which rough-and-tumble behaviours are observed are generally distinct from those in which aggressive behaviours are observed – usually property fights or defence of territory. Although

Figure 9 Group running

the form of some behaviours (e.g. beat, wrestle, flee) seem very similar to analogous behaviours in aggressive situations (film analysis will be necessary for clarification here), others, especially the open-mouth smile, laugh or squeal, and jumps, occur only in obviously friendly situations. A lower intensity open-mouthed smile, and laugh or chuckle, is often associated with conversational play with objects at tables; becoming higher intensity as excitement increases (e.g. saying 'naughty' things to each other; rocking higher in the rocking-boat). Sometimes a child will jump up and down, squealing and arms flapping, while just watching something else exciting going on.

Blurton Jones (1967) suggested that laugh and jumps serve as specific signals ('meta-communications') indicating the non-aggressive nature of rough-and-tumble play. It does sometimes happen that rough-and-tumble behaviours are apparently confused by a child with aggressive behaviours, or vice versa. Sometimes a child is frightened of joining in a rough-and-tumble; or he may react aggressively to a very rough play invitation. Conversely, a child may interpret what the observer interprets as aggressive behaviour (from watching the prior behaviour sequence leading to this) as a play invitation, and attempt to continue rough-and-tumble play, running, jumping or squealing.

It may be that these children who fail to distinguish and react appropriately to rough-and-tumble and aggressive behaviours have had inadequate peer interactions, and either fail to understand the motivational signals, or are too anxious in the nursery situation to join in; or if they try and join in, their play invitations are unintentionally aggressive, and are frequently misunderstood by other children. Smith and Connolly (1972) found a high correlation of laughing and rough-and-tumble play with length of nursery experience, and McGrew (1972b) found frequency of running to increase from a low baseline level when a child was introduced to a new nursery group. Blurton Jones (1967) suggested that there might be a critical period for the development of rough-and-tumble play ending before three years; I personally doubt this, as I have observed a very considerable increase in frequency of the patterns described amongst later three and four year olds; and also three year olds who responded inappropriately on introduction to the group but who subsequently acquired more appropriate behaviours. (However, this does not mean the adjustment was easy; and they may have had some previous experience – with peers or adults.) The situation for five year olds might be different, and this could be a fruitful area in which to examine effects of playgroup or nursery experience. It would also be useful to know more about the earlier (developmental) behaviours preceding these rough-and-tumble patterns; Konner (1972) has described 'gentle-and-tumble' behaviours (gross body movements observed in interactions between under-twos) and also describes the origin of chase/flee behaviours in approach/withdrawal play initiated by an adult to whom the child is attached. Longitudinal studies will be needed to make substantial progress here.

There are important individual differences in children which seem to be relatively unrelated to developmental effects of age or nursery experience. Some older children will rarely or never join in rough-and-tumble play, but appear otherwise quite sociable and able to hold their own in dominance encounters. There is also a sex difference, rough-and-tumble behaviours being more frequent with boys. This difference is more marked for four year olds than three year olds, and also perhaps for contact behaviours (wrestle/tumble) than for non-contact behaviours (chase/flee, group running). It is interesting to compare individual differences with age and sex differences. Are boys who show little rough-and-tumble more like girls in other respects, for example? The difference between children who prefer physically active behaviours and those who prefer less active play, more often with toys, seems to be a very basic one; however there is limited evidence from principal component analysis that sex differences may form an approximately orthogonal dimension to this (Blurton Jones, 1972b; Smith, 1973; Smith and Connolly, 1972).

The frequency with which rough-and-tumble occurs is also affected by environmental variables. McGrew (1972a) found more running and laughing both when a group of children had more space to play in, and also when group size in a given space was decreased from twenty to ten. Smith and Connolly (1972) found more of these behaviours outdoors (more space and less toys) than indoors. Some observations of a playgroup for short periods in a room without toys showed a very high incidence of group running and tumbling about. Smith (1972) also found some evidence for an interaction of sex difference with these environmental variables, the sex difference being greater indoors than outdoors. These are important considerations when interpreting the results of cross-cultural studies.

The only relevant cross-cultural study to date is that by Blurton Jones and Konner (1973) on London and Bushmen children. The study is described in more detail later. Similar behaviours were observed in each culture. Quantitative observations of three to six year olds showed a greater frequency of rough-and-tumble by boys than girls in London, but a non-significant sex difference in the Bushmen children; Bushmen girls scored very much higher than London girls. This would indicate perhaps some cultural inhibition of rough-and-tumble behaviours in the London (middle-class) girls. However, before jumping to conclusions about cultural differences, it should be born in mind that (a) variations in physical environment are probably important, and (b) the evidence for the nature and magnitude of the sex difference in English children over a number of studies is not entirely consistent (Blurton Jones, 1972b; Smith, 1972).

Play fighting and hunting occurs in the young of many mammals. Behaviours similar to rough-and-tumble in human children seem to characterize most of the social play of young primates (Loizos, 1967). Van Hooff (1972) has carried out a motivational analysis of chimpanzee behaviours and found a cluster relating relaxed open-mouth expression to boisterous wrestling, pulling and locomotory movements. He has also argued that the relaxed open-mouth of chimpanzees is a direct homologue of the open-mouth laugh/smile of humans. Loizos suggested that this 'play face' served as a metacommunication in chimpanzees, but Lawick-Goodall (1968) usually observed appearance of a play face *after* a play interaction had commenced (however the 'play walk' may serve as a metacommunication). Social play was observed mostly between infants, but also between infants and juveniles and adults. (She also saw occasional inter-specific play between chimpanzees and baboons.)

Laboratory studies of rhesus monkeys (Harlow, 1969; Young, Goy and Phoenix, 1964) have shown that contact rough-and-tumble especially is very much more frequent in male infants than females; however, two pseudohermaphroditic female rhesus monkeys (whose mothers have been injected with a male sex hormone, testosterone, during pregnancy) engaged in rough-and-tumble much more frequently than two untreated controls. For normal infants, the Harlows have described the development of contact (wrestle, roll, pull, bite) and non-contact (chase, flee) social play. With rhesus, too, inanimate objects are often incorporated in the play sequences. With increasing age, the two patterns intermix and become more violent, with aggressive play and dominance relations appearing at the end of the first year.

Experiments on rhesus infants reared alone with their mothers have shown that mother–infant interaction by itself is inadequate to ensure adjustment when the infant later joins a larger group; in the absence of earlier peer–peer interaction, later interactions were aggressive or fearful rather than playful.

To a lesser extent, the relative lack of peer–peer interaction suffered by many young children in Western societies may be responsible for producing timid children who cannot join in rough social play. While the long-term effects of this are not known, it is clear that for some children their degree of timidity will continue to be a handicap at school. It is interesting to speculate that a more appropriate 'pacing' of social stimulation (Sackett, 1965) may be helpful for such children – for example putting them in a group with younger children, the method Suomi and Harlow used in rehabilitating socially deprived rhesus monkeys (Suomi and Harlow, 1972).

While social experience is clearly established as one important factor in the development of rough-and-tumble play in the individual, it is probable that hormone level, or physiological development influenced by hormonal level, may be a factor in sex differences, as in rhesus monkeys. Individual differences in socially experienced children might be related to this – if so, one might expect co-variance with other sex-related differences. The immediate causation of rough-and-tumble play may be connected with arousal level. Mason (1965) produced evidence that in chimpanzees this kind of play served to increase the arousal state of the animal (whereas activities such as clinging and sucking tended to reduce it). It is very likely that in children, also, this kind of play serves to raise or maintain level of arousal at an appropriate level. This is a partial explanation in terms of a mechanism in the individual. The evolutionary significance of rough-and-tumble play probably relates to practice for adult activities, in this case hunting or fighting – compare how kittens will play at stalking and catching. Loizos (1967) criticizes the view that play is practice for adult activities, since practice itself would be sufficient, and adults play as well as children. However this may be confusing explanation in terms of the individual mechanism with that in terms of species survival. The adult activities of the higher mammals are very varied and it is difficult to see that stereotyped practice would be an efficient way of learning them; the very varied play activities of the higher mammals tend to continue into adult life (often with lesser frequency after dominance relations are established), but this is probably a matter of individual mechanism rather than survival value.

As pointed out by Washburn and Lancaster (1968), the skills of hunting and fighting in children are 'easily learned, satisfying; and have been socially rewarded in most cultures'. Konner (1972) reports that he has seen behaviours typical of rough-and-tumble in Bushmen children when they hunt insects or small animals. Even if the rough-and-tumble play in most primates or mammals functions more in the context of learning dominance relations, in human children (where it seems more distinct from real fighting than in rhesus monkeys, for example) it would seem that the forms it takes, including the group running described earlier, are such as to provide practice for adult hunting activities. A sex difference in rough-and-tumble might reflect, via cultural or genetic/hormonal means, a sex difference in the hunting and gathering roles in paleolithic communities, or the sex division of roles in modern societies.

One result of increasing sex differentiation in social (rough-and-tumble) play in primates with age seems to be increasing segregation of the sexes in social activities (in the latency period in human children). This period often comes to an end when the juvenile acquires a definite status position in adult society; Tiger (1969) has suggested that all-male groups are a characteristic feature of primate and human societies, and this male–male bonding could be facilitated by sexual segregation in the juvenile stage.

A fuller understanding of the causation and function of rough-and-tumble play will await further longitudinal observations of its development and characteristics, as well as wider cross-cultural studies. However, the above discussion will, I hope, give some context to the rather theoretical arguments given earlier.

The present state of the contribution of an ethological approach to child behaviour

The remainder of this chapter will review what applications the ethological approach has had so far in studying children. Topics dealt with in other chapters in this volume (attachment, exploration, language) will only be dealt with briefly. I shall try to convey the 'feel' of the area by describing two recent research projects in some detail; this will also perhaps give some idea of problems facing research of this kind. In the concluding section I shall discuss the potentialities and limitations of the ethological approach.

Kinds of environments in which behaviour has been observed

Most ethologically oriented studies of infants under one year have been made with the infant in the presence of the mother (and/or occasionally a stranger), either at home or in a laboratory or hospital room. A few studies of infants over one year have been made observing mother and infant outdoors, in a large area or park (Anderson, 1972; Rheingold and Eckerman, 1970); in general few studies are available on the age range fifteen to thirty months. The large number of studies of preschool children (roughly thirty to sixty months) have almost all been made in nursery schools or day nurseries. Above five years of age there are again few relevant studies; Esser (1968) studied six- to ten-year-old psychiatrically hospitalized boys in New York; Reynolds and Guest (unpublished) are currently observing behaviour of six to seven year olds in an English primary school.

This limitation of the kinds of situation observed is no doubt due to ease of making observations, and the kinds of behaviours researchers have been especially interested in (mother–infant attachment behaviours in infants, peer–peer interactions in preschoolers); also the increasing complexity of behaviour in older children. Nevertheless, this is only excusable bearing in mind how recently the ethological approach has been taken up. More studies are needed of, for example, peer–peer interaction below thirty months, father–infant interaction (e.g. Ban and Lewis, 1971), and primary-school children. It is worth bearing in mind, even so, that none of these situations corresponds to that in which young children were probably reared in the environment of evolutionary adaptedness (i.e. of hunter-gatherers) – where the young child probably encountered more frequently a wider range of other children of differing ages, or relatives, and, perhaps, relative strangers to the group.

Kinds of behaviour categories described and used; behaviour dictionaries

The kinds of behavioural categories used by ethologists can be of two kinds – those defined in physical terms and those defined in goal-oriented terms. Behaviours defined in physical terms can be considered the most basic; definition is in terms of the muscles involved, intensity and duration of movement. Examples of behaviours defined in this way are: open-mouthed smile, scratch head, cross legs, kneel up. On the other hand, behaviours such as approach adult, press lever, give object, are defined at least partly in terms of what the behaviour achieves.

Ideally, perhaps, the ethologist hopes to bring all description of behaviour down to physical terms. We have already seen how categories such as 'shows attachment' are so motivationally complex as to be of little value, and how the ethologist tries to lay bare the basis on which we make such judgements – the unconscious or semiconscious criteria we use for saying a child 'shows attachment' for example – and develop finer, more useful and more reliable ways of describing and analysing attachment behaviour. The present state of research into attachment behaviour has justified this approach. It is still an open question, however, how far this should be taken. A category such as 'approach mother' is on a more basic level than 'shows attachment behaviour' but is still complex and assumes motivational interpretation on the part of the observer. It could include walking, running, hopping or crawling up to mother, coming slowly or quickly, etc.; on the other hand, one would not normally include a sequence where a child came closer to the mother and stood near her, but only (apparently) because he wanted to pick up an object off the table she was sitting at. It is virtually impossible to justify the omission of this sequence from 'approach mother' by defining the latter in more physical terms, since the criteria we use are so complex; on the other hand, if we include it as 'approach mother' then this category is likely to be less useful, since it confuses what we are pretty sure are motivationally distinct behaviours.

Thus while all ethologists have attempted to be as precise as possible in defining the behaviours they observed, there is usually some degree of compromise between physical and goal-oriented definitions. Researchers concerned with particular problems or situations have tended more towards the latter, but often specifying in considerable detail, e.g. walk up to, run up to, or describing the typical pattern. For example:

'arms up to mother'
the child holds its arms up rather straight, slightly in front of the head–body plane, and usually simultaneously looks at mother (Blurton Jones and Leach, 1972).

'try to keep toy'
in response to another child trying to take a toy, holding on to the toy and/or following the child who has taken it, trying to get it back (Smith and Connolly, 1972).

However, attempts have also been made – especially for preschool children – to produce a comprehensive list of behaviours defined in physical terms. Those published to date are by Blurton Jones (1971), Brannigan and Humphries (1972), Grant (1969), Leach (1972) and McGrew (1970, 1972a). Grant published a list of 118 behaviours, based mainly but not entirely on observations of children. Sixty-two of these were facial expressions and head movements; the remainder comprised twenty-seven limb movements, twenty body and loco-motory movements, six kinds of vocalization and three kinds of autonomic response. McGrew described 111 motor patterns, of the head, hand, limbs and body (postural and locomotory). Blurton Jones has gone into great detail in describing the various muscle movements entering into facial expression, discussing the various positions and movements of mouth, lips, teeth, tongue, eyes, eye-brows, etc. and the combinations in which they tend to occur. Leach has ninety-six different units, including motor patterns, facial expressions and vocalizations. Brannigan and Humphries list 136 behaviour elements, mainly of facial expression and limb movements.

The very detailed nature of these definitions is shown by two examples:

'place'
to move an object to a particular location with a single continuous movement of the arms and trunk, usually in a horizontal direction, then downwards (McGrew, 1970).

'twist mouth'
an asymmetrical unit in which the lips are pressed together and slightly protruded centrally, one corner of the mouth being brought in towards the midline, the other corner being drawn back (Brannigan and Humphries, 1972).

These lists of behaviours are not intended to compete with one another. Although there are some differences in fineness of description, in general there is a considerable amount of agreement between these authors as to which are the basic behaviour units, especially as far as facial expression is concerned. The eventual aim would be to compile an 'ethogram' or 'behaviour dictionary' for the child/ human – a complete list of behaviour units into which more complex behaviours could be broken down.

It is obvious that even if agreement is reached on such a list, the total number of such behaviour units will be very large; this means a correspondingly large task in actually using such detailed units to study child (or human) behaviour. In fact to date there is no published research fully utilizing as many as 100 behaviour units. However it is possible to build up more complex categories from behaviour units – seeing which kinds of behaviour units tend to occur together, and in what order. So far the only attempts at this kind of motivational analysis are by Blurton Jones (1967, 1972b), Grant (1968) and Smith (1973). Grant used thirty-six of his behaviour units and looked at how likely it was that one unit would follow another one in an interview situation (adults, not children). From this he drew a 'flow diagram' for these behaviours, and found four major groups of units which he interpreted as 'contact', 'relaxation', 'assertion' and 'flight'. Blurton Jones and Smith have both carried out analyses on preschool children in nurseries, using categories which were more comprehensive in the range of activities covered, but sometimes less basic than those used by Grant. Blurton Jones used factor analysis on thirty-one behaviours, seeing which behaviours occurred most often together in five-minute periods. He obtained four main factors of 'rough-and-tumble', 'work', 'aggression' and 'social'. Smith used hierarchical cluster analysis on thirty-seven behaviours, seeing which behaviours tended to occur together in half-minute periods. In this case the number of clusters depends on how high up the 'tree' one goes. Four main clusters were obtained, of active play without toys (contact play, non-contact play, play with apparatus), stationary play (usually with objects), agonistic behaviour (aggressive, submissive) and dependency (crying, sucking, behaviour oriented to nursery nurse). Despite the different lists of categories, there is a fair measure of agreement between these two independent studies. It should be emphasized that these more complex groupings or clusters obtained do not have the disadvantages of complex behaviours described earlier, since the behaviour units of which they are comprised are known (however in neither of these two studies was the duration or sequence of behaviour units considered); but larger groupings may be more useful and manageable in many research problems.

Besides describing units or the clusters which they may be grouped into, it is also necessary to interpret their significance. This can be done by situation and form analysis, as well as temporal analysis. A good example here is the analysis by van Hooff (1972) of human smiling. Van Hooff suggests that most smiles are gradations along two independent dimensions, the extremes of which are the wide-mouth laugh and the upper smile; the former expresses playfulness, the latter is affinative and seen for example in greeting situations. The wide-mouth laugh or play face has already been discussed in connection with rough-and-tumble play. The upper smile or broad smile may partly derive from the oblong mouth or bared teeth seen, for example, when a submissive individual is threatened by a dominant one (perhaps an intention bite) – thus there is an element of appeasement, or emphasis of non-hostility, in this kind of smile. Van Hooff bases his analysis on a comparative study of smiling in primates, their form and the situations in which they occur. For alternative discussions see Andrew (1963; primates) and Brannigan and Humphries (1972; children).

Much of the subject matter in this section will be covered in other chapters in this volume (attachment, exploration), so discussion will be brief and will emphasize the ethological aspects of the research described.

A very detailed study of mother–infant interaction in the first weeks of life is being carried out by Richards and his co-workers at Cambridge (Richards and Bernal, 1971). Richards puts considerable emphasis on detailed description of the interactions between mother and infant, and also on collecting sociological data in order to put the behaviour of the group which he is studying in adequate perspective. His published data so far have interrelated behavioural measures (such as 'talk to infant', 'time nipple in mouth') to breast or bottle-feeding, and sociological measures such as father's occupation, intended family size, etc.

Ainsworth and her co-workers at Johns Hopkins University are carrying out a longitudinal study on the development of mother–infant interaction in the first year of life. They emphasize that 'attachment' is not a unitary concept, but can have many age-varying, partially independent measures (e.g. separation anxiety, following, greeting, fear of strangers). Their observational data are based on home visits, and an experimental test situation (the 'strange situation'). Although based on direct observation of behaviour, much of the subsequent analysis is carried out using ratings (e.g. of mother's availability, amount of physical contact) on narrative records of the observation. Recent research by this group (Ainsworth, Bell and Stayton, 1972; Stayton, Hogan and Ainsworth, 1971) suggests that sensitive mothering will in itself lead to a secure mother–infant attachment and infant obedience. For example, a mother who responds promptly and consistently to her baby crying during the first six months, is likely to have a baby who cries *less* during the second six months; the unresponsive mother will have a baby who cries more. The frequency with which babies at nine to twelve months obey the mother's verbal commands correlates more with the general sensitivity of the mother's responsiveness to signals from the child, than it does to how often the mother specifically trains or disciplines the baby (either physically or verbally).

These results are interpreted in the ethological–evolutionary framework proposed by Bowlby (1969). Attachment behaviour is viewed as developing from species-specific reflex-like behaviours such as sucking and crying, the genetic bias of the system being such that in an ordinary expectable social environment (not too different from the environment of evolutionary adaptedness) the stimulus configurations and contingent responses provided by the mother are such that specific attachment will occur. Attachment behaviour in the one year old and subsequently is viewed as a hierarchically organized system of behaviours, the goal of which is to maintain an appropriate balance between exploration and return to a secure base. Bowlby views the function (survival value) of attachment behaviour as being protection from predators. However, predation is a minor cause of death in modern hunter-gatherers (Dunn, 1968) and in most primates (Lawick-Goodall, 1968; Washburn, Jay and Lancaster, 1965), and probably Ainsworth and others are right in giving a wider function to attachment behaviour, namely that of caring for a relatively helpless infant, and providing a secure framework within which exploration and learning (of the external environment and of adult customs and technology) can occur.

Ainsworth and her group have now produced an impressive body of work to support their view of the nature of mother–infant attachment (a view in marked contrast with traditional psychological ideas of learning and reinforcement). The rather global nature of some behaviour categories or ratings, however, may tend to produce an oversimplified picture (though some precautions against 'haloing' have been taken). Most of the studies are also based on the same subject sample of twenty-six mother–infant pairs.

Studies such as those by Lewis (1972) and Moss (1967) indicate that there are important differences between mother–son and mother–daughter interaction. Results tend to suggest that while infant males may receive more stimulation (especially contact stimulation) in the first few weeks or months of life, there is later a cross-over with mothers encouraging greater independence and distance separation in boys than in girls. At thirteen months boys were found to explore further from the mother in a free play situation, and touch and vocalize to the mother less often. These results have been confirmed across social class (Messer and Lewis, 1972). Similar sex-related differences in independence training have been found for other primate species such as pigtailed monkeys (Jensen, Bobbitt and Gordon, 1968) and rhesus monkeys (Mitchell, 1968). Greater maternal attentiveness to the male infant just after birth may have survival value due to the greater fragility of the newborn male. Possibly the nature of these early interactions helps to trigger off the subsequent increased rejection of male infants. Survival value of the latter probably relates to subsequent sex differences in play, and in the roles expected of the adult animal.

Studies of attachment behaviours in older children have been made by Anderson (1972) and Blurton Jones and Leach (1972). Anderson observed one to two and a half year olds with their mothers in a park; he confirmed the goal-oriented nature of attachment as proximity-maintaining behaviour, and discussed the nature and function of the behaviours he observed (for example, pointing to distant objects and looking at mother). Blurton Jones and Leach have described patterns of separation from and greeting of a mother/adult by a child taken to nursery. The relatively fine nature of the behaviour categories they use leads to a considerably more complex picture of attachment behaviour than that suggested by Ainsworth (however, their children were older – two to four years).

Connolly and Smith (1972) described the behaviour of children in a nursery to a strange observer who came and sat in the room. Most responses by the children were investigatory or friendly, virtually none was hostile. This finding, like that of McGrew (1972b) of the absence of hostility to a new child introduced to the group, emphasizes the 'open' nature of the group – a non-hostility to strangers which is not characteristic of primates in general, though it is true of chimpanzees (Lawick-Goodall, 1968) and of surviving hunter-gatherers (Lee and DeVore, 1968), and may well have been an important feature of hominid evolution (Reynolds, 1966).

Studies of child–child interactions

Several studies have been made of children interacting amongst themselves, in schools and playgroups. Using category lists such as those described earlier, records of behaviour have been made usually by time-sampling techniques, using pen-and-paper recordings, tape recordings or videofilm (see Hutt and Hutt, 1970b). Once one has records of chunks of behaviour, there are two obvious things to do. One is to see which behaviour units tend to occur together, in what sequence, etc. This has already been discussed in the section on motivational analysis. The other is to see how children differ in the kinds and amounts of different behaviours which they exhibit. Differences due to the age and sex of the children are important here, and also 'background' factors such as social class, birth order, etc.; and individual differences will remain even if such large-scale variables are factored out.

Effects of variables such as age, sex, length of nursery experience, birth order have been examined for preschool children by Blurton Jones (1967, 1972b), Smith and Connolly (1972), Clark, Wyon and Richards (using measures of friendship preference and choice of activity) (1969) and McGrew (nearest neighbours and spacing behaviour) (1972a). In addition Blurton Jones (1972b) and Smith (1973) have looked at the main kinds of individual difference, using factor analytic methods, and obtained fairly consistent results. The main dimension of individual difference in children at this age (three to five) is one of social maturity, fairly closely correlated with age. This may provide a useful measure of adjustment to the nursery situation. The second main kind of individual difference seems to relate to choice of activity; some children seem consistently to prefer stationary manipulative activities such as table work with beads, paper, etc., whereas others prefer active rough-and-tumble type play. Rough-and-tumble play (discussed earlier) is seen in most young mammals and might be considered as a preparation for hunting or aggressive activities. Manipulative play reflects the genetic potentiality for varied tool-use and tool-making in man and is seen more and to a much higher level in human children than in other primate young. These two kinds of play seem to have fairly distinct motivational contexts, and to have differing degrees of appeal to otherwise equally 'sociable' children.

Although children seem to show the same behaviours, and the same kinds of motivational groupings of these behaviours, both Blurton Jones and Smith found that individual differences do not correspond simply to difference in frequency of occurrence of these behaviour groupings. Thus, almost all children show aggressive behaviour, but individual differences are not just in the frequency with which a child shows aggressive behaviour, but also in the kinds of aggressive behaviour he shows and the way such behaviour patterns are organized (see Figures 10–12). For example, taking an object from another child may be different motivationally from frowning, fixating and hitting or pushing a child; and at a later stage both may be verbally mediated. This emphasizes the need both for fine analysis of behaviour and for longitudinal studies. While it is fairly obvious that longitudinal studies are necessary for examining, say, mother–infant attachment, this is not so obvious for child–child interaction; however, at the present stage of research the need for longitudinal studies seems crucial for further progress. It is this kind of research which will indicate how the fairly clear motivational

Figure 10 Conflict over toy

patterns of the four year old develop, how important certain kinds of experience are for their development, how individual differences in the organization of behaviour relate to age and sex differences; it will also make it easier to get information on the total complex of influences acting on the child – so that instead of using a vague global variable such as 'social class' one examines details of the family environment, adult behaviours, etc. (see Richards and Bernal, 1971).

One short-term longitudinal study has been carried out by McGrew (1972b). He was interested in what happened when a new child was introduced to a nursery group. He observed several children over their first five days, with a follow-up period of five days three months later. The new children initially showed high frequencies of immobile and auto-manipulative behaviour; these later decreased and be-

Figure 11   Hair pulling

Figure 12 Kick

haviours such as running and talking became much more frequent. McGrew also examined changes in behaviour within a morning session, and makes the interesting suggestion that these changes largely parallel those of the initial introduction to the group – so that on arrival at the nursery each morning a child may go rapidly through the same kind of behavioural adjustment that he made over his first days at the nursery.

McGrew (1969), in a study of agonistic behaviour in preschool children, also constructed a 'dominance hierarchy' according to the number of fights won and lost. Esser (1968) constructed a similar 'pecking order' for psychiatrically hospitalized boys in a New York State hospital. In both cases, dominance hierarchy correlated highly with amount of social interaction. Paluck and Esser (1972) related dominance in these children to territorial behaviour (preferred space occupied). These authors have shown that dominance hierarchies can correlate with other observables (e.g. auto-manipulative behaviour, clinical prognosis). However, a one-dimensional characterization of this kind (while fully appropriate for some lower species) would seem to be only a somewhat gross approximation for normal children; the dominance hierarchy concept may be a useful way of summarizing data, but seems unlikely to be a useful tool in further research.

To date, there is no published ethological description of behaviour in school-age normal children. A pilot study has been made by Reynolds and Guest at Bristol of behaviours shown by six- to seven-year-old children in a school classroom. Below the usual nursery age range, Bronson (1973) has made interesting observations on the social behaviour of one year olds.

Ecological studies: extended description of research project

It has become apparent in field studies of primates that aspects of social organization – age/sex/family groupings, dominance relations, spacing patterns – are greatly affected by ecological variables, such as food availability, nature of terrain, presence of predators, even within a single species (Crook and Goss-Custard, 1972). Investigation of such relationships seems a very promising field for human ethology (Crook, 1970), and indeed seems essential for an understanding both of the selection pressures acting on social organization in primitive man, and of present cross-cultural differences. Of course 'cultural' and 'sociological' aspects of behaviour should not be artificially separated from 'psychological' or 'biological' aspects; this has perhaps been brought home forcibly to those studying human behaviour by the complexity of interaction of cultural, sociological and psychobiological factors in chimpanzees and other higher primates.

While one cannot really divorce ecological from cross-cultural studies, this is a convenient section in which to review a small number of studies on the effects of ecological variables on behaviour in young children. These are fairly closely confined experimental studies, and, while not necessarily indicative of how adults would respond to similar variations, do show the kinds of different response produced in children and hence the way in which social learning in childhood might be influenced. In addition, practical results may ensue, as in the playroom designed for autistic children by Richer and Nicoll (1971).

Hutt and Vaizey (1966) looked at children in a hospital playroom, and observed how variations in group size (number of children in the playroom) affected social and aggressive behaviour. Of fifteen children observed, five were normal, five brain-damaged and five autistic. When more children were present in the playroom, the normal and brain-damaged children showed more aggressive behaviour and (at high densities) less social interaction. Autistic children spent more time at the edges of the room. The finding that there is generally less social interaction at higher densities is somewhat surprising, and suggests that the children are definitely acting so as to limit their social encounters in the more crowded conditions; the mechanism may vary with the kind of child.

However, it is possible in Hutt and Vaizey's experiment that the results were, in part at least, due to the relative unfamiliarity of the children to each other (rather than group size *per se*). W. C. McGrew (1972a) examined the effects of group size (which he calls 'social density') in a group of nursery-school children, many of whom had been at the nursery for some time. He observed twelve kinds of behaviour when all the group, and half the group, were in the playroom (on the latter occasions the other half played outside). For both group sizes he also observed effects of spatial density, by sometimes reducing the play area to 80 per cent of its maximum extent. The results for aggressive and fearful behaviours were rather inconclusive, however, and his data do not give much information on non-aggressive social encounters. The amount of play equipment per child was also different in the two group size conditions, so any effects of this would have been confounded with the group size variable.

P. L. McGrew (1970) used the same experimental situation to examine spacing behaviour of the children, and showed that characteristic adjustments were made to the different social and spatial density conditions.

There are many other variables which might be examined for their effects on children's behaviour; for example, the actual size of the group (irrespective of space) might be very important in determining whether certain kinds of rough-and-tumble play emerge. Again the ratio of boys to girls might influence the kind of play considerably. (Such factors could be expected to be much more important in older children, of course.) Rooms with interesting shapes – enclaves, tunnels, stages, etc. – might elicit interesting behaviours; after all, even a well-equipped nursery room differs very considerably from the natural environment containing trees, caves, rocks, other animals, and so on, that, in evolutionary perspective, most human children have grown up in.

In a project at Sheffield[1] being carried out by myself, in collaboration with Professor Kevin Connolly and Mrs Dorothy Fleming, we are examining effects of varying amount of space and toys on children's behaviour in a playgroup. The reason for our interest in this is that space and toys may be considered the most important resources in the physical environment for the preschool child, and we wish to see how variation in the amount of resources available affect behaviour. Effects of varying the social environment will be examined at a later stage. In the course of a three-year project we hope to understand why behaviour varies from one kind of nursery or playgroup to another, by experimentally varying the main physical and social parameters by which they differ (Smith, Connolly and Fleming, 1972). In order to do this we started a playgroup in a large church hall; two groups of twenty-five children were recruited (each attending two mornings a week), so that any reliable findings for one group should be replicated in the other group. The area inside the hall is very large, so that it is possible to use a screen barrier to reduce the available space to one-third of total, while still satisfying regulations that there is a minimum of 25 sq. ft per child (in fact slightly more); the other spatial conditions are two-thirds of total space, and all of total space (about 1950 sq. ft). There is a basic set of toys and equipment available every day; however on some days two of everything is provided, and on yet other days three of everything. Each of the three spatial conditions can occur with each of the three toy conditions, so that there are nine possible environmental conditions for the children; the condition is varied from one morning to the next, and each group of children will be observed in each condition for six mornings throughout an eight-month period. Three experienced

1. This project is supported by the Social Science Research Council.

Peter K. Smith 123

playgroup staff look after the children; there is one and a half hours of unstructured 'free play' each morning during which observations are made, and three-quarters of an hour of structured activities.

Observations are made by means of tape recordings, videotapes and pencil-and-paper recordings of ongoing behaviour. Using a portable tape recorder, four time-samples of behaviour are obtained for each child each morning; these are transcribed on to sheets containing over 100 behaviour units. Many of these are similar or identical to those of the 'behaviour dictionaries', or are simple aggregates of them. It is essential to use a tape recorder to obtain such observations so that one's eyes are never taken off the subject. Even so, rapidly occurring activities such as fights and rough-and-tumbles are difficult to describe accurately *in situ*, as anyone who has tried to do so will know. Here the use of videotape is indispensable. A second observer uses a portable videocamera to film incidents of fights, rough-and-tumbles and other interesting behaviour sequences as they occur; in addition, when fine analysis is not required, pencil-and-paper observations are made for these activities (since incident sampling is preferable to time-sampling for fights, for example, which occur rather rarely).

Once the collection of data is completed, it can be analysed along a number of lines. Firstly, one can analyse using individual behavioural units, or alternatively carry out some motivational analysis to obtain a smaller number of behaviour groupings (these can be examined for consistency across children and across conditions). Differences in frequency of behaviour units or groupings can be related to differences in spatial density, toy density and their various interactions. The change from an inexperienced group of average age three and a quarter to an experienced group of average age four can be documented in behavioural terms, and we shall be able to see if the effects of the density conditions alters with the age and experience of the children. The toy preferences are also being sampled and similar analyses can be worked out for these. Very detailed analyses of rough-and-tumbles and aggressive encounters can be obtained from the videotape records.

Prior to analysis some preliminary impressions may be worth recording: the two groups of children appeared to form distinct group 'identities' a month or two after the study was started, and although matched for age and sex seem appreciably different in character. The extent to which this will affect the replicability of results across groups is as yet undetermined, but this does make the point that results obtained for one group of subjects may be less generalizable than might appear. We were particularly interested to see if aggressive behaviours might decrease when more toys and space were available. There do seem to be less property disputes, for example, with more toys, but the effect does not seem such a very strong one as might have been anticipated; certain toys are still strong favourites and are disputed over. The favourite toy is the tricycle; when there is only one trike there may be more fights over it than when there are three, but even in the latter case disputes still occur. A child sometimes seems to want a particular trike that another child is on, and ignores another one lying idle; or a child may try and acquire two or even three trikes for himself, or for his friends. Such behaviours relate to the dominance relations between the children and show that even at three years dominance behaviours can sometimes lead to a markedly unequal distribution of resources. Nevertheless an environment with a large amount of space, toys and apparatus may provide more opportunity for a less dominant child. We are examining the stability of these dominance relations, and documenting carefully the kinds of behaviours that occur. Some of the rough-and-tumble behaviours observed have been described earlier.

Cross-cultural studies: extended description of research project

To date there are remarkably few observational studies of infant or child behaviour outside the USA or UK. There are some studies of mother–infant interaction in Africa, Mexico and Japan (Ainsworth, 1964; Brazelton, 1972; Caudill and Weinstein, 1969; Goldberg, 1972; Lusk and Lewis, 1972), and Eibl-Eibesfeldt (1971, 1972) has filmed a number of facial expressions and expressive movements in children and adults, some of which show marked similarity across numerous different cultures. Freedman (personal communication) has been studying neonates, and infant play, in some seven different culture areas.

A very comprehensive ethological study of child behaviour in another culture is that being carried out amongst the Zhuŋ/twasi or !Kung Bushmen of Botswana, organized by I. de Vore at Harvard and partially reported by Konner (1972) and Blurton Jones and Konner (1973). An interesting feature of this study is that the Bushmen are one of the few remaining hunter-gatherer cultures still extant; and the study is already yielding insights into the adaptive value of certain child behaviours, in an environment which probably corresponds much more closely to the environment of primitive man for which these behaviours were adapted, than that of present Western civilization. Another important and very valuable aspect of the five-year project is that it is multi-disciplinary; findings on child behaviour can be related to information gathered on subsistence ecology, health and nutrition, population genetics and demography.

In the largely outdoor communal life of the Bushmen, both adult–child and child–child interactions can be readily observed. Konner (1972) has reported a number of interesting findings. He reports that until recently infanticide was practised to ensure three- to four-year spacing between births. Mothers carry their babies in a sling in direct physical contact and in this position (unlike in the European crib) many infant reflexes function to readjust position, or grasp the mother as she rises and walks off. The mother breast-feeds frequently, and often anticipates the child's feeding needs before he gets to the point of crying. Weaning may not occur until six years of age. Very few restrictions are placed on the child, for example with respect to toilet training or playing with objects.

Despite the great cultural differences in child-rearing behaviours, there are notable parallels in child development with that in Western cultures. The infant is born with the same reflexive capabilities: during the first year social experience extends certain reflex abilities into a hierarchical organization of attachment behaviours similar in form across cultures (although amongst the Bushmen children nursing is a more prominent form of attachment behaviour than in Western children). During the second six months fear of strangers develops in most infants, manifested in similar ways (though the reaction seems often more marked, and more prolonged developmentally, amongst the Bushmen). Attachment, once established, provides the context in which most further learning occurs – both exploratory learning, with return to mother as a secure base, and social learning, with proximity to effective models of subsistence behaviour. The importance of parental modelling is especially obvious in the Bushmen context, where there is more opportunity for the child to observe adult activities (infant carried around in upright position by mother; small localized community). Rough-and-tumble and gentle-and-tumble play behaviours develop first from adult–child interactions in an attachment context, and then appear in child–child interactions. Imitation of adult activities occurs both in object play and physical play (in Bushmen children, for example, pounding with mortar and pestle, digging with stick, hunting small animals or insects). Aggressive and fighting behaviours also emerge at this time and in Bushmen children seem more frequent in mother–child than in child–child contexts (tantrum behaviour with parents is not inhibited).

Blurton Jones and Konner (in press) report a quantitative analysis of sex differences, comparing Bushmen and London children. The age range (three to six years) and sex of the children were matched in the two samples. Although sample sizes are small, and direct comparison is rendered difficult by obvious differences in physical and social environment, the authors direct most emphasis on the presence/absence of sex differences and their function within each cultural context.

Two observers observed one child at a time, using pen-and-paper methods and observing for twenty-four half-minute samples in one hour. They recorded the incidence of a wide range of behaviour units; these units were found to occur and to have similar motivational significance in both London and Bushmen children. Analysis was in terms both of behavioural units and behavioural clusters (aggression, rough-and-tumble, sociable interaction, interactions with mother, use of objects, etc.).

It is noteworthy that in no case was a significant reversal of sex differences found between the two cultures. Some sex differences showed very similar trends of sex differentiation – for example, boys showed more aggressive behaviours than girls in both cultures. In the case of interactions with mother and other adults, the picture is rather complex. Boys showed much more rough-and-tumble than girls in London, but this was not so true of the Bushmen children; Bushmen girls showed much more of these behaviours than London girls. Also, unlike London children, Bushmen children do not show a marked sex differentiation in choice of companions (e.g. boys preferring to play with boys). In discussing these results the authors argue that some sex differences have had survival value and are biased before birth by hormonal influences; but that nevertheless Western society may be unduly reinforcing certain sex differences in children, in particular perhaps inhibiting active and rough-and-tumble activities in girls.

Discussion: potential of child ethology

Since ethology has up till now largely been the study of animal behaviour, it relies on observation of behaviour rather than on subjects' verbal reports or introspections of their behaviour. I hope I have shown that the rather broad and nebulous area encompassed by human ethology provides a profitable orientation by which to approach a number of issues in child development. Prominent among these are attachment, exploration, play and aggression – in fact the development of social behaviour on broadly species-specific lines during the first few years of life. The approach may also be useful in studying non-social skills (Connolly and Elliott, 1972). Obviously the ethologist has an advantage in studying young children whose linguistic and cognitive capacities have not vastly outstripped those of other mammals – whose self-awareness and verbal control of behaviour are still not very great; conversely, the 'traditional' psychologist relying on second-hand verbal reports and assessments will be at a disadvantage. However, for children a few years older, the advantages seem to lie the other way; how useful is an ethological approach for understanding the behaviour of, say, sophisticated ten year olds? Or adults? A partial answer is that it is necessary to know the developmental history of the older child or adult, the roots of his behaviour in early infancy; this is a powerful and important argument, but only a partial one. Ethological studies of aggression in young children, for example, may provide some guidelines for the understanding of adult aggression, and indeed may provide some vital clarification of terms. An understanding of the evolution of aggressive behaviours in primate species may also be helpful. But it cannot seriously be contended that these alone provide a sufficient explanation of, say, human warfare (though they will be a necessary ingredient). To say so would be an insult to man's complexity; an unjustified extrapolation from simpler systems. Direct studies of adult human aggression are essential. But ethological studies of older children or adults have so far been restricted to certain sub-systems of behaviour (such as facial expressions or mother–infant interaction), or to psychiatric patients. It is an open question whether an ethological approach *per se* can deal with behaviour involving sophisticated linguistic or cognitive abilities.

It is interesting in this connection to consider the direction of research into human language ability. Studies of language learning in children (although carried out by psychologists and linguists) are obviously of an 'ethological' kind. The actual verbal utterances of children are being recorded in longitudinal studies, using natural as well as experimental situations. The developing structure of the language system is inferred from the combinations of utterances observed. There is discussion as to how this developing structure may be based on species-specific abilities to utilize linguistic information (the problem of linguistic universals – see, e.g., McNeill, 1970). Comparison is possible with the language systems that can be taught to chimpanzees (Gardner and Gardner, 1971; Premack, 1971): for example, the open/pivot class structure of two-word utterances in both species.

There are, of course, sophisticated models of adult language, the most obvious example being Chomsky's (1957, 1965). In principle there seems little reason to doubt that some understanding will be reached of the development of the syntactic structure of language from the simple structures of children (and chimpanzees?) to the complex ones of adults; obviously this is not the whole problem of language but it is a significant one.

Chomsky describes three systems of increasing complexity; finite state systems, phrase structure systems and transformational systems, the latter potentially a more powerful system than is needed to describe language syntax (Lyons, 1972). Vowles (1970) has discussed how similar systems can be used to describe animal behaviour sequences. For example, a finite state system can be used to describe courtship behaviour in the fruitfly *drosophila*. A phrase structure system has been used to describe reproductive behaviour in the male pigeon. Vowles suggests that only in primates does behaviour approach the complexity of that represented by transformational grammars. In these examples the behaviour unit of the ethologist corresponds to the syntactical unit or morpheme of the linguist; the linguistic work suggests that potentially sufficiently complex hierarchical systems are available to provide a useful ethological approach to adult behaviour. Of course it is very controversial whether the structural organization of observed behaviour, or of cognitive abilities, is similar to that of verbal language. Brown (1970) has related stages in syntactic structure to Piaget's stages of cognitive growth. However, others prefer to emphasize the unique and specifically linguistic nature of man's ability for language (Lenneberg, 1967). Nevertheless the systems would appear to be of a comparable order of complexity.

Ultimately the limitations of an ethological approach will only be found from experience; it is sufficient to say they have not yet been reached. There is clearly a need at present for more longitudinal ethological studies of child behaviour, integrating behavioural observations with data from other sources (as in the studies of mother–infant interaction at Cambridge, or of the Bushmen children). There is also now a growing requirement for more sophisticated structural models of behaviour (obviously more complex than those mentioned earlier). Here studies of language syntax may provide a useful source of ideas; and ultimately some link may be possible between the two in terms of the verbal planning of behaviour. This may finally help in the description and understanding of activities most difficult for the child ethologist – the imaginative and role-playing activities so common in children's play by three or four years. Let us take as an example 'mother and baby' play; the 'mother' 'pretends' to hit the baby, the 'baby' 'pretends' to pucker and cry. The behaviour units – hit, pucker, cry – may be similar to or indistinguishable from the 'real' behaviours, but in the imaginative play they are somehow disconnected from their real-life motivational context – just as human language can be similarly disconnected. This may raise similar problems for ethology that the problems of pragmatics and semantics raise for linguistics.

These are mainly theoretical arguments. However the ethological approach may also have something to offer with respect to practical social problems. Essentially the evolutionary perspective of the ethologist provides a framework in which we can examine the adaptability of human behaviour. Here an analogy with animal and plant ecology may be illuminating. Biologists have long been aware of a complex and delicate balance of interrelationships between the animal and plant life forms of a particular environment or ecosystem; small disturbances are compensated for, but large disturbances can lead to a radical restructuring, usually a deterioration, of the potentialities for life support. Similarly, human behaviour patterns might be considered as an equally complex balance of interrelationships, initially adaptive in a paleolithic environment. It is sterile here to talk about whether particular kinds of behaviour are 'innate' or 'learned'. The relevant questions are the adaptability and interrelatedness of behaviours; how easily can a behaviour pattern be modified away from the normal variation in the environment of evolutionary adaptedness? What strain will such changes put on other behaviour patterns? We already know for instance that lack of effective attachment to a mother-figure leads to severe behavioural impairment. As a more controversial example, Blurton Jones (1972c) argues that quasi-continuous feeding and carrying of the baby by the mother is the normal pattern for which humans are adapted (this argument is based mainly on a comparative analysis of milk composition and feeding schedule in different mammalian species). The standard West European pattern clearly differs significantly from this. We do not know the effects of such a variation; but cross-cultural studies such as those by Konner, Goldberg and Brazelton, and longitudinal studies such as that by Richards, will be the way to find out.

This is not to imply a return to the deterministic idea of 'human nature'. One might argue from man's natural behavioural dispositions both 'progressive' and 'reactionary' social changes; perhaps for more extended or communal family life and permissive child rearing; against the effective reduction of hierarchies or sex-role divisions. But essentially such issues as these must be decided at the highest level of awareness of our own value systems, and of the environment we are creating or wish to create for ourselves. The lesson of the ethologist, however, is that meaningful choices should be based on knowledge of how far we can vary our admittedly highly modifiable behaviour patterns, to what extent we can safely tamper with our 'behavioural ecosystem'.

References

AINSWORTH, M. D. (1964), 'Patterns of attachment behavior shown by the infant in interaction with his mother', *Merrill-Palmer Q. Behav. Devel.*, vol. 10, pp. 51–8.

AINSWORTH, M. D., BELL, S. M., and STAYTON, D. J. (1972), 'Individual differences in the development of some attachment behaviors', *Merrill-Palmer Q. Behav. Devel*, vol. 18, pp. 123–44.

ANDERSON, J. W. (1972), 'Attachment behaviour out of doors', in N. G. Blurton Jones (ed.), *Ethological Studies of Child Behaviour*, Cambridge University Press.

ANDREW, R. J. (1963), 'The origin and evolution of the calls and facial expressions of the primates', *Behaviour*, vol. 10, pp. 255–308.

ARDREY, R. (1961), *African Genesis*, Collins.

ARDREY, R. (1967), *The Territorial Imperative*, Collins.

ARDREY, R. (1970), *The Social Contract*, Collins.

BAN, P. L., and LEWIS, M. (1971), 'Mothers and fathers, girls and boys: attachment behavior in the one-year-old', Paper presented to Eastern Psychological Association, New York, April.

BLURTON JONES, N. G. (1967), 'An ethological study of some aspects of social behaviour of children in nursery school', in D. Morris (ed.), *Primate Ethology*, Weidenfeld & Nicolson.

BLURTON JONES, N. G. (1971), 'Criteria for use in describing facial expressions in children', *Hum. Biol.*, vol. 43, pp. 365–413.

BLURTON JONES, N. G. (ed.) (1972a), *Ethological Studies of Child Behaviour*, Cambridge University Press.

BLURTON JONES, N. G. (1972b), 'Categories of child–child interaction', in N. G. Blurton Jones (ed.), *Ethological Studies of Child Behaviour*, Cambridge University Press.

BLURTON JONES, N. G. (1972c), 'Comparative aspects of mother–child contact', in N. G. Blurton Jones (ed.), *Ethological Studies of Child Behaviour*, Cambridge University Press.

BLURTON JONES, N. G., and KONNER, M. J. (1973), 'Sex differences in behaviour of London and Bushmen children', in R. P. Michael and J. H. Crook (eds.), *Comparative Ecology and Behaviour of Primates*, Academic Press.

BLURTON JONES, N. G., and LEACH, G. M. (1972), 'Behaviour of children and their mothers at separation and greeting', in N. G. Blurton Jones (ed.), *Ethological Studies of Child Behaviour*, Cambridge University Press.

BOWLBY, J., (1958), 'The nature of the child's tie to his mother', *Int. J. Psychoanal.*, vol. 41, pp. 350–73.

BOWLBY, J. (1969), *Attachment and Loss, vol. 1: Attachment*, Hogarth Press.

BRANNIGAN, C. R., and HUMPHRIES, D. A. (1972), 'Human non-verbal behaviour: a means of communication', in N. G. Blurton Jones (ed.), *Ethological Studies of Child Behaviour*, Cambridge University Press.

BRAZELTON, T. B. (1972), 'Implications of infant development among the Mayan Indians of Mexico', *Hum. Devel.*, vol. 15, pp. 90–111.

BRONSON, W. C. (1973), 'Competence and the growth of personality', in J. S. Bruner and K. J. Connolly (eds.), *The Development of Competence in Early Childhood*, Academic Press.

BROWN, R. (1970), 'The first sentences of child and chimpanzee', in *Psycholinguistics: Selected Papers*, Free Press.

CAUDILL, W., and WEINSTEIN, H. (1969), 'Maternal care and infant behavior in Japan and America', *Psychiatry*, vol. 32, pp. 12–43.

CHANCE, M. R. A., and JOLLY, C. J. (1970), *Social Groups of Monkeys, Apes and Men*, Cape.

CHOMSKY, N. (1957), *Syntactic Structures*, Mouton, The Hague.

CHOMSKY, N. (1965), *Aspects of the Theory of Syntax*, MIT Press.

CLARK, A. H., WYON, S. M., and RICHARDS, M. P. M. (1969), 'Free-play in nursery school children', *J. child Psychol. Psychiat.*, vol. 10, pp. 205–16.

CONNOLLY, K. (1971), 'The evolution and ontogeny of behaviour', *Bull. Brit. Psychol. Soc.*, vol. 24, pp. 93–102.

CONNOLLY, K., and ELLIOTT, J. (1972), 'The evolution and ontogeny of hand function', in N. G. Blurton Jones (ed.), *Ethological Studies of Child Behaviour*, Cambridge University Press.

CONNOLLY, K., and SMITH, P. K. (1972), 'Reactions of preschool children to a strange observer', in N. G. Blurton Jones (ed.), *Ethological Studies of Child Behaviour*, Cambridge University Press.

CROOK, J. H. (1970), 'Social organization and the environment: aspects of contemporary social ethology', *Anim. Behav.*, vol. 18, pp. 197–209.

CROOK, J. H., and GOSS-CUSTARD, J. D. (1972), 'Social ethology', *Ann. Rev. Psychol.*, vol. 23, pp. 277–312.

DARWIN, C. (1872), *The Expression of the Emotions in Man and Animals*, Murray.

DUNN, F. L. (1968), 'Epidemiological factors: health and disease in hunter-gatherers', in R. B. Lee and I. DeVore (eds.), *Man the Hunter*, Aldine.

EIBL-EIBESFELDT, I. (1970), *Ethology: The Biology of Behavior*, Holt, Rinehart & Winston.

EIBL-EIBESFELDT, I. (1971), *Love and Hate*, Methuen.

EIBL-EIBESFELDT, I. (1972), 'Similarities and differences between cultures in expressive movements', in R. A. Hinde (ed.), *Non-Verbal Communication*, Cambridge University Press.

ESSER, A. H. (1968), 'Dominance hierarchy and clinical course of psychiatrically hospitalized boys', *Child Devel.*, vol. 39, pp. 147–57.

FOX, R. (1967), 'In the beginning: aspects of hominid evolution', *Man*, vol. 2, pp. 415–33.

GARDNER, R. A., and GARDNER, B. T. (1971), 'Two-way communication with an infant chimpanzee', in A. Schrier and F. Stollnitz (eds.), *Behavior of Non-Human Primates*, vol. 4, Academic Press.

GOLDBERG, S. (1972), 'Infant care and growth in urban Zambia', *Hum. Devel.*, vol. 15, pp. 77–89.

GRANT, E. C. (1968), 'An ethological description of non-verbal behaviour during interviews', *Brit. J. med. Psychol.*, vol. 41, pp. 177–84.

GRANT, E. C. (1969), 'Human facial expression', *Man*, vol. 4, pp. 525–36.

HARLOW, H. F. (1969), 'Age-mate or peer affectional system', in D. S. Lehrman, R. A. Hinde and E. Shaw (eds.), *Advances in the Study of Behavior*, vol. 1, Academic Press.

HASS, H. (1970), *The Human Animal*, Hodder & Stoughton.

HINDE, R. A. (1959), 'Unitary drives', *Anim. Behav.*, vol. 7, pp. 130–41.

HINDE, R. A. (1966), *Animal Behaviour: A Synthesis of Ethology and Comparative Psychology*, 2nd edn, 1970, McGraw-Hill.

HINDE, R. A. (ed.) (1972), *Non-Verbal Communication*, Cambridge University Press.

HOOFF, J. A. R. A. M. VAN (1972), 'A comparative approach to the phylogeny of laughter and smiling', in R. A. Hinde (ed.), *Non-Verbal Communication*, Cambridge University Press.

HUTT, C., and VAIZEY, M. J. (1966), 'Differential effects of group density on social behaviour', *Nature*, vol. 209, pp. 1371–2.

HUTT, S. J., and HUTT, C. (eds.) (1970a), *Behaviour Studies in Psychiatry*, Pergamon.

HUTT, S. J., and HUTT, C. (1970b), *Direct Observation and Measurement of Behavior*, C. C. Thomas.

IZARD, C. E. (1971), *The Face of Emotion*, Appleton-Century-Crofts.

JENSEN, G. D., BOBBITT, R. A., and GORDON, B. N. (1968), 'Sex differences in the development of infant monkeys', *Behaviour*, vol. 30, pp. 1–14.

JOUVET, M. (1967), 'The sleeping brain', *Science J.*, vol. 3, pp. 105–10.

KONNER, M. J. (1972), 'Aspects of the developmental ethology of a foraging people', in N. G. Blurton Jones (ed.), *Ethological Studies of Child Behaviour*, Cambridge University Press.

LAWICK-GOODALL, J. VAN (1968), 'The behaviour of free-living chimpanzees in the Gombe Stream Reserve', *Anim. Behav. Mongr.*, vol. 1, pp. 161–311.

LEACH, G. M. (1972), 'A comparison of the social behaviour of some normal and problem children', in N. G. Blurton Jones (ed.), *Ethological Studies of Child Behaviour*, Cambridge University Press.

LEE, R. B., and DEVORE, I. (1968), *Man the Hunter*, Aldine.

LEHRMAN, D. S. (1953), 'A critique of Konrad Lorenz's theory of instinctive behaviour', *Q. Rev. Biol.*, vol. 28, pp. 337–63.

LENNEBERG, E. H. (1967), *Biological Foundations of Language*, Wiley.

LEWIS, M. (1972), 'State as an infant-environment interaction: an analysis of mother–infant behavior as a function of sex', *Merrill-Palmer Q. Behav. Devel.*, vol. 18, pp. 95–121.

LOIZOS, C. (1967), 'Play behaviour in higher primates: a review', in D. Morris (ed.), *Primate Ethology*, Weidenfeld & Nicolson.

LORENZ, K. (1941), 'Vergleichende Bewegungsstudien an Anatinen', *Suppl. J. Ornith.*, vol. 89, pp. 194–294. Eng. trans. in K. Lorenz, *Studies of Animal and Human Behaviour*, vol. 2, 1971, Methuen.

LORENZ, K. (1950), 'The comparative method in studying innate behaviour patterns', *Sym. Soc. Exp. Biol.*, vol. 4, pp. 221–68.

LORENZ, K. (1952), *King Solomon's Ring*, Methuen.

LORENZ, K. (1966), *On Aggression*, Methuen.

LUSK, D., and LEWIS, M. (1972), 'Mother–infant interaction and infant development among the Wolof of Senegal', *Hum. Devel.*, vol. 15, pp. 58–69.

LYONS, J. (1972), 'Human language', in R. A. Hinde (ed.), *Non-Verbal Communication*, Cambridge University Press.

MCCARTHY, D. (1954), 'Language development in children', in L. Carmichael (ed.), *Manual of Child Psychology*, 2nd edn, Wiley.

MCGREW, P. L. (1970), 'Social and spatial density effects on spacing behaviour in preschool children', *J. child Psychol. Psychiat.*, vol. 11, pp. 197–205.

MCGREW, W. C. (1969), 'An ethological study of agonistic behaviour in preschool children', in C. R. Carpenter (ed.), *Behaviour*, Proc. Sec. Int. Congr. Primatol., Karger, Zurich.

MCGREW, W. C. (1972a), *An Ethological Study of Children's Behavior*, Academic Press.

MCGREW, W. C. (1972b), 'Aspects of social development in nursery school children, with emphasis on introduction to the group', in N. B. Blurton Jones (ed.), *Ethological Studies of Child Behaviour*, Cambridge University Press.

MCNEILL, D. (1970), *The Acquisition of Language*, Harper & Row.

MASON, W. A. (1965), 'Determinants of social behavior in young chimpanzees', in A. Schrier and F. Stollnitz (eds.), *Behavior of Non-Human Primates*, vol. 2, Academic Press.

MESSER, S. B., and LEWIS, M. (1972), 'Social class and sex differences in the attachment and play behavior of the year-old infant', *Merrill-Palmer Q. Behav. Devel.*, vol. 18, pp. 295–306.

MITCHELL, G. D. (1968), 'Attachment differences in male and female monkeys', *Child Devel.*, vol. 39, pp. 611–20.

MORRIS, D. (1967), *The Naked Ape*, Cape.

MORRIS, D. (1969), *The Human Zoo*, Cape.

MORRIS, D. (1971), *Intimate Behaviour*, Cape.

MOSS, H. A. (1967), 'Sex, age, and state as determinants of mother–infant interaction', *Merrill-Palmer Q. Behav. Devel.*, vol. 13, pp. 19–36.

OSWALD, I. (1969), 'Human brain protein, drugs and dreams', *Nature*, vol. 223, pp. 893–7.

PALUCK, R. J., and ESSER, A. H. (1972), 'Territorial behavior as an indicator of changes in clinical behavioral condition of severely retarded boys', *Amer. J. ment. Defic.*, vol. 76, pp. 23–9.

PREMACK, D. (1971). 'On the assessment of language competence in the chimpanzee', in A. Schrier and F. Stollnitz (eds.), *Behavior of Non-Human Primates*, vol. 4, Academic Press.

REYNOLDS, V. (1966), 'Open groups in hominid evolution', *Man*, vol. 1, pp. 441–52.

REYNOLDS, V. (1968), 'Kinship and the family in monkeys, apes and man', *Man*, vol. 3, pp. 209–23.

REYNOLDS, V., and GUEST, A., 'The use of ethological methods in educational research', unpublished manuscript.

RHEINGOLD, H. L., and ECKERMAN, C. O. (1970), 'The infant separates himself from his mother', *Science*, vol. 168, pp. 78–83.

RICHARDS, M. P. M., and BERNAL, J. F. (1971), 'Social interaction in the first days of life', in H. R. Schaffer (ed.), *The Origins of Human Social Relations*, Academic Press.

RICHER, J. M., and NICOLL, S. (1971), 'A playroom for autistic children, and its companion therapy project', *Brit. J. ment. Subnormal.*, vol. 17, pp. 1–12.

SACKETT, G. P. (1965), 'Effects of rearing conditions upon the behavior of rhesus monkeys', *Child Devel.*, vol. 36, pp. 855–68.

SMITH, P. K. (1972), 'Social and play behavior of preschool children', *Man–Environment Systems*, vol. 2, pp. 90–91.

SMITH, P. K. (1973), 'Temporal clusters and individual differences in the behaviour of preschool children', in R. P. Michael and J. H. Crook (eds.), *Comparative Ecology and Behaviour of Primates*, Academic Press.

SMITH, P. K., and CONNOLLY, K. (1972), 'Patterns of play and social interaction in preschool children', in N. G. Blurton Jones (ed.), *Ethological Studies of Child Behaviour*, Cambridge University Press.

SMITH, P. K., CONNOLLY, K., and FLEMING, D. (1972), 'Environment and behaviour in a playgroup: effects of varying physical resources', *Man–Environment Systems*, vol. 2, pp. 254–6.

STAYTON, D. J., HOGAN, R., and AINSWORTH, M. D. S. (1971). 'Infant obedience and maternal behavior; the origins of socialization reconsidered', *Child Devel.*, vol. 42, pp. 1057–69.

SUOMI, S. J., and HARLOW, H. F. (1972), 'Social rehabilitation of isolate-reared monkeys', *Devel. Psychol.*, vol. 6, pp. 487–96.

TIGER, L. (1969), *Men in Groups*, Nelson.

TIGER, L., and FOX, R. (1966), 'The zoological perspective in social science', *Man*, vol. 1, pp. 75–81.

TIGER, L., and FOX, R. (1972), *The Imperial Animal*, Secker & Warburg.

TINBERGEN, N. (1951), *The Study of Instinct*, Oxford University Press.

TINBERGEN, N. (1959), 'Comparative studies of the behaviour of gulls (*Laridae*): a progress report', *Behaviour*, vol. 15, pp. 1–70.

TINBERGEN, N. (1963), 'On aims and methods of ethology', *Z. Tierpsychol.*, vol. 20, pp. 410–33.

TINBERGEN, N. (1969), 'Ethology', in R. Harré (ed.), *Scientific Thought 1900–1960: A Selective Survey*, Oxford University Press.

VOWLES, D. M. (1970), 'Neuroethology, evolution and grammar', in L. R. Aronson, E. Tobach, D. S. Lehrman and J. S. Rosenblatt (eds.), *Development and Evolution of Behavior*, Freeman.

WASHBURN, S. L., and LANCASTER, C. S. (1968), 'The evolution of hunting', in R. B. Lee and I. DeVore (eds.), *Man the Hunter*, Aldine.

WASHBURN, S. L., JAY, P. C., and LANCASTER, J. F. B. (1965), 'Field studies of old world monkeys and apes', *Science*, vol. 150, pp. 1541-7.

YOUNG, W. C., GOY, R. W., and PHOENIX, C. H. (1964), 'Hormones and sexual behavior', *Science*, vol. 143, pp. 212-18.

Chapter 4
Forms of Exploratory Behaviour in Young Children

Hildy S. Ross

Within the last decade, developmental psychologists have shown renewed interest in the exploratory behaviour of human infants and children. Children's curiosity about the world around them leads them to explore, and consequently to learn about their environment. Early observers of child behaviour noted that the infant, too, is an active explorer of his surroundings. In one of the first baby biographies Taine (1877, p. 253) vividly described the exploratory behaviour of a twelve-month-old girl:

Any one may observe that from the fifth or sixth month children employ their whole time for two years and more in making physical experiments. No animal, not even the cat or dog, makes this constant study of all bodies within its reach; all day long the child of whom I speak touches, feels, turns round, lets drop, tastes and experiments upon everything she gets hold of; whatever it may be, ball, doll, coral, or plaything, when once it is sufficiently known she throws it aside, it is no longer new, she has nothing to learn from it and has no further interest in it.

Charles Darwin (1877, p. 291), writing in the same issue of *Mind*, concurred: 'Curiosity, as M. Taine remarks, is displayed at an early age by infants, and is highly important in the development of their minds.'

Recent work has borne out the observations of these early investigators, showing that perhaps their only error was placing the origin of exploratory behaviour at five or six months, and ignoring the somewhat less apparent explorations of the younger infant who looks or listens to the things around him.

The developmental importance of curiosity and exploration was emphasized some years later by G. Stanley Hall (1907, pp. v–vi) in a preface to his study of curiosity and interest:

Curiosity and interest are themes of cardinal moment for both psychology and pedagogy. . . . All their outcrops [i.e. exploratory behaviour] represent the way in which the soul of the young strives to expand to the dimensions of that of the race, to know what the life of man in his world is and means, and where each person is to find his place and function in it. In the child there is a sacredness about interest, for when mature in the adult it is this impulse that has created the whole domain of knowledge and made man master of nature. To tell just how to feed it is the whole duty of didactics.

Hall's study itself, done with Theodate L. Smith (Smith and Hall, 1907), pointed to the wide variety of forms exploratory behaviour could assume. Though their methods were primitive, their findings deserve attention and, as they themselves point out, more detailed investigation. They sent a questionnaire to a variety of adults, and in reply received 1247 instances of curiosity in children. Smith and

Table 1 Questions asked about curiosity in children

Curiosity and wonder. Prying, spying, inquiring, asking why, what for, or how, persisting in troublesome questions. Describe the first sign of curiosity or wonder in the infant; sample the growth of the instinct by instances up toward maturity, whether manifested toward natural phenomena, facts, or persons seen or read of, mechanisms, motives, religious teaching, treatment by parents and teachers, etc. Cases of breaking open toys to see what is inside, or experimenting 'to see what it will do'. Later promptings to see the world, know life, travel, read, explore, investigate, etc. What excites chief wonder. Secrecy as a provocative of curiosity. Age of culmination of the chief classes of interest. Utilization and dangers.

Curiosity and interest. I. Give cases of early curiosity or interest shown by infants. State in detail how this was manifested.

II. Give cases of interest or curiosity in children, shown by active observation or experiment.

III. Give instances of destructive curiosity – toys etc. destroyed to find out how they were made.

IV. Give cases of interest or curiosity shown by asking questions.

V. Give instances of strong desire to travel. Did the interest in these cases extend to reading books of travel, etc.?

Source: Smith and Hall (1907)

Hall reported exactly what questions were asked (Table 1) although they were vague about exactly whom they obtained replies from.

The earliest evidence of curiosity in their records was staring, noted as early as the ninth day of life. Nearly half of the 163 cases of staring reported were in infants under three months of age. Smith and Hall considered this earliest manifestation of interest as passive, evoked when the baby was looking around and saw something, often a bright or moving object, that held his gaze for a few seconds. This stage was distinguished from the next, when in the fourth or fifth week of life the baby actively looked for an interesting object.

According to Smith and Hall, exploration through the other senses, including audition, touch, smell and taste, developed later than visual exploration. The infant's interest in sounds apparently rose in the fifth month, and was often accompanied by his repeating acts which gave rise to sound such as crumpling paper or hitting the keys of the piano. During the second half of the first year the infant's interests expanded still further. 'No longer content with merely seeing things, the little investigator desires to touch, taste, smell and handle everything within reach' (Smith and Hall, 1907, p. 97). Exploration thus became increasingly active, as witnessed by the following examples:

Female, nine and a half months.	Being put on the floor, crept to the coal scuttle and upset it.
Female, one and a half years.	When taken up by a lady, began to feel her bracelet and pin, and to smooth the velvet of her dress.

Active exploration itself turned to even more active experimenting, and, as Smith and Hall noted, many instances of experimenting were mistakenly considered naughty (female, five years, used to scratch pictures of people to see if they had life in them), cruel (female, three years, put a kitten's front paws on a very hot stove to see what it would do) or destructive (male, four years, pulled a clock to pieces to find out what made it strike).

The development of language brought another form of exploration, namely, asking questions. Smith and Hall categorized questions according to their topics which included:

1 Forces of nature (female, three and a half years: what makes the sun shine? Who puts the stars in the sky at night?)

2 Mechanical forces (male, three years: what is inside your watch, Auntie, that makes it talk?)

3 Origin of life (female, three and a half years: Mamma, where do the chickens get their eggs?)

4 Theology and Bible stories (male, five years: does God make some little boys good and some bad?)

5 Death and heaven (female, four years: Addie, will you go to heaven whole?).

It should be noted that the responses to the questionnaire were likely to have been influenced by the instructions participants received and by their own notions of what curiosity might involve. The replies were thus only examples of what was considered to be exploration by the investigators and the respondents. In addition, the frequency of exploratory behaviour could not be estimated because the data was compiled from the memories of those who answered the questionnaire rather than from direct observation. Finally, survey data of this type could not establish the determinants of the exploratory responses. This requires that conditions likely to influence the form or prevalence of exploration be systematically varied, and their effects on exploratory behaviour compared. On the other hand, the data did indicate that certain exploratory responses were frequent enough to be noticed by the observers, and many of the suggestions of the authors provided a fertile basis for more direct and objective investigations.

Further studies of exploratory behaviour in children did not resume in earnest until the 1960s, sparked by the extensive study of exploration in rats and monkeys during the previous decade. The work with animals resulted from the realization that much of the behaviour of man and animals (namely, exploration and intellectual curiosity) was left unexplained by traditional theories of motivation based on the notion of primary drive reduction (Harlow, 1953). During the 1950s the pervasiveness of exploration was established in a variety of species, and its determinants, chiefly novelty and complexity, were investigated (for review see Berlyne, 1960). When psychologists returned to the study of exploratory behaviour in children, the variables of novelty and complexity were the major themes.

Up to this point we have been talking about *exploratory behaviour* without defining it. A definition is important, however, because the many forms of exploratory behaviour do not obviously fall together within a single class. We have already mentioned a variety of responses, from staring at objects to questioning, which Smith and Hall (1907) considered manifestations of curiosity in children. To these may be added, for example, the responses of rat and monkey explorers such as sniffing, manipulating and locomoting. This diversity makes exploratory behaviour difficult to define, for it is not similarity in form that draws these different responses together into a common class. Rather, exploratory behaviour constitutes a class by virtue of two factors:

1 The responses are similarly influenced by variables such as novelty and complexity.

2 The apparent functions of the responses are similar.

The effects of novelty and complexity on exploratory behaviour will be documented in a later section of this chapter. The claim that the different responses share a similar *function* is more difficult to establish. What is the function of exploratory behaviour? Berlyne (1960, p. 79), in his masterful review of exploration, stated that its principal function is

to afford access to environmental information that was not previously available . . . by intensifying or clarifying stimulation from objects that are already presented in the stimulus field, and thus reducing uncertainty about the properties of these objects, or else by bringing receptors into contact with new stimulus objects.

Although all the examples of exploratory behaviour mentioned thus far share this function, many other responses not generally classified as exploratory (eating) also bring the receptors into contact with sources of stimulation. However, these other responses have other functions as well (satisfying hunger or supplying the body with nutrition) and thus can be differentiated from exploratory behaviour defined here as those behaviours whose *principal* function is to increase access to environmental information and thereby reduce uncertainty about its properties.

In this chapter, research on the various exploratory responses of infants and children will be reviewed. Responses include looking, listening, cardiac deceleration, manipulating, approaching and questioning. Most of this work has been done since 1960 with the exception of some studies of children's questions conducted in the 1920s and 1930s. The determinants of exploratory behaviour such as novelty and complexity will also be examined. Wherever possible, studies will be highlighted that demonstrate each response at the youngest age at which it has been shown to serve an exploratory function. This will allow us to see the development of different forms of exploration.

Visual exploration

Most recent studies of human infants' exploratory behaviour have been concerned with visual regard or looking. Fantz (1958) found that even newborn infants are selective in what they look at. This was discovered when infants between one and fourteen weeks of age were presented with pairs of patterns. Fantz watched the cornea of each infant's eye for reflections of the different patterns, and thus determined the amount of time subjects spent looking at each one. He found that some patterns consistently attracted more attention than others, and that, furthermore, the particular patterns that were looked at most sometimes changed with age. Thus the newborn does not merely gaze indiscriminately but actually looks more at particular stimuli.

By two or three months, the novelty and complexity of visual patterns control the infant's looking.

Novelty

The dictionary defines *novel* as 'having no precedent' or 'new' (Webster's, 1963); however, closer examination reveals that novelty is a far more subtle and varied concept than it may at first appear. Berlyne (1960) discussed the different ways in which an object or event can be novel. The first distinction was along a temporal dimension; an object is completely novel if it has never been perceived before, but may possess either long-term or short-term novelty if it has not been perceived in either the distant (months or years) or recent (minutes or hours) past of the organism. The second distinction was between absolute and relative novelty; an object that possesses some quality that has never been perceived before is completely novel with respect to that quality, while a new combination or arrangement of familiar elements or qualities is only relatively novel.

It is not possible, however, to claim that an object is completely and absolutely novel, because it is impossible to determine that some aspect of it (if only a line, angle or colour) has not been perceived before (Lewis, 1970). Similarly, an object is never completely known or familiar, because each time it is perceived some aspect of it may change, if only because the perceiver is examining it from a slightly different point of view.

For these reasons psychologists have studied novelty by means of a comparative technique. Although it is not possible to measure the precise degree of novelty, it is possible, through experimental manipulation, to order objects according to their relative degree of novelty. Experimental investigations of novelty have generally taken the following form: a stimulus is presented either repeatedly or for a specified period of time, and then the organism's reactions to this more familiar (previously exposed) stimulus are compared to those to a more novel (not exposed) alternative.

One of the earliest demonstrations that infants look longer at novel stimuli was a study conducted by Fantz in 1964. The visual patterns were eleven different photographs and advertisements cut from magazines. One of the patterns (though not the same one for all subjects) served as a constant stimulus and was presented to the infant ten times, for one minute each time. The other ten stimuli (variable patterns) were presented once each, simultaneously with the constant pattern. Again, the time that the pattern was reflected in the subject's cornea was the measure of visual regard. The stimuli were presented to twenty-eight infants who ranged in age from six to twenty-five weeks. All the age groups initially spent between 45 and 55 per cent of the time looking at the constant stimulus; for those over two months, however, the percentage of the time they looked at the constant pattern progressively decreased as the pattern became more familiar (Figure 1). The total time looking at both stimuli did not decline (it averaged forty-seven out of every sixty seconds), which meant that decreasing regard of the familiar or constant pattern was accompanied by increasing regard of the variable or novel ones. This basic finding has since been repeated for infants over two months of age with many different stimuli and procedures (e.g. Fagan, 1970, 1971; Fantz and Nevis, 1967; McGurk, 1970; Saayman, Ames and Moffett, 1964; Schaffer and Parry, 1970).

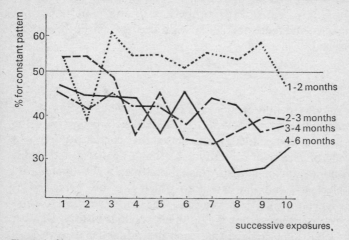

Figure 1 Change in relative duration of fixation of a repeatedly exposed (constant) pattern relative to a novel (variable) pattern during a series of exposure periods. From Fantz (1964). © 1964 by the American Association for the Advancement of Science

Subjects under two months of age did not show any change in the percentage of time they looked at the familiar and novel patterns. As there were only six subjects in this age group, further verification of this finding was appropriate. A recent paper by Fagan, Fantz and Miranda (1971) again found that infants under two months did not look more at novel patterns. Furthermore, this study was conducted with both premature and term infants and demonstrated that the age of transition to a preference for novelty was best measured in terms of gestational age rather than age since birth, an indication that for premature infants experience outside the womb may not play a major part in the development of a preference for novel stimuli.

The research of Fantz and others demonstrated more than the fact that human infants over two months look longer at novel stimuli. It showed that, by looking, the infants learn about the properties of the objects and events in their environment. They had, in this instance, learned about the familiar or constant pattern – learned enough to recognize it as it was repeatedly presented. This recognition was demonstrated by the infants' looking more at the novel than at the familiar pattern in subsequent trials. To distinguish the two, the infant must have learned the properties of the pattern he had previously seen, and remembered those properties when both patterns were presented.

Complexity

While novelty by definition depends on the previous history of the child, complexity may be better characterized as a property of the stimulus itself. Berlyne (1960, p. 38) stated that complexity refers to 'the amount of variety of diversity in a stimulus pattern' and that it depends on the number of distinguishable elements, the dissimilarity between elements, and the extent to which they are perceived as separate elements rather than as a unit. The child's reaction to complexity may, nevertheless, depend upon his previous history. Dember and Earl (1957) hypothesized that each individual has its own level of complexity, and that he tends to prefer stimuli that just exceed his individual level of complexity (pacers). Through the exploration of pacers, an organism increases his own personal complexity level, and thus grows to prefer increasingly complex stimuli. Evidence for this theory comes from studies which show that following appropriate experience (the exploration of pacer stimuli), the preferred complexity level shifted from less to more complex stimuli (Dember, Earl and Paradise, 1957; May, 1963; Thomas, 1969).

Research findings with infants in the first weeks of life are consonant with the Dember and Earl model. Newborns looked longer at checkerboard patterns with fewer elements (Hershenson, 1964) and at random figures with an intermediate number of turns (Hershenson, Munsinger and Kessen, 1965), rather than at the more complex patterns (which may have exceeded their personal complexity level). In addition, during the first eight weeks of life, infants looked longer at more and more complex stimuli (Brennan, Ames and Moore, 1966), perhaps because experience with pacers in the early weeks of life increased the infants' personal complexity levels.

On the other hand, infants older than two months of age have generally shown more exploration of stimuli with a greater number of distinguishable parts. Infants of two, three and four months of age looked longer at checkerboards with more elements (Caron and Caron, 1968, 1969) and at patterns with a greater number of black lines or of white areas created by the arrangement of the black lines (Moffett, 1969). When complexity was manipulated by varying the number of positions of a light in a 4×4 matrix (1, 4, 8 or 16) the results were less clear (Cohen, 1969). When each stimulus was presented by itself the infants looked longest at the one with four position changes; however, when the light stimuli were presented in pairs, the infants looked more at the stimulus with the greater number of position changes (the more complex stimulus). Finally, older infants (nine to fourteen months) who were shown pairs of random shapes which varied in number of turns or corners in the perimeter (5, 10, 20, 40) looked longer at the stimuli with the greater number of turns (Munsinger and Weir, 1967).

Complexity, however, can be defined in ways that do not involve a change in the number of elements of a stimulus. When defined as the irregularity of arrangement of elements within a visual array, complexity did not affect infants' viewing time (Karmel, 1969a, 1969b; McCall and Melson, 1970b; Moffett, 1969). Thus, different forms of complexity may not be psychologically equivalent and any experimental test or review of data must differentiate between the definitions used.

Cardiac deceleration

Cardiac deceleration is a response that has recently been used to measure attention. Heart rate decreases by about six to ten beats over a four- to six-second interval when an unexpected event, or one that differs from those that preceded it, occurs (Kagan, 1971). These heart rate changes seem to be accompanied by motor quieting and visual attentiveness to the stimulus (though the relation here is far from perfect). Furthermore, cardiac deceleration attenuates when the same stimulus is presented repeatedly, but recovers when a new or different pattern is presented (Lewis and Goldberg, 1969; McCall and Kagan, 1967; McCall and Melson, 1969).

McCall and Kagan used the visual stimuli illustrated in Figure 2. The standard was placed over the crib in the infant's home for thirty days when he was between three and four months old. At the end of this period the infant was taken to the laboratory where he was shown the standard and each of the rearranged stimuli. The infant showed a larger cardiac deceleration to the rearranged stimuli than to the standard that had become familiar. A control group of infants, who did not have the standard at home, did not differ in their cardiac deceleration to the standard and rearranged stimuli.

Similar experimental techniques have been used to study attention to auditory stimuli in infants (McCall and Melson, 1970a; Melson and McCall, 1970). In the case of visual stimuli, the infants' fixation

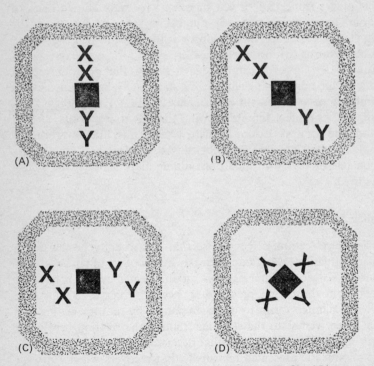

Figure 2 The stimuli used as standard (A) and rearranged (B, C and D) patterns. From McCall and Kagan (1967)

or regard of the stimuli (often measured by the reflection of the stimulus on his cornea) tells the investigator that the infant is looking at the pattern. No similar responses exist to assure us that the infant is listening to an auditory stimulus. For this reason, the use of cardiac deceleration as an index of attention was even more important for the study of auditory than visual exploration.

In one study (McCall and Melson, 1970a) the same set of eight tones were combined in either an ascending or a random order, and half of the subjects heard each of the sequences repeatedly as a standard. The standard was presented to three groups of five-and-a-half-month-old boys either three, seven or eleven times, and then standard (S), rearranged (R) and standard sequences were presented three times each so that the entire sequence was: S (three, seven or eleven times) S R S S R S S R S. Cardiac deceleration was greatest to the rearranged stimuli, and the amount of deceleration depended on the number of times the standard had been presented. The more familiar the standard, the greater the amount of cardiac deceleration to the rearranged sequence. Thus novel sequences received more attention, as measured by cardiac deceleration, than did familiar sequences, and the extent of the effect depended on the relative novelty of the two sets of auditory stimuli.

The studies of cardiac responses to visual and auditory stimuli have almost exclusively dealt with a variable that corresponds to Berlyne's definition of relative novelty; a new combination or arrangement of familiar elements. The one exception is a recent study by McCall and Melson (1970b) in which complexity, defined by the regularity of arrangement of stimuli, did not influence the cardiac deceleration of five-month-old females. Thus, the infant's cardiac reaction to complex visual and auditory stimuli has yet to be thoroughly investigated and could yield interesting new findings.

Instrumental responding

As mentioned previously, the particular physical form of a response does not mark it as exploratory. Almost any designated response can be exploratory if the situation is arranged correctly, that is, by having that response increase exposure to or clarify environmental information. The situation just described is similar to an instrumental learning paradigm, where the response (pressing a bar or pushing a panel) leads to a reinforcer – in this case some form of sensory stimulation. Siqueland (1969) conducted such a study with one- and four-month-old infants. If sensory stimulation can act as a reinforcer, then presenting it after a given response should change the rate of response. The response Siqueland selected was high-amplitude sucking. A pressure-sensitive tube was placed in the infant's mouth, and his rate of sucking was automatically recorded. For some infants high-amplitude sucking led to the presentation of visual stimuli; for others, *the absence* of high-amplitude sucking produced the stimuli. In this way Siqueland controlled for the possibility that any corresponding increase in responding was a result of general excitement rather than because the stimulation was reinforcing. The results showed that infants did change their rate of high-amplitude sucking when the visual stimuli were presented. As one stimulus became increasingly familiar, the sucking rate returned to normal, only to change again (either increasing or decreasing) when a novel stimulus replaced the familiar one. A similar study by Siqueland (1969) used sounds rather than visual patterns as reinforcers, and found similar results. When 'gah' replaced 'bah' as a contingent reinforcer, the rate of high-amplitude sucking changed appropriately. Thus the *novelty* of both visual and auditory stimuli was crucial for changing the frequency of an arbitrarily designated response.

Manipulation

During the second half of the first year the infant is not content to merely look and listen, but feels, touches and manipulates any objects he can reach. This occurs most persistently if the object is new. Hutt (1967) made what parents often consider an annoying childhood game into an experiment that demonstrated the infants' greater interest in new objects. A seven-month-old infant was seated at a table and Hutt repeatedly handed the baby a 'toy' (household items such as a coffee jar lid or an empty film roll along with children's rattles, beads and rings served as toys). With each successive presentation of the same object, the baby manipulated it less, and dropped it on the floor more quickly. The presentation of a novel object evoked renewed manipulation and inhibited dropping.

Other studies of infants between eight and thirteen months gave them a choice between novel and familiar objects. The infants reached first for the novel object and spent a greater proportion of their time manipulating it (Collard, 1962; Ross, Rheingold and Eckerman, 1972; Schaffer and Parry, 1970). Schaffer and Parry did not find this same phenomenon with six-month-old infants. These younger subjects looked longer at the novel than the familiar object, but manipulated both equally, a result which is not easily interpreted. The authors suggested that in the six-month-old child the responses involved in manipulating the toy are not controlled by the perceptual system which can discriminate novel from familiar. Further, the ability to carry out selective manipulation of novel and familiar objects under the guidance of the perceptual system is a separate development, which occurs shortly after this age period.

Complexity also controls manipulation; infants of ten and twelve months spend more time manipulating complex objects or arrays than simple ones. McCall and Garratt (1971) compared objects (a circle, square and irregular star) that contained varying numbers of sides or angles, and were judged to be more or less complex; Ross (1972) used varying numbers of toys in simple (one toy) or complex (four toys) arrays. In both cases the infants spent more time manipulating the more complex arrays.

Thus both novelty and complexity influence the manipulatory exploration of infants. The information the child receives is tactual, auditory and visual; he may learn about the texture and shape of the object, how it sounds when moved or hit against the floor and how it looks when it is turned.

Approach and entry

Toward the end of the first year of life infants become proficient at moving about, and, when they approach objects to explore them, crawling or walking also become exploratory responses. The twelve-month-old infant's approach to novel and familiar rooms and toys has been a topic of study (Ross, Rheingold and Eckerman, 1972). During a five-minute familiarization trial the infants were placed with their mothers in a large empty room, and a second smaller room contained a toy. They were free to leave their mothers, enter the other room and play with the toy. All but one of the twelve infants crawled or walked to the toy – and did so rather rapidly; on the average it took them only twenty-nine seconds to travel seventeen feet (5·2 metres) and reach the toy. On a second trial, these same infants were given a choice between the room and toy that had been available on the familiarization trial (familiar room and toy) and another similar adjacent room which contained a toy they had not yet played with (Figure 3). Ten of the eleven infants who had left their mothers on the familiarization trial entered the novel room and approached the novel toy *first* when given the choice. Although some later entered the familiar room and played with the familiar toy, the infants on the average spent a greater proportion of their time in the novel room and playing with the novel toy.

In this study (Ross, Rheingold and Eckerman, 1972) the novel room and toy combination were compared with a familiar room and toy; there was no way to separate the influence of environment (room) and object (toy), except to say that the infants went rapidly

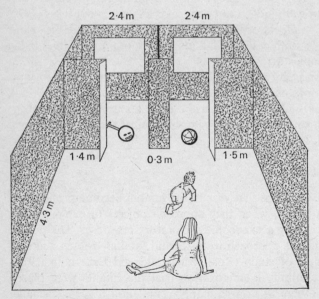

Figure 3 The experimental environment during the choice trial.
From Ross, Rheingold and Eckerman (1972)

to the toy once they entered the room, and that therefore the role of the novel object seemed pre-eminent. A second similar study (Ross, 1972) showed that even when the two rooms were equally novel, infants approached the novel toy first.

At the same time, novel rooms or environments also influence the exploratory behaviour of human infants and children. Both studies mentioned above (Ross, 1972; Ross, Rheingold and Eckerman, 1972) and a previous study with ten month olds (Rheingold and Eckerman, 1969) demonstrated that infants will leave their mothers and enter a novel environment. For some of the infants in the latter study the room they entered was empty, and yet these infants entered it readily and without distress, travelled out of sight of their mothers and explored the environment. Moreover, Ross (1972) found that infants spent more time in novel rooms than in familiar ones. Thus novel environments, as well as novel objects, increased the exploratory behaviour of human infants.

Novelty, complexity and the function of exploratory behaviour

The influence of novelty and complexity on a variety of exploratory responses can further elucidate the function of exploratory behaviour. If the function is to increase access to environmental information, as was previously suggested, then it follows that greater novelty or complexity should lead to increased exploration. When an object is novel, the organism must explore to gain new information about its properties; when an object is familiar its properties are already well known. Thus novelty should enhance exploration. Complexity should also enhance exploration because a complex stimulus contains more information (i.e. a greater number of distinguishable parts) than a simple one. As we have seen, the research findings with infants have generally confirmed these assumptions.

Questioning

The last form of exploration with which we will deal has not often been studied in relation to the others. In the first place its history is quite distinct. While other forms of exploratory behaviour were relatively neglected during the 1920s and 1930s, children's questions were the subject of a fair amount of empirical investigation. During this period the questions that children spontaneously asked were recorded, and efforts were made to classify them systematically as well as to trace the occurrence of various types of questions among children of different ages. By the time the exploratory behaviour of animals had become a popular topic in the 1950s, children's questions were no longer a subject of much interest. Some studies of their questioning were undertaken in the late 1960s; however, few of them have emerged from studies of other forms of exploration. I know of only one investigation that has studied the role of variables such as novelty or complexity in determining the number and kind of questions asked.

Questioning has always been considered a sign of curiosity. Woodworth (1922) stated that the primary motivation for questioning is 'curiosity regarding some particular thing' (p. 122). It meets our definition of increasing the exposure of the various senses to environmental information, for questions usually receive answers which clarify, for the questioner, some aspect of the environment about which he has expressed his uncertainty. While it has been pointed out that some questions may serve to draw attention to the questioner, and others may be designed to test the knowledge of the respondent, it is still probably true that questions function chiefly to add information about some portion of the environment.

The third and fourth years have often been designated as the age of questioning, for the young child's questions seem endless and demanding. Estimates vary as to the frequency of questions at different ages. For this age group, questions constitute from 11 to 28 per cent of all utterances (Fahey, 1942). Furthermore, questioning is an important means of obtaining information. In many instances asking a question can be a more rapid and efficient means of gathering information than other forms of exploration. Information about environmental events removed in either time (future or past) or space (not immediately accessible to the sense organs) can be transferred from respondent to questioner. In addition, there are some aspects of the world that can only be explored through questioning. What do you think about . . .? How do you like . . .? Why did you . . .?

One of the earliest methods of classifying children's questions was by the form of the question. The age of appearance of 'what', 'who', 'when', 'where', 'how' and 'why' have been carefully marked in more than one language (Fahey, 1942). More recently questions have been classified according to the linguistic capacities they required (Cazden, 1972). The earliest questions are single word utterances with rising intonation. These are followed by *yes–no* questions in which a single transformation moves the auxiliary verb to the beginning of the sentence. Thus 'The boy can drive the car' becomes 'Can the boy drive the car?' Finally, *wh– questions* develop which require two transformations: selecting an appropriate question word to begin the sentence and placing the auxiliary immediately after that word in the sentence, 'Where is he going?'

Another method of classification has been in terms of the objects of the questions. Smith and Hall's (1907) report represents one of the first classifications of questions according to topic or subject matter. Other similar studies were used to design curricula that met the interests expressed by children in their questions.

A more difficult classification system was proposed by Piaget (1928). It was designed to reflect the thought processes of the child. For Piaget, questions were an important means of studying thought. 'There is no better introduction to child logic than the study of spontaneous questions' (Piaget, 1928, p. 163). The data Piaget based his system on were 1125 questions gathered over a ten-month period by the teacher of one six-year-old boy. The teacher recorded the questions that the boy asked during their daily two-hour talks. The data based on the records of only one child may not be representative of many others. While the boy was not aware that his questions were being recorded, the teacher was, and she may have influenced (by her answers or other means) the frequency, form or content of the boy's questions. Nevertheless, later studies using Piaget's system of classification have eliminated these problems and corroborated many of Piaget's findings (Davis, 1932).

Piaget's classification scheme was based first on the presence or absence of the word 'why' and second, on the anticipated answer to the question. 'Whys' were classified as:

1 'Whys' of causal explanation that refer to physical objects.

2 'Whys' of motivation that seek understanding of the motives of various acts.

3 'Whys' of justification of various laws, rules or customs.

The 'whys' of causal explanation include such questions as: '*Why* do they [bodies] fall?' 'Has it rained last night? – No – Then *why* have they [weeds] grown?' '*Why* is it [pigeon] like an eagle, *why*?' Piaget felt that many questions in this class were a result of the child's inability to understand and hence to attribute some events to chance. Thus the child will 'look for the why and wherefore of all fortuitous juxtapositions which he meets with, in experience' (Piaget, 1928, p. 174). According to Piaget, many 'whys' which seem to fall in this category really sought understanding of the motives of the creator of the event, and perhaps belonged to the next category.

The majority of the questions asked by this child were 'whys' of motivation. Questions like '*Why* is she frightened?' and '*Why* are angels always kind to children?' are examples.

'Whys' of justification are similar to 'whys' of motivation in that they can be interpreted as seeking to determine the motives of whoever imposed the rule. This class is further divided into 'whys' relating to rules and customs, 'whys' relating to lessons like those learned in school and 'whys' relating to definitions. Piaget claimed that this last subclass eventually led to the use of 'whys' of logical reason although such forms were only rarely found among this child's questions. For example, he asked '*Why* "black coffee", all coffee is black?'

Each of the methods of classification has its merits and problems. While those that use either the particular interrogative or the topic of the question as their basis are precise and easy to use, they are not as meaningful, and their psychological implications are greatly reduced. Piaget's system, on the other hand, while rich in detail is based largely on his inferences about the type of answer expected; consequently it is difficult to know if any question has been properly classified.

Despite the absence of any entirely satisfactory classification scheme, it seems obvious that children's questions represent a more varied and diversified form of exploratory behaviour than the others we have discussed. In addition, when the child asks a question, the information he seeks usually seems far more specific than what he seeks to know when he looks at a picture or approaches a new toy. At least, it seems easier to determine (if not to classify) exactly what information is sought with a question, and what information is received in an answer, than it is with other forms of exploration.

Perhaps we should determine whether visual or auditory exploration actually seek more specific information about the environment than we presently think. Does the explorer 'ask' about an object when he just looks at or touches it? Is he guided by the 'question' he wants to answer? If such specific exploration does occur, is the activity different in some way, depending on the presence and nature of the question that guides exploration? It would seem that if other forms of exploration were guided by questions, expectations would emerge about the form the answer might take. Visual or tactual exploration might then consist of scanning the stimulus until a particularly relevant piece of information was found, followed by closer attention to the particular information that could help to answer the question. Such a suggestion is of course highly speculative, but if questioning is another form of exploration, we should be able to build bridges from one area of inquiry to the other.

One more recent study of children's questions does relate the two areas of research. Berlyne and Frommer (1966) looked at environmental determinants of the incidence and form of children's questions, focusing on those conditions that increased other forms of exploration in animals and man. The subjects of this study were children in kindergarten, and grades 3, 4, 5 and 6. They were exposed to stimuli that consisted of stories, pictures and stories accompanied by pictures. After each stimulus the children were asked: 'Is there anything that you would like to know about this story (picture)? Are there any questions you would like to ask? . . . Anything else?' (Berlyne and Frommer, 1966, p. 179). The stimuli themselves were varied along dimensions that typically lead to differences in exploratory behaviour including novelty, surprisingness, incongruity, uncertainty and amount of information. Novelty (unusual animals substituted for familiar ones in a fable), surprisingness (an unlikely ending to a story, or magic tricks) and incongruity (the combination of various parts of different animals or distortion of a familiar animal) are closely related to our prior definition of novelty; uncertainty (the number and relative probability of outcomes of a story) and amount of information (a picture either accompanied by additional verbal information or not accompanied by additional information about it) are related to complexity. The greater the novelty, incongruity, uncertainty and surprisingness (magic tricks only) of the items, the more questions the children asked. Thus it would seem that, at least in some instances, novelty and complexity produced more exploration in the form of questioning. The children asked more questions about novel and complex stimuli than about familiar and simple ones.

One unexpected finding, however, suggests some intriguing possibilities for the study of the child's questioning as an exploratory response. Berlyne and Frommer (1966) answered the questions of only half their subjects; those of the other subjects remained unanswered. Furthermore, answers were not provided immediately after the questions were asked, but after all questions on a given item were elicited and before proceeding to the next item. In general, there were no differences in the number of questions asked by children who did not receive answers. This result is unusual, given the present conceptions of questioning. In questioning, the child seeks information to fill gaps in his knowledge. Questioning is exploratory behaviour because it increases the subjects' access to environmental information. But if questions are unanswered, then they do not affect the amount of information the children receive. They do not reduce uncertainty. It might, therefore, be expected that unanswered questions would decline in frequency but they did not. How can this result be explained? First, it is possible that the subjects weren't really exploring when they asked questions in the Berlyne and Frommer study. They may have been only complying with the experimenter's request for questions. Why then did novelty and complexity lead to increased questioning? Possibly because it is easier to think of questions concerning novel or complex stimuli, rather than familiar or simple ones. Another possibility is that by delaying the answer until all questions about a given item had been asked, the experimenter reduced the child's interest in the answer. The gap in knowledge upon which the child focused when he asked the question has been passed over, while he considered other possible questions. As a result the delayed answer was not as important to him as an immediate answer might have been. A third alternative is that questioning is such a common form of exploration, and the failure to have one's questions answered so unusual, that within the relatively short time span of the current study, it did not affect the frequency of the children's questions. Perhaps prolonged questioning that is never answered would eventually lead to decreases in children's questions.

On the surface this problem may not seem crucial. Nevertheless, if questions are inspired by a lack of information, it is essential that providing or not providing the information should influence the questioning activity. Otherwise further motives must be invoked to explain questioning. The possibility this procedure points to is that of observing exploratory responses and withholding their natural consequences. Looking, listening, manipulating and approaching all have consequences for the explorer (in the form of the information that they provide) that are not easily eliminated. On the other hand, the answers to questions could always be either withheld, or varied in some other manner, so that their effect on further exploration could be investigated.

The development of exploratory behaviour

Exploratory responses, defined as those that increase access to environmental information, have been found to vary in a remarkably similar manner in situations involving differing amounts of novelty and complexity. Whenever new or a greater amount of information exists in a particular situation (novel or complex), more exploratory behaviour, be it looking, listening, approach, manipulation or asking, usually occurs.

These different responses come to serve an exploratory function at various times in the child's life, with the exact timing controlled more by the child's growing motor capacities than by any other factor. The infant cannot approach a new toy until he can crawl; and questioning awaits the child's growing linguistic abilities. It might be the case that as soon as the child is capable of a response, it is likely to be used for exploration. As soon as he can use the behaviour to investigate his surroundings, he does.

This proposal needs to be tempered by some contradictory evidence. The newborn is capable of selective fixation of various stimuli (Fantz, 1958) and yet it is not until he is more than two months old that novelty and complexity systematically influence where he looks. Similarly, at six months the infant can manipulate objects, but novelty does not yet influence which objects he will manipulate (Schaffer and Parry, 1970). Similar lags may appear as other exploratory responses enter the infant's repertoire. Although an explanation of this phenomenon at the present time can hardly be more than a guess, it might be the case that when a response is *new*, it is practised repeatedly and indiscriminately on any available object and the novelty of the *activity* supplies the child with sufficient new information. When the response is more familiar, the *stimuli* to which it is directed, and not the response itself, are the sources of new information, and novel and complex objects are explored. It would, therefore, be interesting to know if other exploratory responses, such as approaching and questioning, follow patterns similar to vision and manipulation.

This brief review demonstrates that the child is an active, involved explorer of his environment. Exploratory behaviour encompasses a wide variety of his responses and a significant proportion of his day. In particular his appetite for new facts and complex situations is enormous and by exploring he increases his knowledge and understanding of the world. His learning is motivated by curiosity, not the stern dictates of his elders. His learning is constantly changing in form as more and more responses come to serve an exploratory function. It is as if the child has accepted the advice of one of the great thinkers of our time:

The important thing is not to stop questioning. Curiosity has its own reason for existence. One cannot help but be in awe when one contemplates the mysteries of eternity, of life, of the marvelous structure of reality. It is enough if one tries merely to comprehend a little of this mystery each day. Never lose a holy curiosity (Albert Einstein in Clark, 1971, p. 623).

References

BERLYNE, D. E. (1960), *Conflict Arousal and Curiosity*, McGraw-Hill.
BERLYNE, D. E., and FROMMER, F. D. (1966), 'Some determinants of the incidence and content of children's questions', *Child Devel.*, vol. 37, pp. 177–89.
BRENNAN, W. M., AMES, E. W., and MOORE, R. W. (1966), 'Age differences in infants' attention to patterns of different complexities', *Science*, vol. 151, pp. 354–6.
CARON, R. F., and CARON, A. J. (1968), 'The effects of repeated exposure and stimulus complexity on visual fixation in infants', *Psychonom. Sci.*, vol. 10, pp. 207–8.
CARON, R. F., and CARON, A. J. (1969), 'Degree of stimulus complexity and habituation of visual fixation in infants', *Psychonom. Sci.*, vol. 14, pp. 78–9.

CAZDEN, C. B. (1972), 'Children's questions: their forms, functions, and roles in education', in W. W. Hartup (ed.), *The Young Child*, vol. 2, National Association for the Education of Young Children, Washington.

CLARK, R. W. (1971), *Einstein: The Life and Times*, World.

COHEN, L. B. (1969), 'Observing responses, visual preferences, and habituation to visual stimuli in infants', *J. exp. child Psychol.*, vol. 1, pp. 419–33.

COLLARD, R. R. (1962), 'A study of curiosity in infants', unpublished Ph.D. dissertation, University of Chicago.

DARWIN, C. (1877), 'A biographical sketch of an infant', *Mind*, vol. 2, pp. 285–94.

DAVIS, E. A. (1932), 'The form and function of children's questions', *Child Devel.*, vol. 3, pp. 57–74.

DEMBER, W. N., and EARL, R. W. (1957), 'Analysis of exploratory, manipulatory and curiosity behaviors', *Psychol. Rev.*, vol. 64, pp. 91–6.

DEMBER, W. N., EARL, R. W., and PARADISE, N. (1957), 'Response by rats to differential stimulus complexity', *J. comp. physiol. Psychol.*, vol. 50, pp. 514–18.

FAGAN, J. F. (1970), 'Memory in the infant', *J. exp. child Psychol.*, vol. 9, pp. 217–26.

FAGAN, J. F. (1971), 'Infants' recognition memory for a series of visual stimuli', *J. exp. child Psychol.*, vol. 11, pp. 244–51.

FAGAN, J. F., FANTZ, R. L., and MIRANDA, S. B. (1971), 'Infants' attention to novel stimuli as a function of postnatal and conceptual age', Paper presented to the Society for Research in Child Development, Minneapolis.

FAHEY, G. L. (1942), 'The questioning activity of children', *J. genet. Psychol.*, vol. 60, pp. 337–57.

FANTZ, R. L. (1958), 'Pattern vision in young infants', *Psychol. Rec.*, vol. 8, pp. 43–7.

FANTZ, R. L. (1964), 'Visual experience in infants: decreased attention to familiar patterns relative to novel ones', *Science*, vol. 146, pp. 668–70.

FANTZ, R. L., and NEVIS, S. (1967), 'Pattern preferences and perceptual–cognitive development in early infancy', *Merrill-Palmer Q. Behav. Devel.*, vol. 13, pp. 88–108.

HALL, G. S. (1907), *Aspects of Child Life and Education*, Ginn.

HARLOW, H. F. (1953), 'Mice, monkeys, men and motives', *Psychol. Rev.*, vol. 60, pp. 23–32.

HERSHENSON, M. (1964), 'Visual discrimination in the human newborn', *J. comp. physiol. Psychol.*, vol. 58, pp. 270–76.

HERSHENSON, M., MUNSINGER, H., and KESSEN, W. (1965), 'Preference for shapes of intermediate variability in the newborn human', *Science*, vol. 147, pp. 630–31.

HUTT, C. (1967), 'Effects of stimulus novelty on manipulatory exploration in an infant', *J. child Psychol. Psychiat.*, vol. 8, pp. 241–7.

KAGAN, J. (1971), *Change and Continuity in Infancy*, Wiley.

KARMEL, B. Z. (1969a), 'Complexity, amount of contour, and visually dependent preference behavior in hooded rats, domestic chicks, and human infants', *J. comp. physiol. Psychol.*, vol. 68, pp. 649–57.

KARMEL, B. Z. (1969b), 'The effect of age, complexity and amount of contour on pattern preferences in human infants', *J. exp. child Psychol.*, vol. 1, pp. 339–54.

LEWIS, M. (1970), 'Attention and verbal labeling behavior: a study in the measurement of internal representation', *Research Bulletin, Educational Testing Service*, Princeton, New Jersey.

LEWIS, M., and GOLDBERG, S. (1969), 'The acquisition and violation of expectancy: an experimental paradigm', *J. exp. child Psychol.*, vol. 7, pp. 70–80.

MCCALL, R. B., and GARRATT, C. R. (1971), 'Qualitative aspects of exploratory behavior in infants', unpublished manuscript.

MCCALL, R. B., and KAGAN, J. (1967), 'Stimulus-schema discrepancy and attention in the infant', *J. exp. child Psychol.*, vol. 5, pp. 381–90.

MCCALL, R. B., and MELSON, W. H. (1969), 'Attention in infants as a function of magnitude of discrepancy and habituation rate', *Psychonom. Sci.*, vol. 17, pp. 317–19.

MCCALL, R. B., and MELSON, W. H. (1970a), 'Amount of short-term familiarization and the response to auditory discrepancies', *Child Devel.*, vol. 41, pp. 861–70.

MCCALL, R. B., and MELSON, W. H. (1970b), 'Complexity, contour and area as determinants of attention in infants', *Devel. Psychol.*, vol. 3, pp. 343–9.

MCGURK, H. (1970), 'The role of object orientation in infant perception', *J. exp. child Psychol.*, vol. 9, pp. 363–73.

MAY, R. B. (1963), 'Stimulus selection in preschool children under conditions of free choice', *Percept. mot. Skills*, vol. 16, pp. 203–6.

MELSON, W. H., and MCCALL, R. B. (1970), 'Attentional responses of five-month girls to discrepant auditory stimuli', *Child Devel.*, vol. 41, pp. 1159–72.

MOFFETT, A. (1969), 'Stimulus complexity as a determinant of visual attention in infants', *J. exp. child Psychol.*, vol. 8, pp. 173–9.

MUNSINGER, H., and WEIR, M. (1967), 'Infants' and young children's preference for complexity', *J. exp. child Psychol.*, vol. 5, pp. 69–73.

PIAGET, J. (1928), *The Language and Thought of the Child*, Harcourt, Brace & World.

RHEINGOLD, H. L., and ECKERMAN, C. O. (1969), 'The infant's free entry into a new environment', *J. exp. child Psychol.*, vol. 8, pp. 271–83.

ROSS, H. S. (1972), 'Novelty and complexity as determinants of exploratory behavior in 12-month-old infants', unpublished dissertation, University of North Carolina.

ROSS, H. S., RHEINGOLD, H. L., and ECKERMAN, C. O. (1972), 'Approach and exploration of a novel alternative by 12-month-old infants', *J. exp. child Psychol.*, vol. 13, pp. 85–93.

SAAYMAN, G., AMES, E. W., and MOFFETT, A. (1964), 'Response to novelty as an indicator of visual discrimination in the human infant', *J. exp. child Psychol.*, vol. 1, pp. 189–98.

SCHAFFER, H. R., and PARRY, M. H. (1970), 'The effects of short-term familiarization on infants' perceptual–motor coordination in a simultaneous discrimination situation', *Brit. J. Psychol.*, vol. 61, pp. 559–69.

SIQUELAND, E. R. (1969), 'The development of instrumental exploratory behavior during the first year of human life', Paper presented to the meeting of the Society for Research in Child Development, Santa Monica, California.

SMITH, T. L., and HALL, G. S. (1907), 'Curiosity and interest', in G. S. Hall (ed.), *Aspects of Child Life and Education*, Ginn.

TAINE, H. (1877), 'Acquisition of language by children', *Mind*, vol. 2, pp. 252–9.

THOMAS, H. (1969), 'Unidirectional changes in preference for increasing visual complexity', *J. comp. physiol. Psychol.*, vol. 68, pp. 296–302.

Webster's Seventh New Collegiate Dictionary (1963), Merriam.

WOODWORTH, R. S. (1922), *Dynamic Psychology*, Columbia University Press.

Chapter 5
Infant Attachments

Carl Corter

Responses between infant and mother come first in accounts of social development. The mother is the primary target of the infant's looking, smiling and reaching as these responses emerge in his first months; the mother merits such early attention not because the infant 'knows' she is mother, but simply because she, more than any other, is there and responsive. Towards the end of his first year, however, the infant 'chooses' to direct some of his social responses to the mother as he establishes a special tie to her, a tie psychologists label 'attachment'.

Not only is the mother the main target of the infant's responses, but she is the chief source of modification of his behaviour; her responses modify his. In turn, the infant's behaviour can have powerful effects on the mother, as any mother of a crying baby can testify. The infant socializes his mother just as she socializes him (Bell, 1971); although this chapter concentrates on the infant side, attachment is nevertheless a complex interaction between mother and infant.

Still more importance must be assigned to the mother since her decisions greatly affect the extent and character of the child's world beyond the family. For example, the mother may choose to stay at home, or to place her child in day-care. In these points the mother's importance is clear; to a large extent she controls and is controlled by her infant's behaviour in the here and now. More controversial is Freud's assertion that the nature of the mother–child dyad sets the child's behaviour for practically all subsequent social interactions. Why the controversy if most laymen and most developmental psychologists subscribe in some degree to the theory that bent twigs produce bent trees – that early experience has pervasive later effects?

A few words about methods of studying early social behaviour are in order.

Freud made his guesses from the recollections of troubled adults; neither the behaviours which were thought to result from the early mother–infant experience, and certainly not the early experience itself, were quantified or related to each other in any systematic way. Clinical hunches may be good starting points for scientific analysis; how have Freud's ideas about early experience fared? One approach, similar to Freud's but more objective, has been to correlate parents' retrospective reports of the child's early experience with objective measures of the child's later behaviours. Studies of this nature have not found clear relationships between early experiences in feeding, weaning and toileting with later social behaviours such as aggression (see Orlansky, 1949). These studies, however, have a methodological weakness, the use of retrospective reports. Psychologists have found that parents' reports are often inaccurate, especially when the reports concern events in the past (Robbins, 1963). Perhaps with reliable measures of both the early experience and the later behaviour, studies might be able to verify the importance of what happens early upon how the child behaves later. Nevertheless, the influence of early experience would probably not be as pervasive as Freud thought; even psychoanalysts now question Freud's belief that wars result from the mother–son love affair and the ensuing jealousy the son feels towards the father.

Another problem in the Freudian legacy is that casting early social development only in questions about subsequent social behaviour may serve to cloud understanding of the young child. An understanding of early social behaviour is valuable in its own right, not simply as an adumbration of adulthood. Direct observation of social behaviour in young children is therefore needed. Once a basic understanding of the early forms takes shape, we may ask about their later effects.

The call for direct observation of the infant–mother dyad is no rallying cry, for the number of recent studies on the topic shows that it is already one of the most popular topics in the study of child development.

Before these studies are reviewed, a brief apology to liberated fathers and mothers is in order. So far only the *mother*–infant relationship has been mentioned, but the mother is not magic. She achieves her special status with the infant only through hours of caretaking and general stimulation, not by birthing or even necessarily by breast feeding. With the erosion of traditional sex roles, more and more fathers may become 'mothers'. In fact, even in many 'traditional families' infants develop a special relationship with their fathers or grandmothers as well as with the mother (Schaffer and Emerson, 1964). In the following discussion, the word 'mother' applies to all those who fit the mother role and who establish a special relationship with the infant.

Attachment responses

What is this special relationship between mother and infant? The newborn is undiscriminating. He cries in hunger or pain regardless of who is present. He seeks to suck whatever brushes his cheek, a paediatrician's finger or the mother's nipple. In the first few months, people come to be preferred to things. During the remainder of the first year of life, certain of the infant's social responses gradually come to be directed more to the mother than to others; these attachment responses are usually characterized as proximity-maintaining – they serve to keep the mother and infant close. These points are generally accepted by investigators of early social behaviour, but there is less unanimity on other questions such as what accounts for the development of the selective responding to the mother and which behaviours are important in the tie. One list of attachment behaviours named sixteen responses that the infant comes to direct selectively to the mother (Ainsworth, 1967). John Bowlby (1958) named sucking, clinging, following (by looking and by locomotion), crying and smiling. These behaviours fall into two classes: by sucking, clinging and following, the infant actively maintains or seeks proximity to his mother; by smiling and crying, the infant signals the mother so that she becomes the active partner in maintaining proximity. Again there is the emphasis on partnership, the two-way character of social interaction.

The partnership between mother and child is evident even in the earliest responses of the infant to his mother – rooting and sucking.

Though both are well-coordinated responses at birth, the mother acts very quickly to modify them. The manner in which she holds her infant partly determines the success of his rooting for the breast (Blauvelt and McKenna, 1961). The particular shape of the mother's nipple may very quickly modify the sucking response (Gunther, 1961). Usually the modification allows successful feeding, but with certain nipple shapes sucking may actually be extinguished. This is likely to happen when the infant is smothered by the breast.

Besides modifying her infant's early feeding behaviour, the mother may learn that her infant's rooting is a signal for feeding and respond with preparation for feeding and even with the 'let-down reflex' (Newton, 1951); an impressive sight is to see a mother's blouse become sopping shortly after she hears her infant cry. Of course the harmony between infant and mother does not function perfectly from feeding to feeding (Ainsworth and Bell, 1971). On the infant's part, for example, whether he is brought to his mother drowsy or alert will affect his success at feeding. In turn, the mother is affected by unsuccessful feeding and may feel rejected (Levy, 1958). In some cases she may modify her part in the feeding, perhaps inappropriately so that subsequent feedings are hindered. Because some mothers who want to breast-feed cannot and because others choose not to in the first place, it is fortunate that the special relationship between mother and infant can be established though a bottle comes between them. Even Freud, who argued that feeding was the well-spring for attachment, gradually saw the overwhelming evidence that bottle-feeding did not necessarily hinder attachment formation (Freud, 1926). In addition it is now widely accepted that the association of the mother with the satisfaction of the infant's hunger, whether by breast or bottle, is not critical to the formation of an attachment relation. The evidence for this conclusion will be reviewed later.

Furthermore, sucking may not qualify as an attachment response. By seeking and holding the breast, the infant facilitates proximity to the mother, and he gains general stimulation by touching, hearing, smelling and looking at her. Such stimulation may facilitate the development of the infant–mother tie, but there is no evidence that sucking is selective. In fact, many breast-fed babies in Western cultures are weaned before the time when the infant is thought to be able to discriminate between mother and stranger. Thus sucking is best thought of as a precursor of attachment rather than as a sign that the infant discriminates the mother from others and seeks her proximity.

In contrast to sucking, other responses between infant and mother continue to be important throughout early childhood and beyond. Two of these behaviours, looking and smiling, are well developed at birth or soon after. Others, such as following, naturally appear later as the infant develops in motor capacity.

The analysis of findings on looking as a social response requires consideration of the infant's visual capacities. The infant is not blind at birth. Although he lacks some of the finer visual capabilities, these develop rapidly over the first few months. For example, the newborn can focus sharply only on objects about seven inches from his eyes, but by four months his ability to accommodate, or focus, is close to that of an adult (Haynes, White and Held, 1965). Other visual capabilities also develop rapidly in the first months; among them are the capacity to perceive brightness differences, depth, pattern and movement (Doris, Casper and Poresky, 1967; Fantz, 1964; Fantz and Nevis, 1967; Haith, 1966). This early competence contrasts with the slower development of some of the other senses (Peiper, 1963) and indicates that vision is a very important source of general stimulation and information about the infant's social world. Furthermore, vision continues to be important later since social behaviour in children and adults is often maintained at a middle distance where vision and hearing predominate (Walters and Parke, 1965).

The responses of fixation and visual pursuit are present soon after birth and rapidly become important in the infant–mother tie (Moss and Robson, 1968). The human face is likely to be looked at often since it has characteristics that evoke looking: it is complex and variable, always changing. Early looking is not limited to familiar faces, however, or even to faces. Complexity and change in objects also evoke looking.

Young infants are, therefore, promiscuous lookers, but the suggestion has been made that they gradually come to look more often at the mother than at a stranger. At present, however, there is no convincing evidence that looking is a response that shows mother is special. One study showed that ten-month-old infants who had a choice of looking at mother or stranger looked equally at both

(Corter, 1973). Looking no doubt serves different functions, and is directed to the new as well as to the familiar. Infants may gaze inquisitively as well as fondly. On present evidence, it can only be said that looking does not seem to distinguish between mother and others, although looking may provide the information whereby other responses are directed selectively to the mother or stranger.

Smiling, in contrast, provides a different wrinkle; by six months the infant smiles more to the mother than to others (e.g. Schaffer, 1966; Spitz and Wolf, 1946). Even so, smiling also has unselective beginnings. In the first day of life, smiling may occur in the absence of any obvious external stimulus, usually when the infant is in a state of drowsiness or irregular sleep (Wolff, 1963). Generations of mothers have attributed such smiles to 'gas' but science offers no supporting evidence; other internal stimuli or even unobserved external stimuli could be responsible. During the second week, the infant begins to smile when his eyes are open, and by the fourth week his smiles seem to be evoked by specific stimuli in the environment (Wolff, 1963). The stimuli may be the sight of a toy (Piaget, 1952; Rheingold, 1961) or of a human face, familiar or strange (Laroche and Tcheng, 1963). Some studies suggest that the human face has characteristics that are especially likely to evoke smiling; movement, for example, has been suggested as an important variable in evoking smiles (e.g. Wolff, 1963). Other studies have suggested that particular 'parts' of the face, especially the eyes, become powerful controllers of smiling (Spitz and Wolf, 1946). Finally there is evidence that touching the infant by either social or non-social objects may produce smiling; one study (Freedman, 1964) found that blind infants smiled to touch or voices.

People often combine the qualities of sight, sound and touch in their interactions with the infant; social stimuli therefore evoke smiling more readily than do non-social stimuli. The greater responsivity to people in general continues until the infant is four or five months old (Ambrose, 1961; Gewirtz, 1965); thereafter smiling is restricted more and more to the mother (Schaffer, 1966).

The other side of the infant–mother interaction should not be overlooked; the infant's smiles may control his mother's behaviour. Some writers have pointed out that the infant's smile may serve to keep the mother near the infant; the smile is gratifying to the mother so she stays close, thereby ensuring that the infant receives the care he needs. Some writers have gone so far as to suggest that the smile of the human infant is *the* most important response in the mother–infant tie, analogous to the following response that binds an attached (imprinted) duckling to its mother (e.g. Gray, 1958). These suggestions, however, are merely conjecture; the effects of the infant's smile on the mother have not been studied. Furthermore, most mothers can no doubt tell us that infants receive care even when they are unsmiling, even when they screw their faces up in a cry. Smiling is directed selectively to the mother, but it is probably not *the* critical link of the infant–mother tie.

Crying has also been shown to be directed selectively to the mother, and it too may serve to bring the mother close. Although crying may sometimes be a reflexive response to painful physical stimulation, the infant may learn that crying controls his caretaker. As in the case of smiling, however, there is no experimental evidence on the effects of the infant's cry on the mother's behaviour.

The infant's crying selectively to the mother has been demonstrated in situations in which the mother leaves the infant; in this instance crying is labelled 'separation protest'. Studies of separation protest by Fleener (Fleener and Cairns, 1970) and Schaffer (Schaffer and Emerson, 1964) offer an interesting contrast in method and will serve to illustrate some of the different methods that researchers of child development use to gain knowledge about social behaviour.

Both studies asked the same questions: does the infant protest more when his mother, rather than a stranger, leaves him, and if so, at what age does the discrimination begin? Schaffer studied a group of infants monthly over much of their first year and then again at eighteen months; because his was a pioneering study he chose to 'cast his nets widely' by obtaining his information from the mothers' reports concerning separation protest in various situations in the everyday life of the child. For example, the mother was asked whether her infant protested when he was 'left in his pram outside shops' or 'in his cot at night'. By using interviews, Schaffer was able to obtain data more easily than if he had carried out observations of the actual behaviour, but this gain must be weighed against the possibility of bias in the mothers' reporting. Schaffer was nevertheless able to make several improvements on the usual interview study. First, the mothers' reports were of behaviours that had occurred within a few weeks of the interview, not years before. Second, he showed that two people could agree in transforming the mothers' verbal reports into numbers that could then be analysed statistically. Finally, he found that the mothers' reports actually agreed substantially with what he observed of the infants' actual behaviour during the interview. Specifically, he recorded the infant's behaviour when the mother left the room during the course of the interview and compared these findings to the mother's reports about protest in the same situation. With such careful checks, interview studies may provide provocative leads for studies of actual behaviour.

Even though the study was carefully done, Schaffer's conclusion that selective protest at the mother's departure begins at an average of eight months may be questioned. Although Schaffer saw for himself that the older infants protested when the mother left, they might also have protested at the departure of a stranger. A clear test of the mother's control over separation protest would require an experimental study in which the departures of the mother and of a stranger are systematically manipulated and the effects on the infant's behaviour measured. By manipulating a variable such as whether the mother or stranger departs, an experimental study can establish a cause-and-effect relationship between that variable and the behaviour of interest. In contrast, a descriptive study, such as Schaffer's (whether interview or observation), cannot establish a causal relationship since there is no controlled manipulation that allows a gauging of the effects of a variable upon behaviour.

Fleener's experimental study manipulated the departure of the mother and of a stranger so that the mother's selective control of protesting could be tested. Fleener studied different infants at each of six age levels from three to nineteen months and recorded fussing and crying as the adults alternatively left the room. The results showed that only the infants over twelve months protested more when the mother, rather than the stranger, left. Both Fleener's study and Schaffer's study therefore suggested that separation protest was selective, but found different average ages for the onset of the discrimination.

Fleener's experimental data are not necessarily more valid than Schaffer's interview data; there is only a greater probability that the experimental manipulation and direct recording of behaviour provide a more reliable picture of selective protest behaviour than do mothers' reports. On the other hand, another experimental study of ten-month-old infants (Corter, 1973) showed that the mother's leaving evoked crying sooner than a stranger's leaving. Thus, the development of differential protest has not been charted as clearly as the development of selective smiling to the mother.

Following is a final behaviour suggested as an attachment response and shown to be directed selectively to the mother. In contrast to the infant's early prowess in smiling and crying, his mastery of moving about well enough to follow generally takes the better part of his first year of life. In one study of following (Corter, 1973), ten-month-old infants were selected as subjects because most infants of that age can move about efficiently. Infants were placed by the mother in one room, and the mother and a stranger then walked away, each going into a different adjoining room, sitting down where the infant could see. Given the choice of following the mother or stranger, almost all infants followed the mother. In contrast, infants looked almost equally at the mother and stranger before following. The infants were faithful followers but promiscuous lookers. Following therefore qualifies as an attachment response soon after the capacity for loco-motion develops; it is selective and it increases the infant's proximity to the mother.

Other responses such as clinging and vocalizing have also been suggested as part of the complex of behaviours that ties the child to his mother, but as yet the selectivity of these responses has not been studied; only smiling, crying and following have been established as behaviours that the young child directs selectively to the mother.

Attachment as a construct

For some psychologists the concept of attachment is more than the sum of the responses that are directed selectively to the mother. In particular, some psychologists have stressed the importance of the interrelationships among attachment behaviours (e.g. Lewis and Ban, 1971). Others have argued that attachment behaviours can be understood only in relation to hypothetical states or structures within the organism – personality structures (Freud, 1926), emotion or affect (Ainsworth, 1971), or cognitive structures (Bell, 1970).

Several recent studies have tested the interrelations among responses to the mother in an effort to tie the responses together at the empirical level. The theme of these studies is that the different attachment responses should be correlated if attachment is unitary or more than the sum of its parts. A representative finding from these studies is that visual regard is related to other responses such as active approach to the mother in ten-, fourteen- and eighteen-month-old infants (Coates, Anderson and Hartup, 1972). Since the general finding is that responses to the mother are related, the results are offered as evidence that the child's tie to his mother is unitary.

The meaningfulness of these findings may be questioned, however. The evidence reviewed earlier showed that the mother had no special control over looking, but she did evoke active approach (following) more than a stranger. This evidence must be reconciled with the findings from the studies that show looking to be related to active approach. A simple explanation would be that infants look where they are moving. A correlation between looking and moving would therefore result from the mechanics of moving towards the mother rather than from a unitary attachment to her. The present search for a unitary attachment is somehow reminiscent of the psychologist's search for a general, or g, factor underlying intelligence; that search has long been abandoned but the diverse behaviours subsumed under the label of intelligence are still under study.

Extending the concept of attachment to include hypothetical states or structures within the child has produced volumes of speculation but little research. The lack of research is no doubt due to the difficulty, if not impossibility, of studying internal states or structures. Freud's personality structures have traditionally eluded any sort of objective study. Emotion has proved equally slippery and recent attempts to use indexes of autonomic arousal, such as pupil dilation (Fitzgerald, 1968), have not given us a clear window to the inner emotions of the child.

In contrast, some studies have claimed success in relating cognitive structures to attachment; nevertheless, these studies (e.g. DeCarie, 1965) define the cognitive structures in terms of observable behaviours. Bell (1970), for example, related attachment behaviour to the infant's cognitive ability to 'conserve' objects, an ability that Piaget (1952) outlined in his descriptions of the growth of intelligence. The infant conserves an object when he retains some representation of the object in mind, even though it disappears from the reach of his senses. The representation in the infant's mind cannot be studied; it is inferred from the infant's searching for an object that has disappeared. Infants in the first half-year of life do not seek objects that disappear. During the second half of the first year the infant begins to search for objects put away in drawers, spoons that fall from his plate and even his mother who leaves the room. Bell found that the infant's ability to conserve inanimate objects and people was correlated with his attachment responses to his mother. Since the study was descriptive, the correlation cannot be taken as evidence that there is a causal relationship between the ability to conserve objects and attachment behaviour. Another problem with the study is that the 'conservation of people' was tested by observing the infant's response to his mother's disappearance. This procedure was similar to the situation in which 'attachment behaviours' were observed. Consequently the distinction between 'attachment' and 'conservation of people' was blurred. Perhaps this is an illustration that psychological concepts may order the real world in artificial ways, particularly when the concepts grow at a greater rate than the empirical knowledge which should be at their base.

Present evidence is not sufficient to confirm elaborate concepts of attachment based on internal states and structures. The research on attachment is mainly limited to studies of the separate responses to the mother; the evidence is that several of the infant's responses come to be controlled by the mother, more than by others, over the first year of the infant's life.

Theories of attachment

What accounts for the development of this selectivity? There is general agreement that it depends on the development of sensory capabilities that allow the infant to differentiate between mother and stranger and on motor capabilities that allow him to express the differentiation. Nevertheless, the discrimination alone does not explain attachment. The attached infant can 'tell the difference' between mother and stranger but, in addition, seeks the company of the mother in preference to the stranger; the mere fact of discrimina-

KARMEL, B. Z. (1969b), 'The effect of age, complexity and amount of contour on pattern preferences in human infants', *J. exp. child Psychol.*, vol. 1, pp. 339–54.

LEWIS, M. (1970), 'Attention and verbal labeling behavior: a study in the measurement of internal representation', *Research Bulletin, Educational Testing Service*, Princeton, New Jersey.

LEWIS, M., and GOLDBERG, S. (1969), 'The acquisition and violation of expectancy: an experimental paradigm', *J. exp. child Psychol.*, vol. 7, pp. 70–80.

McCALL, R. B., and GARRATT, C. R. (1971), 'Qualitative aspects of exploratory behavior in infants', unpublished manuscript.

McCALL, R. B., and KAGAN, J. (1967), 'Stimulus-schema discrepancy and attention in the infant', *J. exp. child Psychol.*, vol. 5, pp. 381–90.

McCALL, R. B., and MELSON, W. H. (1969), 'Attention in infants as a function of magnitude of discrepancy and habituation rate', *Psychonom. Sci.*, vol. 17, pp. 317–19.

McCALL, R. B., and MELSON, W. H. (1970a), 'Amount of short-term familiarization and the response to auditory discrepancies', *Child Devel.*, vol. 41, pp. 861–70.

McCALL, R. B., and MELSON, W. H. (1970b), 'Complexity, contour and area as determinants of attention in infants', *Devel. Psychol.*, vol. 3, pp. 343–9.

McGURK, H. (1970), 'The role of object orientation in infant perception', *J. exp. child Psychol.*, vol. 9, pp. 363–73.

MAY, R. B. (1963), 'Stimulus selection in preschool children under conditions of free choice', *Percept. mot. Skills*, vol. 16, pp. 203–6.

MELSON, W. H., and McCALL, R. B. (1970), 'Attentional responses of five-month girls to discrepant auditory stimuli', *Child Devel.*, vol. 41, pp. 1159–72.

MOFFETT, A. (1969), 'Stimulus complexity as a determinant of visual attention in infants', *J. exp. child Psychol.*, vol. 8, pp. 173–9.

MUNSINGER, H., and WEIR, M. (1967), 'Infants' and young children's preference for complexity', *J. exp. child Psychol.*, vol. 5, pp. 69–73.

PIAGET, J. (1928), *The Language and Thought of the Child*, Harcourt, Brace & World.

RHEINGOLD, H. L., and ECKERMAN, C. O. (1969), 'The infant's free entry into a new environment', *J. exp. child Psychol.*, vol. 8, pp. 271–83.

ROSS, H. S. (1972), 'Novelty and complexity as determinants of exploratory behavior in 12-month-old infants', unpublished dissertation, University of North Carolina.

ROSS, H. S., RHEINGOLD, H. L., and ECKERMAN, C. O. (1972), 'Approach and exploration of a novel alternative by 12-month-old infants', *J. exp. child Psychol.*, vol. 13, pp. 85–93.

SAAYMAN, G., AMES, E. W., and MOFFETT, A. (1964), 'Response to novelty as a indicator of visual discrimination in the human infant', *J. exp. child Psychol.*, 1, pp. 189–98.

SHAFFER, H. R., and PARRY, M. H. (1970), 'The effects of short-term familiarization on infants' perceptual–motor coordination in a simultaneous discrimination situation', *Brit. J. Psychol.*, vol. 61, pp. 559–69.

CAZDEN, C. B. (1972), 'Children's questions: their forms, functions, and roles in education', in W. W. Hartup (ed.), *The Young Child*, vol. 2, National Association for the Education of Young Children, Washington.

CLARK, R. W. (1971), *Einstein: The Life and Times*, World.

COHEN, L. B. (1969), 'Observing responses, visual preferences, and habituation to visual stimuli in infants', *J. exp. child Psychol.*, vol. 1, pp. 419–33.

COLLARD, R. R. (1962), 'A study of curiosity in infants', unpublished Ph.D. dissertation, University of Chicago.

DARWIN, C. (1877), 'A biographical sketch of an infant', *Mind*, vol. 2, pp. 285–94.

DAVIS, E. A. (1932), 'The form and function of children's questions', *Child Devel.*, vol. 3, pp. 57–74.

DEMBER, W. N., and EARL, R. W. (1957), 'Analysis of exploratory, manipulatory and curiosity behaviors', *Psychol. Rev.*, vol. 64, pp. 91–6.

DEMBER, W. N., EARL, R. W., and PARADISE, N. (1957), 'Response by rats to differential stimulus complexity', *J. comp. physiol. Psychol.*, vol. 50, pp. 514–18.

FAGAN, J. F. (1970), 'Memory in the infant', *J. exp. child Psychol.*, vol. 9, pp. 217–26.

FAGAN, J. F. (1971), 'Infants' recognition memory for a series of visual stimuli', *J. exp. child Psychol.*, vol. 11, pp. 244–51.

FAGAN, J. F., FANTZ, R. L., and MIRANDA, S. B. (1971), 'Infants' attention to novel stimuli as a function of postnatal and conceptual age', Paper presented to the Society for Research in Child Development, Minneapolis.

FAHEY, G. L. (1942), 'The questioning activity of children', *J. genet. Psychol.*, vol. 60, pp. 337–57.

FANTZ, R. L. (1958), 'Pattern vision in young infants', *Psychol. Rec.*, vol. 8, pp. 43–7.

FANTZ, R. L. (1964), 'Visual experience in infants: decreased attention to familiar patterns relative to novel ones', *Science*, vol. 146, pp. 668–70.

FANTZ, R. L., and NEVIS, S. (1967), 'Pattern preferences and perceptual–cognitive development in early infancy', *Merrill-Palmer Q. Behav. Devel.*, vol. 13, pp. 88–108.

HALL, G. S. (1907), *Aspects of Child Life and Education*, Ginn.

HARLOW, H. F. (1953), 'Mice, monkeys, men and motives', *Psychol. Rev.*, vol. 60, pp. 23–32.

HERSHENSON, M. (1964), 'Visual discrimination in the human newborn', *J. comp. physiol. Psychol.*, vol. 58, pp. 270–76.

HERSHENSON, M., MUNSINGER, H., and KESSEN, W. (1965), 'Preference for shapes of intermediate variability in the newborn human', *Science*, vol. 147, pp. 630–31.

HUTT, C. (1967), 'Effects of stimulus novelty on manipulatory exploration in an infant', *J. child Psychol. Psychiat.*, vol. 8, pp. 241–7.

KAGAN, J. (1971), *Change and Continuity in Infancy*, Wiley.

KARMEL, B. Z. (1969a), 'Complexity, amount of contour, and visually depe preference behavior in hooded rats, domestic chicks, and human infants', *J. comp. physiol. Psychol.*, vol. 68, pp. 649–57.

Hildy S.

that the social behaviours of infants may be reinforced by the responsiveness of adults. For example, the infant smiles increasingly often when his smiles are followed by the touching, talking and smiling of an adult (Brackbill, 1958; Wahler, 1967). Similarly, the infant vocalizes more when his sounds produce responses from adults (Rheingold, Gewirtz and Ross, 1959; Weisberg, 1963). These experiments suggest that the operant model might account for the development of attachment in real-life situations.

The ethological theory of attachment is another theory in current favour with some psychologists. The theory evolved from ethology, the study of animal behaviour by zoologists. This orientation makes the ethological theory of attachment quite different from learning theories of attachment. In particular, ethological theory emphasizes the importance of genetic determinants of attachment behaviour, rather than the environmental determinants emphasized by learning theorists.

Some of the first attempts to apply ethological theory to attachment were made by those who saw an analogy between the imprinting phenomenon in precocial birds and the development of attachment in human infants (e.g. Gray, 1958). According to the ethologists, precocial birds follow and rapidly become attached to the first large, salient object in their post-hatch world, normally the mother. This innate approach response, unselective at first, is quickly focused on the mother. At the same time a tendency to avoid other objects is on the increase, so the young bird avoids competing attachments and predators and sticks with his mother. Thus there is a critical period when the bird is ripe to become attached but which is ended by the onset of fear of new objects.

Perhaps the human infant's attachment is analogous to this imprinting process. According to this line of reasoning, the human infant is equipped with innate, proximity-promoting responses which are initially released by any person but which gradually become focused on the mother. Carrying the imprinting analogy further, some have proposed that there is a critical period for attachment learning in infants and that its end is marked by the onset of fear of strangers sometime during the latter part of the first year. Supporting this proposal are studies (e.g. Provence and Lipton, 1962) which show that institutionalized infants fail to develop normal attachments if placed with adoptive parents after a certain age. However, such infants may be deprived in so many ways that it is difficult to pin their problems solely on missing a critical period.

There are other problems with the imprinting and critical-periods analogies. The attachment responses of human infants are not released nearly so automatically as the following response of an imprinted duckling. Ducklings follow the departing mother as if tied to her by an invisible string; the human infant may poke and play with a toy even as his mother leaves him alone in a strange place (Corter, Rheingold and Eckerman, 1972). Furthermore, fear of strangers by human infants does not seem nearly as universal as the imprinted duckling's fear of strange objects (Corter, 1973). Even in infants who show fear, there is no clear attachment between the time at which attachment behaviours develop and the time at which fear responses develop (e.g. Yarrow, 1967).

Bowlby's theory of human attachments (1969) is an ethological account which goes beyond the simple avian analogies. He suggests a model in which the separate instinctive attachment responses become linked in complex 'control systems' that are constantly modified by environmental feedback so that the infant stays within a safe distance of his mother. The control systems work to maintain a cosy degree of proximity in a manner analogous to a thermostat-furnace system which uses feedback on temperature changes to maintain a set temperature. The degree of proximity for which the control systems are 'set' depends on factors such as whether the child is tired or hungry, whether the environment he is in is familiar or strange. Another step beyond the duckling-on-a-string model of attachment is Bowlby's consideration of field studies of infant–mother relations in monkeys and apes and their implications for human attachment.

Bowlby still retains the ethological emphases on innate determinants of attachment behaviour and on the adaptive value that such behaviour might have in the evolution of the species. One of the less compelling features of his theory is that the primary function of attachment behaviour for our primitive ancestors was to protect the infant from predators; attachment could give the infant numerous advantages including opportunities for learning or caretaking and there is no way to determine if any one advantage was particularly important in man's evolution. Though Bowlby uses the term *in-*

stinctive to describe attachment behaviour he also says that maternal responsiveness is important in augmenting and maintaining the instinctive social responses. The importance of maternal responsiveness thus emerges as an important point of agreement between Bowlby's theory and the operant-learning theory of attachment.

Although operant and ethological theory are the most promising of the four theories reviewed here, the theoretical speculation about attachment is far ahead of the empirical knowledge.

Detachment

Besides the mother's special control over some of the infant's social responses, she is special in another way: her presence facilitates the infant's exploration of new things and places. Many studies have shown that in unfamiliar places, infants with their mothers move away and explore and that infants with a stranger cry and do not explore (e.g. Rheingold, 1969). Important though attachment may be, the child's detachment (Rheingold and Eckerman, 1970), or leaving his mother's side, is also important if the child is to begin to learn about the larger world and achieve the independence necessary to function as a mature member of society. Concern with the infant–mother tie should not be allowed to obscure the importance of the infant's interactions with the inanimate environment and with members of his social environment other than the mother.

Summary

The infant establishes a special tie to his mother during the first year of his life. The behaviours comprising the tie include at least smiling, crying and approach. Possible emotional, personality and cognitive concomitants of these behaviours have not proved easy to study, and elaborate conceptions of attachment are not warranted by present evidence. The conditions necessary for the formation of attachment are not known, but biological drive-reduction or need-satisfaction appears not to be necessary. The evidence suggests that the social stimulation provided by the mother is the critical variable in the formation of the infant–mother tie. Apart from the mother's importance in the attachment relationship, she is also important by her facilitation of the infant's exploration of his world outside the infant–mother interplay.

A great deal of empirical research must precede putting order into the conceptual and theoretical issues entangled in attachment. Some of the responses, such as clinging, have hardly been studied. For others, little is known about the immediate determinants of the responses, much less about long-term determinants such as how child-rearing practices affect their development. In general, very little is known about the maternal side of attachment. Future research will fill these gaps. At the same time, implications from other areas of infant research will spill over into the study of early social behaviour; the trickle of studies relating attachment to perceptual and cognitive development will likely become a deluge. Much research to come will have a practical bent; social issues such as day-care and infant education will require answers about the responses between infant and mother. Eventually research may find its way back to Freud's concern with how the infant–mother tie affects later behaviours.

References

AINSWORTH, M. D. (1967), *Infancy in Uganda: Infant Care and the Growth of Love*, Johns Hopkins University Press.

AINSWORTH, M. D. (1971), 'The development of infant–mother attachment', in B. M. Caldwell and H. N. Ricciuti (eds.), *Review of Child Development Research*, vol. 3, University of Chicago Press.

AINSWORTH, M. D., and BELL, S. M. (1971), 'Some contemporary patterns of mother–infant interaction in the feeding situation', in J. A. Ambrose (ed.), *Stimulation in Early Infancy*, Academic Press.

AMBROSE, J. A. (1961), 'The development of the smiling response in early infancy', in B. M. Foss (ed.), *Determinants of Infant Behaviour*, Methuen.

BELL, R. Q. (1971), 'Stimulus control of parent or caretaker behavior by offspring', *Devel. Psychol.*, vol. 4, pp. 63–72.

BELL, S. M. (1970), 'The development of the concept of the object as related to infant–mother attachment', *Child Devel.*, vol. 41, pp. 291–311.

BIJOU, S. W., and BAER, D. M. (1965), *Child Development: II. Universal Stage of Infancy*, Appleton-Century-Crofts.

BLAUVELT, H., and MCKENNA, J. (1961), 'Mother–neonate interaction: capacity of the human newborn for orientation', in B. M. Foss (ed.), *Determinants of Infant Behaviour*, Methuen.

BOWLBY, J. (1958), 'The nature of the child's tie to his mother', *Int. J. Psychoanal.*, vol. 39, pp. 350–73.

BOWLBY, J. (1969), *Attachment and Loss vol. 1: Attachment*, Hogarth Press.

BRACKBILL, Y. (1958), 'Extinction of the smiling response in infants as a function of reinforcement schedule', *Child Devel.*, vol. 29, pp. 115–24.

CAIRNS, R. B. (1966), 'Development, maintenance, and extinction of social attachment behavior in sheep', *J. comp. physiol. Psychol.*, vol. 62, pp. 298–306.

COATES, B., ANDERSON, E. P., and HARTUP, W. W. (1972), 'Interrelations in the attachment behavior of human infants', *Devel. Psychol.*, vol. 6, pp. 218–30.

CORTER, C. M. (1973), 'A comparison of the mother's and a stranger's control over the behavior of infants', *Child Devel.*, vol. 44, pp. 705–13.

CORTER, C. M., RHEINGOLD, H. L., and ECKERMAN, C. O. (1972), 'Toys delay the infant's following of his mother', *Devel. Psychol.*, vol. 6, pp. 138–45.

DECARIE, T. G. (1965), *Intelligence and Affectivity in Early Childhood*, International Universities Press.

DORIS, J., CASPER, M., and PORESKY, R. (1967), 'Differential brightness thresholds in infancy', *J. exp. child Psychol.*, vol. 5, pp. 522–5.

FANTZ, R. L. (1964), 'Visual experience in infants: decreased attention to familiar patterns relative to novel ones', *Science*, vol. 146, pp. 668–70.

FANTZ, R. L., and NEVIS, S. (1967), 'Pattern preferences and perceptual-cognitive development in early infancy', *Merrill-Palmer Q. Behav. Devel.*, vol. 13, pp. 77–108.

FITZGERALD, H. E. (1968), 'Autonomic pupillary reflex activity during early infancy, and its relation to social and nonsocial visual stimuli', *J. exp. child Psychol.*, vol. 5, pp. 470–82.

FLEENER, D. E., and CAIRNS, R. B. (1970), 'Attachment behaviors in human infants: discriminative vocalization on maternal separation', *Devel. Psychol.*, vol. 2, pp. 215–23.

FREEDMAN, D. G. (1964), 'Smiling in blind infants and the issue of innate v. acquired', *J. child Psychol. Psychiat.*, vol. 5, pp. 171–84.

FREUD, S. (1915), 'Instincts and their vicissitudes', *Standard Edition*, vol. 14, Hogarth Press.

FREUD, S. (1926), 'Inhibitions, symptoms and anxiety', *Standard Edition*, vol. 20, Hogarth Press.

GEWIRTZ, J. L. (1961), 'A learning analysis of the effects of normal stimulation, privation, and deprivation on the acquisition of social motivation and attachment', in B. M. Foss (ed.), *Determinants of Infant Behaviour*, Methuen.

GEWIRTZ, J. L. (1965), 'The course of infant smiling in four child-rearing environments in Israel', in B. M. Foss (ed.), *Determinants of Infant Behaviour*, vol. 3, Methuen.

GRAY, P. H. (1958), 'Theory and evidence of imprinting in human infants', *J. Psychol.*, vol. 46, pp. 155–61.

GUNTHER, M. (1961), 'Infant behaviour at the breast', in B. M. Foss (ed.), *Determinants of Infant Behaviour*, Methuen.

HAITH, M. (1966), 'The response of the human newborn to visual movement', *J. exp. child Psychol.*, vol. 3, pp. 235–43.

HARLOW, H. F., and ZIMMERMAN, R. R. (1959), 'Affectional responses in the infant monkey', *Science*, vol. 130, pp. 421–32.

HAYNES, H., WHITE, B. L., and HELD, R. (1965), 'Visual accommodation in human infants', *Science*, vol. 148, pp. 528–30.

LAROCHE, J. L., and TCHENG, P. (1963), *La sourire au nourisson*, University of Louvain.

LEVY, D. M. (1958), *Behavioral Analysis*, C. C. Thomas.

LEWIS, M., and BAN, P. (1971), 'Stability of attachment behavior: a transformational analysis', Paper presented to the meeting of the Society for Research in Child Development, Minneapolis.

MOSS, H. A., and ROBSON, K. (1968), 'Maternal influences in early social visual behavior', *Child Devel.*, vol. 39, pp. 401–8.

NEWTON, H. R. (1951), 'The relationship between infant feeding experience and later behavior', *J. Pediatrics*, vol. 38, pp. 28–40.

ORLANSKY, H. (1949), 'Infant care and personality', *Psychol. Bull.*, vol. 46, pp. 1–48.

PEIPER, A. (1963), *Cerebral Function in Infancy and Childhood*, Consultants Bureau.

PIAGET, J. (1952), *The Origins of Intelligence in Children*, International Universities Press.

PROVENCE, S., and LIPTON, R. C. (1962), *Infants in Institutions*, International Universities Press.

RHEINGOLD, H. L. (1961), 'The effect of environmental stimulation upon social and exploratory behaviour in the human infant', in B. M. Foss (ed.), *Determinants of Infant Behaviour*, Methuen.

RHEINGOLD, H. L. (1969), 'The effect of a strange environment on the behaviour of infants', in B. M. Foss (ed.), *Determinants of Infant Behaviour*, vol. 4, Methuen.

RHEINGOLD, H. L., and ECKERMAN, C. O. (1970), 'The infant separates himself from his mother', *Science*, vol. 168, pp. 78–83.

RHEINGOLD, H. L., GERWITZ, J. L., and ROSS, H. W. (1959), 'Social conditioning of vocalizations in the infant', *J. comp. physiol. Psychol.*, vol. 52, pp. 68–73.

ROBBINS, L. E. (1963), 'The accuracy of parental recall of aspects of child development and child rearing practices', *J. abnorm. soc. Psychol.*, vol. 66, pp. 261–70.

SCHAFFER, H. R. (1966), 'The onset of fear of strangers and the incongruity hypothesis', *J. child Psychol. Psychiat.*, vol. 7, pp. 95–106.

SCHAFFER, H. R., and EMERSON, P. E. (1964), 'The development of social attachments in infancy', *Mongr. Soc. Res. Child Devel.*, vol. 29, no. 3.

SCOTT, J. P. (1967), 'The development of social motivation', in D. Levine (ed.), *Nebraska Symposium on Motivation: 1967*, University of Nebraska Press.

SEARS, R. R., MACCOBY, E. E., and LEVIN, H. (1957), *Patterns of Child Rearing*, Row, Peterson.

SLUCKIN, W. (1965), *Imprinting and Early Learning*, Aldine.

SPITZ, R. A., and WOLF, K. M. (1946), 'The smiling response: a contribution to the ontogenesis of social relations', *Genet. Psychol. Mongr.*, vol. 34, pp. 57–125.

SUTTIE, I. D. (1935), *The Origins of Love and Hate*, Matrix House edn, 1966.

WAHLER, R. G. (1967), 'Infant social attachments: a reinforcement-theory interpretation and investigation', *Child Devel.*, vol. 38, pp. 1079–88.

WALTERS, R. H., and PARKE, R. D. (1965), 'The role of distance receptors in the development of social responsiveness', in L. P. Lipsitt and C. C. Spiker (eds.), *Advances in Child Development and Behavior*, vol. 2, Academic Press.

WEISBERG, P. (1963), 'Social and nonsocial conditioning of infant vocalizations', *Child Devel.*, vol. 34, pp. 377–88.

WOLFF, P. H. (1963), 'Observations on the early development of smiling', in B. M. Foss (ed.), *Determinants of Infant Behaviour*, vol. 2, Methuen.

YARROW, L. J. (1967), 'The development of focused relationships during infancy', in J. Hellmuth (ed.), *Exceptional Infant*, vol. 1, Special Child Publications.

Chapter 6
The Development of Language and Cognition: The Cognition Hypothesis

Richard F. Cromer

That was when I learned that words are no good; that words don't ever fit even what they are trying to say at . . .

William Faulkner, *As I Lay Dying*

That thought might be possible without language does not strike most people as an unreasonable idea. In fact, some artists claim that they cannot express themselves in a purely verbal medium. Even writers, whose life work immerses them in the very task of arranging words and sentences to convey meaning, often complain that their thoughts 'will not enter words'. It may come as a surprise, then, to find that the predominating view by psychologists over the last half century has been precisely the opposite; namely, that thought is dependent upon language and not possible without it. How can such a state of affairs be? What has brought about an adherence to a view which seems to go against our intuition?

Before tracing the intellectual currents which influenced the adoption of this view, it may be well to note that psychologists have not always believed that language was necessary for thought. According to William James, thinking would tend to make use of the kind of 'mind-stuff' which is easiest for the purpose. In his famous textbook, *The Principles of Psychology* (1890), he asserted that words, whether uttered or unexpressed, are the handiest mental elements we have, and thus would be the material usually used for thinking. However, he also noted that the deaf and dumb can weave their tactile and visual images into 'a system of thought quite as effective and rational as that of a word-user'. To support this claim, James quoted at length an extract of reminiscences of childhood by a Mr Ballard, a deaf-mute who was an instructor in the National College at Washington. For our purposes, a few excerpts will suffice:

I could convey my thoughts and feelings to my parents and brothers by natural signs or pantomime, and I could understand what they said to me by the same medium; our intercourse being, however, confined to the daily routine of home affairs and hardly going beyond the circle of my own observation. . . .

My father adopted a course which he thought would, in some measure, compensate me the loss of my hearing. It was that of taking me with him when business required him to ride abroad; and he took me more frequently than he did my brothers; giving, as the reason for his apparent partiality, that they could acquire information through the ear, while I depended solely upon my eye for acquaintance with affairs of the outside world. . . .

It was during those delightful rides, some two or three years before my initiation into the rudiments of written language, that I began to ask myself the question: *How came the world into being?* When this question occurred to my mind, I set myself to thinking it over a long time. My curiosity was awakened as to what was the origin of human life in its first appearance upon the earth, and of vegetable life as well, and also the cause of the existence of the earth, sun, moon and stars. . . .

I have no recollection of what it was that first suggested to me the question as to the origin of things. I had before this time gained ideas of the descent from parent to child, of the propagation of animals, and of the production of plants from seeds. . . .

I think I was five years old when I began to understand the descent from parent to child and the propagation of animals. I was nearly eleven years old when I entered the Institution where I was educated; and I remember distinctly that it was at least two years before this time that I began to ask myself the question as to the origin of the universe.[1]

We will see, further on, that evidence of thinking by the deaf in controlled, experimental situations has been used as support by more recent exponents of the view that thinking is independent of language. But before we leave William James, it is worth noting one more short passage from his argument (1890, pp. 269–70) that thinking is not dependent on language, for this idea is only currently becoming acceptable again, and James has been able to render it in words more ably than most others:

1. This passage is excerpted from a longer version quoted by William James and attributed by him to Samuel Porter, 'Is thought possible without language?', *Princeton Review*, 57th year, pp. 108–12 (Jan. 1881?) [*sic*].

Let *A* be some experience from which a number of thinkers start. Let *Z* be the practical conclusion rationally inferable from it. One gets to the conclusion by one line, another by another; one follows a course of English,

another of German, verbal imagery. With one, visual images predominate; with another tactile. Some trains are tinged with emotions, others not; some are verry abidged, synthetic and rapid, others hesitating and broken into many steps. But when the penultimate terms of all the trains, however differing *inter se*, finally shoot into the same conclusion, we say and rightly say, that all the thinkers have had substantially the same thought. It would probably astound each of them beyond measure to be let into his neighbour's mind and to find how different the scenery there was from that in his own.

A view directly contrary to this arose in the 1920s and 1930s, primarily through the writings of two men – Edward Sapir, an anthropologist and linguist, and Benjamin Lee Whorf, who was a fire prevention engineer for an insurance company but who spent his non-business hours working in linguistics. The new viewpoint, which became known as the Sapir–Whorf Hypothesis, basically asserted that the commonly held notion that all human beings possess a common logical structure and think in similar ways was incorrect. Indeed, the Sapir–Whorf hypothesis claims that individuals are not even able to observe the world in the same way. Rather, they are constrained to certain modes of interpretation by the language they speak. The grammar of one's language leads one to different types of observations and different evaluations of external experience. As Whorf (1952) put it, 'We cut up and organize the spread and flow of events as we do largely because, through our mother tongue, we are parties to an agreement to do so, not because nature itself is segmented in exactly that way for all to see. Languages differ not only in how they build their sentences but in how they break down nature to secure the elements to put in those sentences. . . .'

Whorf claimed, for example, that European languages (which he lumped together as SAE or Standard Average European), treat 'time' as an objective entity, as if time were a ribbon with equal spaces marked off, presumably because of the use of past, present and what can be called the future tense. The Hopi Indian language of

North America, however, gets along without tenses for its verbs, and it has no words, grammatical forms, constructions or expressions that refer directly to what we call 'time'. Consequently, the Hopi speaker's conception of 'time', or more precisely 'duration', is very different from that of SAE speakers. Whorf believed that while Hopi speakers would have trouble with concepts such as simultaneity, which we find easy, they would easily be able to deal with concepts of relativity, which we often find difficult. Whorf (1958) has indeed noted several ways language affects our scientific views.

If all this seems a bit abstruse, a passage from Sapir (1949) will perhaps serve to clarify the claim that the Sapir–Whorf hypothesis makes:

... when we observe an object of the type that we call a 'stone' moving through space towards the earth, we involuntarily analyse the phenomenon into two concrete notions, that of a stone and that of an act of falling, and, relating these two notions to each other by certain formal methods proper to English, we declare that 'the stone falls'. We assume, naïvely enough, that this is about the only analysis that can be properly made.

[However], in German and in French we are compelled to assign 'stone' to a gender category – perhaps the Freudians can tell us why this object is masculine in the one language, feminine in the other; in Chippewa we cannot express ourselves without bringing in the apparently irrelevant fact that a stone is an inanimate object. If we find gender beside the point, the Russians may wonder why we consider it necessary to specify in every case whether a stone, or any other object for that matter, is conceived in a definite or an indefinite manner, why the difference between 'the stone' and 'a stone' matters. 'Stone falls' is good enough for Lenin, as it was good enough for Cicero. And if we find barbarous the neglect of the distinction as to definiteness, the Kwakiutl Indian of British Columbia may sympathize with us but wonder why we do not go a step further and indicate in some way whether the stone is visible or invisible to the speaker at the moment of speaking, and whether it is nearest to the speaker, the person addressed, or some third party. 'That would no doubt sound fine in Kwakiutl, but we are too busy!' And yet we insist on expressing the singularity of the falling object, where the Kwakiutl Indian, differing from the Chippewa, can generalize and make a statement which would apply equally well to one or several stones. Moreover, he need not specify the time of the fall. The Chinese get on with a minimum of explicit formal statement and content themselves with a frugal 'stone fall'.

These differences of analysis, one may object, are merely formal; they do not invalidate the necessity of the fundamental concrete analysis of the situation into 'stone' and what the stone does, which in this case is 'fall'. But this necessity, which we feel so strongly, is an illusion. In the Nootka language the combined impression of a stone falling is quite differently analysed. The stone need not be specifically referred to, but a single word, a verb form, may be used which is in practice not essentially more ambiguous than our English sentence. This verb form consists of two main elements, the first indicating general movement or position of a stone or stonelike object, while the second refers to downward direction. We can get some hint of the feeling of the Nootka word if we assume the existence of an intransitive verb 'to stone', referring to the position or movement of a stonelike object. Then our sentence may be reassembled into something like 'It stones down.' In this type of expression the thing-quality of the stone is implied in the generalized verbal element 'to stone', while the specific kind of motion which is given us in experience when a stone falls is conceived as separable into a generalized notion of the movement of a class of objects and a more specific one of direction. In other words, while Nootka has no difficulty whatever in describing the fall of a stone, it has no verb that truly corresponds to our 'fall'.

It would be possible to go on indefinitely with such examples of incommensurable analyses of experience in different languages (pp. 157-9).

Various aspects of the language we speak, then, and of which we are normally unaware, restrict the way we view the world and the ways we are able to think. This is what is meant by the 'strong' form of the Sapir–Whorf hypothesis. However, it is interesting to note that we can translate concepts expressed in one language into another, although the expression of those concepts may be more tortured – we may have to use long phrases where the original language uses a single word. And certainly, even if our language is resistant to the concept of relativity, we can come to grasp its meaning by attending lectures or reading on the subject. (It is also interesting to note in this regard that Einstein was somewhat of a slow child and acquired language rather late; he claims that language did not play much part in his thought processes.) Roger Brown (1956), in an essay on the relation between language and thought, offered a suggestion which somewhat undermines the extreme position of linguistic determinism. Brown noted that languages differ in their 'codability' of certain concepts, and he reasoned that codability of a concept would affect the 'availability' of that concept to the speakers of that language. He thus held that languages do not *determine* thinking, ~~but only that they~~ _predispose_ people to think in particular ways. A number of experiments using memory for variously coloured discs examined this 'weak' form of the Sapir–Whorf hypothesis. Brown and Lenneberg (1954) forced subjects to place greater emphasis on verbal cues when remembering colours they had seen by two methods. In one, they increased the delay interval between the time the colours were first seen and the time when an array was presented from which the subject had to choose the remembered colours. In the second method, they merely increased the number of colours to be remembered. When the subjects' reliance on verbal memory was increased in these ways, Brown and Lenneberg found that the colour was more easily and accurately picked out of a large array, the more codable it was in language. Lenneberg and Roberts (1956) examined the memory for colours by Zuni and English speakers. The Zuni language has only a single term for yellows and oranges, and as predicted, Zuni speakers had difficulty with these colours and often confused them, a mistake English speakers rarely made; and the number of errors made by bilingual Zuni/English speakers was midway between monolingual Zuni and monolingual English subjects' error scores. A review of these results is found in Brown and Lenneberg (1958). The same type of task has also been approached using a concept of communication accuracy instead of codability (Lantz and Stefflre, 1964), and there is a full discussion in Miller and McNeill (1969).

There are several good reviews of the Sapir–Whorf hypothesis (e.g. Henle, 1958; Hoijer, 1954; Slobin 1971c), and Adams (1972) has republished a number of interesting readings on language and thought. The writings of both Sapir and Whorf used to be difficult to obtain, but many of them are now more readily available. Sapir's writings have been collected by Mandelbaum (1949, 1961), and Whorf's essays have been brought together by Carroll (1956).

It is clear that the common-sense notion that thought is independent of language, and that thinking runs its own course, indeed encountering difficulty when it must be put into words, is severely challenged by the Sapir–Whorf hypothesis whether in its strong or weak form. But there was a second intellectual current, one which stirred directly in the mainstream of psychological theory, which has played a major part in inducing most psychologists to adopt the view that language determines thought. We can label this influence the 'behaviourist' tradition. By 'behaviourist' we will mean here a conjunction of intellectual trends the most important of which, for our purposes, are the empiricist theory of mind, the emphasis on objective, publicly observable events, and the associationistic theory of the connection of ideas. These trends which affected the study of psychology at the end of the nineteenth century are discussed and put into historical perspective by George Miller in his introductory text, *Psychology: The Science of Mental Life* (1962). The infant's mind was believed to be a blank slate upon which experience inscribed its lessons. The only events which could be observed were those impinging from outside the organism, and the possibility of internal organization of these events was discounted as being unscientific speculation. The outside events were analysed in terms of their elements and these were seen to combine by the laws of association. At this point we should note that as far as the issue of the relationship between thought and language is concerned, there was no necessity to equate the two. When the two are equated, however, it is easier to conceptualize language as the determiner of thought since speech units are observable phenomena which impinge on the child, who is seen as essentially passive. This view has certain consequences for a theory of language acquisition, and these will be discussed in more detail further on. The consequence for the thought/language controversy is simply that in the behaviourist view speech units are heard and imitated by the child, acquired through the process of selective reinforcement, and thereby become the means of thought. One did not have to hypothesize any unobservable events in thinking. The extreme position was put forward by John B. Watson, the founder of American behaviourism, in 1912. He held that all thought processes are really motor habits which would be observable as movements in the larynx during so-called 'silent' thought. This is in some sense an ironic claim by Watson since at the time he made it instruments sufficiently precise to measure these movements were not available, and their existence was based on speculation. Nevertheless, movements of the larynx have since been recorded during silent thought. But whether they *are* thought or are even necessary for thought is another matter. Experiments using the drug curare leave no doubt that movements of the larynx are not necessary for thought processes to occur. A dose of d-Tubocurarine chloride two and a half times that necessary for complete respiratory paralysis and adequate for complete skeletal muscular paralysis was given intravenously to a subject. He was, of course, kept breathing by artificial means. While in this state, with the speech musculature completely immobilized, the individual was still capable of thought and was later able to report his thoughts and perceptions (Smith *et al.*, 1947). Lenneberg's demonstration (1962, 1964) of the ability of a child unable to speak due to congenital anarthria (impairment of the speech organs) but nevertheless able to understand language propositions and concepts, as well as the common observation of the ability of the deaf to think (see Furth, 1966, for experimental support of such observations), would seem to indicate that this extreme view is unwarranted. It is easy to see, however, the reasons why a less extreme theory is appealing. Thoughts and their acquisition are difficult to observe, but speech units and the acquisition of productive language is scientifically observable and quantitatively measurable. Any kind of thinking which appears to be more elaborated than could be explained by the mere acquisition of immediate motor habits can be seen in the same theoretical framework as these habits, if words serve as a mediating influence but are themselves acquired as habits.

There has been a good deal of study of language serving a mediating function in thought and in the development of children's concepts (see e.g. Kendler, 1963; Spiker, 1963). The question which is of central concern to us, however, is not whether verbal materials can facilitate performance on some tasks, but whether certain cognitive abilities are actually dependent on language. Crossmodal transfer between different sensory modalities was thought at one time to be limited to human beings and that, therefore, language served as the device which mediated between differing modalities. Hermelin and O'Connor (1964) found, however, that normal, subnormal and autistic children showed crossmodal transfer from vision to touch. As these groups differed markedly in their verbal ability, but not in their capacity to transfer from one modality to another, Hermelin and O'Connor rejected the view that crossmodal effects were due to verbal coding. Looking at the effects of language from the other way round, O'Connor and Hermelin (1971) found in another experiment that normal, subnormal and deaf children were unable to transfer a touch discrimination to another modality even though most subjects could verbalize the solution. In other words, these results indicate that verbal coding and crossmodal transfer are independent processes. Furthermore, the initial assumption on which the importance of language was based, i.e. that other animals, because they lack language, are unable to transfer information from one modality to another, seems to be unwarranted, and some crossmodal transfer has, in fact, been demonstrated in other species (Davenport and Rogers, 1970; see also studies reported by Koehler, 1972).

A strong claim for the importance of language in higher thinking processes was made in 1956 in the Soviet Union by A. R. Luria and F. Ia. Yudovich. They separated a pair of identical twins who were retarded in their language and mental development in order to force them to communicate with others. The ensuing improvement in their mental abilities was attributed to the improvement in their language. However, whether such a causal relationship can be asserted between the two processes, as Luria and Yudovich have done, is questionable. Indeed, Luria and Yudovich report that special speech training for one of the twins, while accelerating the conscious application of speech, nevertheless played only a subsidiary role in intellectual improvement, since both twins made great gains.

A more extended version of the importance of language in thinking has been proposed by Bernstein (1961). He has claimed that children from working-class backgrounds have a restricted language code while children from middle-class homes possess an elaborated code. Bernstein asserts that since the relationship between potential and developed intelligence is mediated through the language system, the lack of an elaborated code by the working-class child prevents him from developing his intellectual faculties to their fullest capacity. There are a number of problems in such a view, particularly in the assessment of intelligence itself in groups from differing backgrounds. But even the basic assumption that working-class children possess a less elaborated code than middle-class children has come under criticism (Houston, 1970). It is probably true to say that while Bernstein's proposal concerning the relation between language and cognition is an interesting one, the direction of causation is still undetermined. If Bernstein's ideas on language are interpreted in the sense that certain linguistic abilities in an individual (regardless of what social group he belongs to) are facilitative of particular forms of thought, one is still left with the question of whether that individual's intellectual capabilities in fact provided the ability necessary to master those linguistic forms. It is this question – whether language precedes cognition or whether cognition precedes language – which will be the central concern of this chapter, but we will be looking at the problem in terms of the young child first acquiring his native language.

What has been characterized as the behaviourist tradition in psychology has been shown to influence the view that language precedes thought because of its emphasis on the empiricist theory of mind and its beliefs concerning the mechanisms by which knowledge, including language, is acquired. As has been pointed out, the behaviourist viewpoint does not exclude the possibility of cognition prior to language, but the application of behaviourist principles to the study of the acquisition of language has led most adherents of that position to conceptualize language acquisition in a vacuum, with the organism passively being exposed to the language about him, being reinforced for his imitations (which occur first to those items which are most frequent in the language behaviour about him) and of thus slowly approximating the language spoken in his community. Probably the clearest and strongest expression of this view was by Skinner (1957), although others had expressed similar positions (e.g. Mowrer, 1954). As is now well known by students in the field, the linguist Noam Chomsky (1959) wrote a devastating criticism of the stimulus–response, learning-theory view expressed by Skinner.

There are many psychologists who still adhere strongly to the Skinnerian viewpoint on the acquisition of language, and there are many others whose thinking is still coloured by an over-riding interest in processes such as frequency, imitation, reinforcement, and generalization as explanatory principles in the child's acquisition of his native language. There is increasing evidence, however, that such principles, while possibly important in explaining some aspects of language learning, are nevertheless by themselves inadequate to account for the linguistic changes occurring in children acquiring language. It is beyond the scope of this chapter to review the arguments and the evidence against these stimulus–response principles, although some of the findings concerning cognitive processes preceding and in some cases directing language acquisition, which will be discussed further on, also serve as warnings against a too simplistic view of the language-acquisition process. The reader who is interested in both the theoretical reasoning and the empirical evidence against stimulus–response theories of language acquisition can find excellent reviews by Bellugi (1967, 1971), Bever, Fodor and Weksel (1965a, 1965b), Brown, Cazden and Bellugi-Klima (1969), Ervin-Tripp (1966), McNeill (1966, 1970a, 1970b), Miller and McNeill (1969), Sachs (1971), Slobin (1971b) and Vetter and Howell (1971).

One of the main points of contention has centred on the problem of what exactly the child brings with him to the language-acquisition task if he is not an empty organism with a 'blank slate'. Chomsky's viewpoint (1962, 1965, 1966, 1968) is that the child has, innately, a number of formal and substantive linguistic mechanisms which are part of his 'language-acquisition device' (LAD). These mechanisms are, of course, universal since they are innate, and they provide schema which are applied to the particular language to which the child is exposed. McNeill has attempted to describe several possible innate features. He claims, for example, that the basic grammatical relations are innately part of the child's grammatical competence (McNeill, 1966, 1970a, 1970b). More recently, he has asserted that the grammatical category of 'nouns' is a strong linguistic universal and that this category is based on a strictly linguistic ability as a necessary cause (1970c). The claim, then, by this school of thinking, is that language has its own specific roots which are observable in the linguistic universals which can be recorded in children's language acquisition everywhere in the world regardless of the particular language being acquired. Some loose writing has occasionally seemed to indicate that what was being claimed was the illogical view that because these features are found universally, they are therefore innate. However, the actual claim is that certain linguistic features are innate and can, therefore, be observed universally.

This theory has been subjected to severe criticism by adherents to the empiricist theory of mind. And there are others less committed to the 'blank slate' theory who nevertheless are distrustful of assuming any processes as innate since such suppositions, in the past, have sometimes served as cloaks to cover the ignorance of the details of particular developmental phenomena. Theories of innate analysers and inborn organizational properties are, however, more acceptable today than they were just a few years ago. For example, advocates of innate organization of perception have found support in the discovery of specific perceptual receptors in the cortex of the cat for horizontal and vertical orientation (Hubel and Wiesel, 1962). The prospect of discovering similar 'real entities' for language functions, however, is slim – and the necessity to do so logically dubious in any case. The argument between those linguists and psycholinguists who posit the existence of innate language functions, and psychologists who refuse to consider the possibility of any 'innate ideas', seems destined to continue for some time. The notion that language has its own roots has, however, been attacked by a second group who have little in common with the behaviourist school of thought in psychology as sketched earlier. This new attack on the Chomskyan position has come from Piagetian psychologists in Geneva, who claim that language reflects thought, i.e. that language is, in fact, structured by thought.

It would be impossible to summarize succinctly Piaget's view of development. There are a number of good reviews of Piagetian theory, however (e.g. Flavell, 1963; Furth, 1969), and Piaget himself has recently published some excellent overviews of his theory (Piaget, 1970a, 1970b; Piaget and Inhelder, 1966). The point to note for our purposes is that in the Piagetian view of development, the child for his first two years of life has represented the world to himself through sensori-motor actions, and his 'prelinguistic thought' (for we can call it that from the Piagetian point of view) is characterized by sensori-motor intelligence. According to Piaget, the accomplishments of this period include a number of striking cognitive attainments – for example, the achievement of object permanence, imitation of actions seen sometime previously, the anticipations of the future position of an object before its movement, etc.

The Piagetian view on language is a very complex one. Piaget notes that when language begins, it obviously plays a major part in the person's representation of the world and in the interiorization of action into thought. But he also points out that language is only one factor of the symbolic function as a whole – other factors being deferred imitation, mental imagery, symbolic games, drawing and the like.

Richard F. Cromer 195

When the symbolic or semiotic function begins to be operative, it has the advantage of being able to detach thought from action. It therefore has several important effects on sensori-motor thought. Piaget notes, for example, that language, in particular, allows for three developments: a speeding up of representation over that possible by sensori-motor representation, an ability to transcend immediate space and time, and the ability to represent a number of elements simultaneously rather than by means of successive, step-by-step thought. The semiotic function, then, detaches thought from action, and language plays a particularly important role in this formative process (see Piaget and Inhelder, 1966). But the main point for us is the claim that language builds on and affects a number of cognitive abilities which have already arisen in the sensori-motor period.

What about thought in the more traditional sense? Even though it may be true that there are a number of cognitive structures which are built up during the first two years of life which have little relationship to language, what about the kind of thinking which has been characterized by Piaget as operational thinking, which arises at about the age of seven years? Surely, it could be argued, this type of more elaborated thought is dependent on language, especially in view of the importance which Piaget has attributed to language in freeing representation from its reliance on immediate action. Indeed, it has been claimed by some (e.g. Bruner, 1964) that language transforms experience by lifting it to a new plane of symbolic manipulation. According to this view, language frees the individual from the immediate perceptual qualities of a situation (as in the traditional conservation experiment where water transferred from one of two identical beakers to a taller but thinner one is thought by the younger child to change in amount and become 'more') and enables him to give correct adult-like answers in such situations. But Piaget denies that language is responsible for the new logical structures which define the stage of 'operational thinking' (see e.g. Inhelder and Piaget, 1959, p. 282). Further, he cites evidence (Piaget, 1970a, 1970b; Piaget and Inhelder, 1966) that the deaf are as capable of operational thinking as those who have language, although the particular studies he mentions show the deaf to be greatly delayed in the emergence of operational thought. Furth (1966) has conducted a number of studies of the development of thought in the deaf using Piagetian techniques.

Although his results are also ambiguous in that operational thinking is somewhat delayed as compared to non-impaired children, he too concludes that language does not appear to be necessary for operatory functioning. Piaget contrasts the studies of the deaf with studies of the blind. The deaf have complete sensori-motor schemes but lack language, while the blind are in full possession of normal language but are impaired in their sensori-motor experiences. Yet while the deaf are said not to be deficient in the development of their operational thinking, the blind (on evidence by Hatwell, 1966) are said to be severely delayed in the emergence of operational thought. Piaget claims that this comparison especially well illustrates that language is not the source of operational thinking. The actual evidence on which this claim is made is very shaky in that the experimental studies showed a considerable delay in the emergence of operational thinking in the deaf, which was, however, attributed by the experimenters to other factors. Furthermore, new evidence (Cromer, 1973) indicates that the blind may not be delayed in the emergence of operational structures, as had previously been suggested. Nevertheless, the claim that operational thinking precedes particular linguistic changes finds support in the study of non-handicapped children. We will see later on, for example, revealing experimental evidence by Sinclair on this point.

Finally, there is the period of formal operations which arise at adolescence according to the Piagetian school. Formal operations are manifested in propositional thinking. That is, these operations consist of a combinatorial system which allows the construction of hypothetical possibilities, so that the individual is enabled to envisage all the possible relationships which could hold true in a set of data. Is it possible that at least this type of thinking is dependent on language and the elaboration of verbal categories? Those who have studied thinking by the deaf seem to feel that this is a real possibility. Furth and Youniss in a recent review of their studies (1971) assert:

Whereas language is never a sufficient or necessary condition of operatory functioning, the evidence from our work with linguistically deficient persons indicates that it may have, at best, an indirect facilitating effect for concrete operations, but can have a direct facilitating effect on certain formal operations precisely because of the close relation between formal operations and symbolic functioning (p. 64).

Richard F. Cromer 197

Piaget also notes that the propositional operations are closely related to 'a precise and flexible manipulation of language' but also warns that it would be a mistake to assume that the only advances at that stage are those marked by an advance in language. Indeed, Piaget conceives the formal operational structures which allow formal thinking in a way which goes quite beyond a mere linguistic ability to manipulate propositions, and he makes this clear in his writings on that topic (see chapters 16 and 17 in Inhelder and Piaget, 1955). I think one would not be far wrong in characterizing Piaget's position by saying that language may possibly be necessary for the propositional manipulations of formal thought but that language itself is not a *sufficient* condition for that type of thinking. Indeed, it is difficult to see in what way the language of the individual at the stage of formal operational thought significantly differs from that of the individual who has not yet attained this stage of thinking, except in the use he makes of his linguistic structures.

It would appear then, that in Piaget's view, at all stages of thought, the later as well as the earlier, it is cognition which affects language and not the reverse. It is in this context that Piaget, though supporting much of what Chomsky has to say, finds fault with him. Chomsky does not make any specific claims about the relation between language and thought, and it is not here that the controversy between Piaget and Chomsky lies. Rather, Piaget takes issue with the Chomskyan view that certain linguistic mechanisms are innate. Piaget claims:

Chomsky goes so far as to say that the kernel of reason on which the grammar of language is constructed is innate, that it is not constructed through the actions of the infant as I have described but is hereditary and innate (1970a, p. 47).

And

Chomsky's transformational structures are facilitated by the previous operation of the sensori-motor schemes, and thus . . . their origin is neither an innate neurophysiological program (as Chomsky himself would have it) nor in an operant or other conditioning 'learning' process [as Chomsky (1959) has shown conclusively] (1970b, p. 711).

In the next section, we will return to some evidence which Piaget offers on this.

Up to this point, an attempt has been made to sketch in a bit of the more recent historical background of the position psychologists have held on the issue of the relation between language and thought. We have seen that psychologists did not always oppose the view that thought and cognitive processes preceded language. We then reviewed two contributions to the opposite point of view – the Sapir–Whorf hypothesis which directly asserted the formative role of language, and the behaviourist tradition in psychology which has significantly influenced the types of experimentation and observation carried out by psychologists. I have purposely left one significant figure, Vygotsky, for the conclusion. We have also seen two more recent contributions to the controversy. The Chomskyan linguistic position has emphasized the independence of the origins of language and maintained that these linguistic roots are innate. This view has met with opposition by the Piagetian psychologists who, though not at all in the behaviourist tradition, reject the nativist assumption of inborn linguistic mechanisms and argue instead that cognitive properties which are built up through interaction with the environment precede language and directly influence its acquisition.

The remainder of this article will be based on experimental evidence bearing on these issues. In the next section we will examine the evidence for cognition preceding language. The studies will be subdivided into three subsections which will deal with the effects of cognitive factors on babbling and first words, the acquisition of grammar, and later acquisitions. We must also note, however, that there is a good deal of evidence to support the linguists' claims that language has its own roots. There will, therefore, follow a section concerned with the evidence that language progresses according to its own developmental rules and is not wholly dependent on cognition. Finally, we will put forward two forms of a 'cognition hypothesis' and take a measure of the distance we have covered.

Evidence for cognition preceding language
Cognitive effects on babbling and first words

One can observe the influence of behaviouristic psychology, as outlined earlier, in the way psychologists have until recently theorized about the babbling of the very young infant and his later acquisition of words. It has often been observed that the infant, in one stage of his babbling, produces all of the sounds which are available to all of the world's languages and only in later childhood narrows his repertoire so that it includes only those sounds which are present in the language he hears about him. Indeed, it is very difficult at later ages even to produce certain sounds of foreign languages, but we are assured that we easily did so during our initial babbling stage. The processes by which the narrowing occurs are said to be a combination of imitation and differential reinforcement. According to this view, the child in his babbling occasionally stumbles across sounds which are similar to those occurring in the adult speech around him. It was hypothesized by some that when the child does this, the adult reinforces the child by attention of some kind, such as smiling. Thus the child tries to imitate the sounds around him and makes successively closer approximations to them. A slightly different version of this type of theory was that the child finds the production of the sounds reinforcing itself, rather than requiring some adult reinforcement directly, and the reason this sound production is reinforcing is due to association with adult comforting, attention and the like. In either case, the important principles for phonological acquisition were thought to be imitation and reinforcement. It is somewhat ironic that this learning-theory view of the acquisition of phonology has often paid so little attention to the empirically observable facts. Linguists, looking far more closely at the child's phonological acquisitions, have come to a very different point of view.

The linguistic position is that the child does not imitate sounds; instead, he produces them according to a systematic set of phonological rules. In 1941, Roman Jakobson put forward a theory concerning the features of sounds used in language. This was only translated into English in 1968 and has not yet served as the basis for many empirical studies. Basically, his theory is that the infant discriminates features of sounds which are represented by phonological contrasts such as vocalic/non-vocalic, voiced/voiceless, nasal/oral, grave/acute, etc. The child seems first to dichotomize all sounds on the basis of one feature, and he thus begins making sound distinctions with that single contrast. Later, he adds features to his system and by this means he progressively separates sounds until all of those in the language have been identified on the basis of the distinguishing features. The features are rules which act across particular sounds. For example, when the child acquires the contrast voiced/voiceless, he creates not one but a number of distinctions based on the voicing feature – for example /g/ versus /k/, /b/ versus /p/, /d/ versus /t/, and /v/ versus /f/. It is also said that these contrast rules appear in the child's productions in a constant order, and that this order will correspond to the number of languages in the world which contain the particular feature. The details of theories of this type can be found in Chomsky and Halle (1968), Jakobson (1941), Jakobson and Halle (1956) and Jakobson, Fant and Halle (1952). Good short introductory summaries of the linguistic position are available by David Palermo in his chapter on language acquisition in Reese and Lipsitt (1970), and by Kaplan and Kaplan (1971). There are not yet very many studies which have been carried out with this linguistic view in mind. Ervin-Tripp (1966) has examined the data from several diary studies of language acquisition by individual children in terms of the distinctive features, and Neil Smith (1973) has been making a longitudinal study of phonological acquisition in this light. In these, there is strong evidence for the acquisition of phonology according to a set of rules like those described. In general, there is a rough correspondence with Jakobson's predictions, but there are individual variations as well.

The identification of the full set of phonological rules by linguists is not complete, but the evidence nevertheless indicates that imitation as traditionally conceived does not appear to be the process whereby the infant acquires the sounds of his language. Lenneberg, Rebelsky and Nichols (1965) have found that vocalizations of children born to deaf parents do not differ from those of babies born to hearing parents in the first three months of life. Thus, at least in early vocalization, the types of sounds made are identical. This is not surprising, and it is really the later stages of babbling which are crucial for an imitation theory. Barbara Dodd (1972) has made a study of infant vocalizations at the peak of their babbling period (age nine to twelve months). Against a baseline of the sounds each individual infant was already producing, she compared the sounds produced after a period of concentrated vocal stimulation. This stimulation by an adult included sounds not found in the child's babbling during the base period. Dodd found that with purely vocal stimulation, there was no imitation of the adult, and indeed not even an increase in the amount of babbling by the infant. In a group which received both social and vocal stimulation, however, the infant increased his *amount* of vocalization. But, there was no increase in the range of the *types* of sounds made. Thus, imitation was not produced even in situations which combined social and concentrated vocal stimulation, although the *amount* of babbling was increased.

There is the further consideration, too, that at least for receptive language competence, the child need never have imitated sounds made by adults. Lenneberg's study mentioned earlier (1962, 1964) indicated that children with impaired speech apparatus are able to acquire language and understand linguistic propositions. But even among non-impaired children normally acquiring productive speech, the notion of imitation in the traditional sense is now disputed. As we have seen, modern linguistic theory holds that the child progresses through a series of contrastive phonological features by which he analyses the sounds he hears, and he produces his own sounds in accordance with those rules. Neil Smith (1971, 1973) reports an amusing observation which shows how the young child's application of particular phonetic rules in fact prevents him from being able to imitate accurately certain words, even when it can be shown that he has the ability to do so. When the child, playing an imitation game, was asked to say *puddle* he replied *puggle* since his phonological rules at that stage required him to replace /t/ or /d/ before syllabic /l/ with a velar sound, e.g. /g/ or /k/. But when the same child was asked to say *puzzle*, he then replied *puddle*, since his rules require the replacement of non-continuant sonorants by /d/ or its allophones.

The fact that children universally apply the same type of phonological feature analysis to the sounds they hear, would seem to indicate that the phonological aspects of language are not acquired from external sources in the way usually hypothesized by psychologists (imitation and reinforcement). At the same time, however, the application of these features universally would be strong evidence that at least some aspects of language obey their own developmental laws, and this is a question to which we will return in the next major section. But what is interesting for our purposes here is an idea put forward by Eleanor and George Kaplan (1971) that *meaning* also affects the acquisition of early sounds. Before looking at their proposal, however, let us look at the possibility of 'meaning' in the very first cries of the newborn infant.

It has been proposed that infant cries contain a set of differentiated messages. Lind (1965) has edited a number of studies of the crying sounds of the newborn infant, and Wolff (1969) has demonstrated that these different cries communicate distinct messages. Derek Ricks (1972) has carried out a very interesting study on communicative aspects of the cries of normal children of eight to twelve months of age and the cries of autistic children of age three to five years. Under controlled conditions, Ricks elicited four types of messages: a requesting sound, a frustrated sound, a greeting sound, and a sound expressing pleased surprise (e.g. a novel and exciting event). This was done by setting up actual situations which stimulated the child to produce the appropriate 'message'. The cries were recorded on tape and, in addition to the English children, the cries of Italian and Spanish children in the four situations were also recorded. In the experiment, six parents of normal children and six of autistic children each listened to the tape-recorded sounds of four babies each giving the four cries in the situations just noted. Thus, each parent had sixteen cries to identify. The four babies that the parents of normal children heard included their own baby, one non-English baby and two infants randomly selected from the other normal English babies. The four children that the parents of autistic children listened to included their own autistic child, one non-autistic subnormal child and two other autistic children randomly selected from the other autistic children. The task of the parents was four-fold: they had to identify and label all four sounds for each of the four children; they had to identify their own child; the parents of normal children had to identify the non-English child while the parents of autistic children had to identify the non-autistic child; finally, the parents heard the request cries of six babies and had to pick out their own child from amongst these. The results were that the parents of normal children could identify the messages, but to their surprise were not able to pick out their own child. Furthermore, these parents correctly identified the messages of the cries of the non-English babies but were not able to pick out which child was non-English. The parents of autistic children, on the other hand, could only identify the messages of their own child or of a non-autistic child, and they could easily recognize which child was their own. In other words, it appears that while autistic children do not use the vocabulary of intonated signals of normal children and instead have their own distinctive cries, the cries of normal children show a marked similarity converging on the same message, and these signals seem to be independent of language background. This would again be evidence of universal phonological laws, but here these are tied to a function of communicating specific meanings.

Kaplan and Kaplan (1971) propose that the child's semantic system develops out of the early distinctions present in his communication system. They feel that with adequate data one will be able to identify a set of semantic features and chart the developmental order of their emergence. For example, when the infant makes the early distinction between human and non-human sounds, the Kaplans suggest the feature '± human' has become operative. When the infant differentiates himself from others, as observable in the effect of delayed auditory feedback on crying (i.e. indicating that the infant can distinguish between his own voice and other sounds), he is credited with the feature '± ego'. As the child develops his knowledge of object properties he adds such features as '± existence' and '± presence'. Other later acquisitions would include '± agent', '± past' and the like. These semantic features would place constraints on the child's language acquisition. Although the Kaplans have formulated this theory with reference to the infant's first sounds, it would be possible to extend a similar kind of analysis to grammatical acquisitions at later ages.

On the acquisition of first words, Ricks (1972) has conducted an experiment which has a bearing on the issue of imitation and acquisition. He first made the interesting observation that the child's first words were of two major types. Between eleven and eighteen months, the infant begins to produce a number of early words which have either loose referents or are used in babble without any referents at all. Furthermore, they are imitated when spoken by the adult to the child. These first utterances include words like 'dada' and 'mama' and Ricks calls them 'dada words'. However, at some point, a second type of word appears and this type is used concurrently with the 'dada words'. This second type, which he calls 'label words', has an interesting set of characteristics which separates them clearly from 'dada words'. For example:

1 The 'label words' are not found in the babbling like the 'dada words' are.

2 The 'label word' occurs only in the context with the stimulus for which it is a label, and is used by the child only when related to that particular stimulus or event.

3 When the 'label word' is repeated, it is not modified by the child to resemble a more conventional term. Indeed, Ricks points out that the parents often begin using the child's term in context so that it is the parental language which is modified!

4 Once utilized, a 'label word' frequently generalizes to other objects, e.g. 'bow wow' used for a dog soon becomes used for any four-legged animal.

5 The child always expresses the 'label words' with a great deal of excitement and zeal.

6 Mention of a 'label word' usually captures the child's attention and alerts him to look for the object to which, to him, it refers.

7 Mention of a 'label word' by the parent produces very ready repetition by the child.

In an imitation experiment, infants heard three tapes, each played on different days. On each tape, the words were spoken by the child's mother, his father and by two adults, unknown to the child, one male and one female. One tape was made up of a 'dada word' of the individual child, and each adult uttered it five times at ten-second intervals. A second tape consisted of one of the child's own 'label words'. The third tape had the adults uttering a meaningless combina-ation such as 'dibby' which the child was capable of uttering, but as far as could be ascertained had never actually uttered. Thus, each child was presented with one of the types of words twenty times on each tape (each of four adults uttering it five times) for a total of eighty times during the day (each tape was played four times during the day). The child's imitations were carefully recorded, and the results showed that although there was some imitation of all three word types, it was fairly low for the meaningless words; 'dada words' were moderately imitated, but 'label words' elicited by far the greatest number of imitations. In other words, the child seems to imitate mainly the sounds which he already spontaneously applies to the world about him. He also shows some moderate imitation of words which he already uses but which do not constitute a label which he, in some sense, invented. Meaningless but phonetically possible combinations are imitated practically not at all. It would appear, then, that the child does not *learn* words, but that he *invents* them for the things he wants to communicate. Furthermore, imitation does not appear to be a mechanism of acquisition. This does not mean that these inventions are totally independent of the language he hears about him; they are closely related to it, but are nevertheless independent of it in important respects, the most important appearing to be the creativity which he brings to bear on the acquisition process, and this creativity has to do with the communication of concepts which he is cognitively able to handle.

In fact, just prior to the time when the child begins to utter his first multi-word combinations, are the words he utters merely labels at all? There is some evidence that they may not be. Many investigators have noticed that the words young children utter are more like complete sentences or thoughts and these early words have been called 'mot-phrases', 'sentence words', or 'holophrases'. For example, in 1927, Grace de Laguna noted that the proper names uttered by a child were not used by him simply to designate or label that individual; rather they were used to make all sorts of comments about that person or even about objects and events connected with him. The child might, for example, point at a pair of slippers and say 'Papa'. More recently, McNeill (1970a, 1970b) has argued that holophrastic speech is evidence that children possess basic grammatical relations. That is, he claims that since most of the utterances express predication (i.e. they are *comments* on the situation in which the speech occurs), the basic grammatical relations such as subject, predicate, verb, object, modifier and head are being honoured in this earliest speech. There is some dispute over whether these one-word utterances should be considered grammatical (see e.g. Bloom, 1970), but the fact that they express such relations as predication, direct and indirect object relationships, and modification indicates that children are able to express meaning from the onset of language acquisition. In other words, the child does not arrive at a meaning of these relationships because he has learned linguistic categories which then restructure his thinking; instead, he brings certain meanings to the task of language acquisition, and these affect even his very first words. But the child's intellectual accomplishments are not complete at this time. Do continuing developments in cognition affect language acquisition at later stages?

Cognitive effects on grammar

In a theoretical paper on the cognitive bases of language learning, Macnamara (1972) has claimed that the child cannot discover many syntactic structures without the aid of meaning. He proposes a specific theory of acquisition in which children determine the referents for main lexical items in sentences that they hear and then use their knowledge of these referents to decide what the semantic meaning of the structures intended by the speaker must be. In other words, once the child is able to determine the meaning of particular words, he will be able to work out the intended meaning of a speaker's utterances using them on the basis of what he knows about the world. Whether this particular theory is true can only be determined by evidence from language-acquisition studies. We will see further on that there is some evidence that when children acquire a new cognitive category, they acquire both the syntactic structures for it and associated lexical items simultaneously – and that would seem to be at odds with the particular mechanism of acquisition which Macnamara proposes. Nevertheless, in a more general sense Macnamara's proposal that acquisition is dependent on cognitive prerequisites is an intriguing one.

In a recent review of language-acquisition studies, Susan Ervin-Tripp (1971) has suggested that language could never be learned unless the meanings were obvious to the child when he heard sentences expressing them. If this is true, she argues, then the study of the categories, features and relations available to children at the very outset of language acquisition is crucially important in the explanation and prediction of language learning. In addition, if one could establish a developmental order of cognitive growth, then one would be better able to account for developments within language. And one would also be able to specify which properties of input are incomprehensible to children due to limitations of their cognitive development at particular stages. One is reminded here of the developmental theories of the Piagetian psychologists whose claims have already been dealt with in a general way. It will be recalled that when language acquisition begins, the foundations of sensori-motor thought have already been laid. This in itself is of very great interest, for if language has its own independent developmental laws, why does it appear only at the close of the sensori-motor period?

Hermine Sinclair, a linguist working in the Piagetian framework, believes that the child begins to acquire language only at the conclusion of the sensori-motor period because language is dependent on some of the intellectual accomplishments of that period. Not until then has the child reached a stage where he is an active person distinct from the objects he acts upon. This allows a differentiation between himself and others and therefore calls for communication. After about eighteen months of age, there is evidence that the child can achieve problem solutions cognitively, i.e. prior to carrying out actions. In other words, it is inferred from behavioural observations that the child of about eighteen months comes to possess the ability to represent reality mentally. Such representation includes the ability to recapitulate actions in the past and to anticipate actions in the future. It should be especially noted that this representation is said initially to occur in non-verbal form. Piaget's example of his daughter's use of motor representation at the age of one year four months is often cited. A small chain was placed in a matchbox, the opening of which was made so small that little Lucienne could not retrieve it by poking her finger into the box as she had been doing previously. After manipulating the box, she suddenly stopped, opened and shut her mouth several times more and more widely, and then immediately pushed the box open to retrieve the chain. Piaget interpreted this as evidence of motor symbolism, in which could be seen the beginnings of anticipatory thought.

Sinclair (1971) notes a number of sensori-motor schemes which she feels can account for corresponding linguistic abilities observed in language acquisition. The child's ability to order things both spatially and temporally would have its linguistic equivalent in concatenation of linguistic elements. The child's ability to classify in action (i.e. to use a whole category of objects for the same action, or to apply a whole category of action schemes to one object) has, as its linguistic counterpart, categorization of linguistic elements into the major categories like noun phrase and verb phrase. The ability to relate objects and actions to one another provides the underpinnings for the functional grammatical relations such as 'subject of' and 'object of'. The ability to embed action schemes into one another allows a linguistic recursive property such that phrase markers can be inserted into other phrase markers. These serve as examples, then, of the types of sensori-motor abilities which have been achieved when the symbolic function begins to make possible the acquisition of language, and these schemes account for the ability to acquire particular aspects of that linguistic system. In Sinclair's words, 'The child possesses a set of coordinations of action schemes which can be shown to have certain structural properties which will make it possible for him to start comprehending and producing language' (Sinclair, 1971, p. 127). The linguist, John Lyons, who incidentally has written a short book which serves as an excellent introduction to Chomsky's ideas (see Lyons, 1970), makes much the same point as Sinclair:

By the time the child arrives at the age of eighteen months or so, he is already in possession of the ability to distinguish 'things' and 'properties' in the 'situations' in which he is learning and uses language. And this ability seems to me quite adequate as a basis for the learning of the principal deep structure relationship between lexical items (the subject–predicate relationship), provided that the child is presented with a sufficient amount of 'primary linguistic data' in real 'situations' of language use (Lyons, 1966, p. 131).

There seems to be a growing interest on the part of linguists and psychologists in the possibility of underlying meanings which affect the surface structures of language. Fillmore (1968), for example, has put forward a case theory of grammar in which underlying meanings play a primary role. McCawley (1968) has suggested a directly semantic deep structure. Schlesinger (1971a, 1971b) has proposed a theory taking into account the speaker's intentions and these are based on cognitive capacities. Sinclair's Piagetian analysis, in a sense, goes somewhat further than these since it incorporates not only the idea of cognitive principles underlying language acquisition but also specifies some *developmental* features of these cognitive abilities. Her analysis of the sensori-motor schemes and their relationship to particular linguistic abilities may be very useful, and the sensori-motor schemes may indeed eventually be shown to be *necessary* to make language acquisition possible, but we are entitled to ask whether such structures are *sufficient* to account for human linguistic abilities. This question will be put off until later, however, as it is the topic of the next major section; and it will be our task now to examine instead the available evidence that supports the view that cognitive properties precede grammatical distinctions.

For some years now, Roger Brown and his associates at Harvard University have been carrying out a detailed study of the acquisition of language by three children. Basically, the research workers recorded the child's utterances in his natural home situation for two hours at fortnightly intervals. Any adult speech was also recorded; this was usually speech by the mother. Pertinent situational cues were also noted. Detailed descriptions of the study itself and analyses of various parts of the linguistic data have been reported in several papers (Brown and Bellugi, 1964; Brown and Fraser, 1964; Brown and Hanlon, 1970; Brown, Cazden and Bellugi-Klima, 1969; Brown, Fraser and Bellugi, 1964). Most of these papers have been reprinted in Brown (1970b). These reports have dealt almost entirely with purely linguistic changes occurring as the child acquired language. More recently, however, Brown (1973) has turned his attention to the semantic or meaning aspects of the child's utterances.

In looking at the children's utterances at Stage I of their language acquisition (a stage defined not by age but by a comparable mean utterance length in the three children ranging from approximately one and a half to two morphemes, and thus constituting a very early stage in multi-word constructions), Brown noted that for all three children the verb was initially in an unmarked form, i.e. it did not have any inflectional endings. Nevertheless, such a verb was understood by the parents in one of four ways, depending not only on the utterance itself but on the situational context in which the utterance occurred. One of these was the *imperative*, as in 'Get book.' A second meaning which was communicated at this stage was reference to the *past*, as for example, in 'Book drop' where the book had just dropped. A third meaning ascribed to the child was that of *intention or prediction*, as in 'Mommy read' in a context where Mommy was about to read to the child. Finally, there was the expression of *present temporary duration* as in 'Fish swim' where the context would call for an adult utterance using a progressive, such as 'The fish is swimming.' Brown reports that after Stage I, the children gradually learned to modify the generic verb in three ways. They began marking the past, with -ed or an irregular allomorph, producing such utterances as 'It dropped' and 'It fell', with the time range at first limited to a very immediate past. Another way they modified the verb was to use it in conjunction with a semi-auxiliary or catenative such as 'gonna', 'wanna' and 'hafta'. Although it was not possible to judge when the use of these was necessary, Brown notes that their meaning can be mainly characterized by intentionality or imminence, a kind of immediate future of the child's intentions or of actions about to occur (e.g. 'I wanna go', 'it's gonna fall'). A third modification was that the child began to use a primitive progressive form, i.e. he used -ing endings on the verb but without an auxiliary. It is startling to note that these first three operations that children perform on the verb just after Stage I encode three of the four semantic intentions attributed by adults to the child (past, intention or prediction, and present temporary duration) when he was only using the unmarked, generic form of the verb at the earlier stage. The fourth semantic intention, the imperative, has no specific grammatical marker in English, but Brown notes that the children began to use 'Please' at this time along with the other three markers. It would appear, then, that the first grammatical distinctions the child makes with verbs in his utterances after Stage I are those which encode the types of *meaning* he had been credited with expressing just prior to the acquisition of his new linguistic abilities.

Brown also traced the development of prepositions, but found that in the earliest stages only two were used with a great enough frequency to yield analysable data. These were the prepositions 'in' and 'on'. When Brown listed all occurrences of these along with the nouns with which they were used by the children, a semantic principle motivating their differential use was revealed. The nouns used with 'in' were objects which could contain other objects, i.e. they were objects having cavities or containing internal spaces such as 'bag', 'box' and 'briefcase'. The nouns used with 'on' were all objects which had flat surfaces which could support other objects, such as 'floor', 'shelf' and 'table'. In addition, one of the children had a meaning for 'in' which was used to denote intermingling, and was used in such utterances as 'in my hair' and 'in the snow'. The parents of these children were similarly using 'in' and 'on' to denote the same spatial locations, but interestingly, they were also using them in phrases with abstract non-spatial forms (as in 'in' in '*in* phrases with abstract non-spatial forms'). Yet the children, while exposed to these, did not give evidence of using them in this abstract way (except in the case of a few idiomatic expressions). Although there is not a careful study of the spatial relations children use at their first stages in speech, it is clear that they are able to express the spatial concepts encoded by 'in' and 'on' before they acquire any prepositions. In particular situational contexts, phrases like 'put box' can be reliably interpreted by adult observers as encoding 'in'; and 'pot stove' uttered while pointing to a pot on the stove will be interpreted as encoding 'on'.

The prepositions 'in' and 'on' used to encode spatial relations are locatives whose meaning can be described in terms of simple topological notions. This is not true of all locatives. There are some, like 'in front of', 'below' and 'beside', in which dimensional space notions (Euclidian) are prominent. There is also a third type which encodes more complex spatial notions, as in 'along' and 'through'. Parisi and Antinucci (1970) predicted an order of acquisition of these three types of locatives based on the Piagetian order of the development of spatial notions, an order beginning with topological space and only later encoding Euclidian spatial concepts (see Piaget and Inhelder, 1948). The study they report, while not longitudinal, showed that Italian children had least trouble with words indicating simple topological concepts, slightly more trouble with locatives concerned with Euclidian space, and most trouble with terms encoding complex spatial notions. Comparing this study on the acquisition of locative prepositions with Brown's study of 'in' and 'on', it is interesting that Brown's children, at the very earliest stages of language acquisition, seem to have acquired only the prepositions which refer to the cognitively simplest spatial relations – those to do with topological relations. And other studies also seem to indicate that children are expressing these relations in their two-word utterances, even before they have acquired the particular prepositions which encode them.

Brown also studied the acquisition of the possessive inflection, the 's in 'Adam's bike', for example. Using a criterion of 90 per cent use in contexts where this inflection was obligatory, he found that the children did not fully control this inflection until after what he called Stage III, based on a mean utterance length above two and a half morphemes. What is interesting, however, is that the child has been indicating possession quite clearly before this time, that is, he has been doing so before acquiring the grammatical inflection. Thus, the child has made many constructions like 'Adam chair' in contexts where possession is indicated. That these are not rote-learned seems indicated when, for example, the child said 'Fraser coffee' the first time Colin Fraser was ever served coffee by the mother. Brown gives other evidence that the concept involved in possession preceded its grammatical marking. One day Eve went round pointing and appropriately saying 'That Eve nose', 'That Mommy nose right there', 'That Papa nose right there.' Bloom (1970) also presents evidence from three other children acquiring language which clearly shows that they possess the genitive relation (concept of possession) well before they ever begin to use the grammatical inflection proper for its linguistic expression. Brown reports several other observations on the acquisition of semantic categories and their relation to the grammatical features which encode them, and those who are interested in this topic should consult his work (1973) as it is a most comprehensive examination of the relation between particular concepts and their grammatical expression during the acquisition of language.

Both Bloom (1970) and McNeill and McNeill (1968) have studied the growth of the concept of negation, and as it happens, in children acquiring very different languages – English and Japanese. Bloom's study of three unrelated children in America paid particular attention to the situational contexts of the children's utterances and thus focused on meaning. One part of her study was concerned with the syntactic development of negation. She identified negative utterances in two ways: all utterances containing a negative element such as 'no', 'no more ', 'not', 'don't', etc., signalling negative intent were analysed, as well as all utterances in which a negative intent was expressed by such means as shaking the head, pushing the object away or refusing to follow a direction, even though no negative element was expressed. From the contexts of the utterances, Bloom found that three basic types of negation were occurring: non-existence, rejection and denial. Non-existence, as the term indicates, was used by the child in situations where the referent was non-existent. For example, when the child uttered 'no pocket' while handling a piece of clothing where there was no pocket, the category 'non-existence' was scored. Rejection seemed indicated when the child used actions which appeared to be rejecting in nature – such as pushing away the rejected object. Bloom gives an example of this category which illustrates the kinds of cues the researcher can use in determining the meaning of an utterance. While being given a bath, the child said 'no dirty soap', and as he did so, he pushed away the soap which was being offered. The researcher did not rely on the evidence of the pushing motion alone, however, but noted both the existence of the soap and the fact that it was dirty. The utterance of 'no dirty soap', in context then, was not being used to indicate that there was no soap, nor that there was no *dirty* soap. Therefore, through a combination of cues – the pushing away, the fact that a dirty piece of soap was present – the utterance could be reasonably classified as an instance of rejection. In this manner, Bloom was able to categorize many of the children's utterances. The third type of negation, denial, asserted that some predication was not the case. If we say 'That's not an apple' when someone has said that it is, we are using this third type of negation.

Bloom noted a fairly constant developmental order of the syntactic expression of the three types of negation. For all three children, non-existence was the first category to be syntactically elaborated, usually with the words 'no more' as in 'no more lights', 'no more people'. Rejection was the next category to emerge, and the children mainly came to use 'don't' in contexts where this meaning seemed called for; examples include 'I don't need pants off', 'don't eat it'. Denial was the last meaning to appear and it came to be marked mainly by the use of 'not', as in 'that not lollipop' and 'it's not cold out'. The developmental order – non-existence, rejection, denial – was constant in the syntactic development across the three unrelated children. But Bloom's study was concerned solely with the emergence of *syntactic* negative reference and not with negative reference itself. It is not clear in her report whether the child was able to refer to other types of negation at earlier stages with the non-syntactically elaborated 'No.' We are told, for example, that when syntactic expression was limited to non-existence, the child's use of rejection and denial was limited to the single word 'no', and this would seem to imply that all negative meanings might have been available from the very beginning. However, this may be a misinterpretation since each new category emerged, as we will see, with the simplest forms for expressing it. It may be that the non-elaborated 'no' was only being used to indicate rejection and denial sometime *after* non-existence was being *syntactically* expressed.

McNeill and McNeill (1968) had a somewhat easier time as they were studying the development of negation in Japanese where the different meanings are expressed by different vocabulary items. Their analysis of the acquisition of negative meaning is made in terms of three binary dimensions labelled existence/truth, external/internal, and entailment/non-entailment. The McNeills' examples of each category, however, make it possible to translate their terminology into that used by Bloom, and I will use that latter terminology in order to facilitate comparison. According to the McNeills, 'nai' (adj.) is used to express non-existence. An example would be, 'There's not an apple here.' 'Nai' (aux.) indicates falsity of statements, or what we will call denial$_1$, a simple form of denial. The example given by the McNeills is the utterance 'That's not an apple' when someone pointing to a pear claimed it was an apple. What they call 'internal desire or lack of it', which we will call 'rejection', is indicated by 'iya' and would be used in contexts similar to 'No, I don't want an apple.' Finally, the form 'iiya' is said to be used in a contrastive sense, as in 'No, I didn't have an apple; I had a pear.' This is called 'entailment' in that its use indicates that one alternative is false while the other is true; we will call this denial$_2$ for it is a more complex type of denial.

The McNeills report the emergence of these negative items in a Japanese child. At the earliest stage (twenty-seven months), no semantic contrasts are observable, although *nai* (adj.) is used from the beginning and always where called for, that is, in situations of non-existence. At this stage *iya* is also used but inconsistently in that it is often replaced by *nai* (adj.). During the next stage, at twenty-nine months, the child begins to use *iya*, but always in contexts calling for *nai* (aux.) and *iiya*. McNeill and McNeill interpret this as evidence that the child is really using a shortened form of *iiya*, for the contexts are always those where denial is called for. At the third stage (thirty-one months), the child has acquired the real *iya*, and its replacement by *nai* (adj.) ceases. The child is now credited with the external/ internal dimension, that is, he is now able to express rejection. But the long form, *iiya*, and *nai* (aux.) are still being used as synonyms. Finally, at thirty-two months, the child begins to distinguish *nai* (aux.) from *iiya* and is said to have acquired the entailment/non-entailment dimension. The order of acquisition for the Japanese child, then, is said to be non-existence, denial$_1$, rejection and finally denial$_2$. This closely parallels Bloom's findings for English-speaking children, where the order of emergence was non-existence, rejection and denial. The only difference is the insertion of the category denial$_1$ into the developmental order found by Bloom. I find it very difficult to specify contexts where denial$_1$ and denial$_2$ are differentiable. It is, of course, impossible to check the reliability of coding, but it may be that what Bloom has called 'denial' occurs in situations that the McNeills would have labelled denial$_2$ where a closer distinction is called for in Japanese. And if we look at some of Bloom's examples of 'non-existence', we may perhaps begin to question the validity of her coding of that category. There are, for example, many instances of the use of 'can't' listed under non-existence – such utterances as 'I can't put this here', 'I can't get out', 'I can't fix it', and 'I can't reach it.' There are also several entries using other lexical items: 'This don't fit in', 'I didn't make dirty', etc. I wonder if other investigators would have listed all of these as instances of non-existence, even if they had all the contextual material available on which to base their decision. Many of these seem to me not to be examples of non-existence, but a kind of denial, although, as I have said, I would find it difficult to separate the two types of denial in most real-life situations. In any case, there is a close parallelism in the emergence of the types of negation in the two unrelated studies in two unrelated languages, and I suspect that the parallelism might be closer if the data of both studies were examined together using explicit and reliable coding procedures.

It is interesting that Bloom's children slowly began to use particular lexical items to express the different kinds of negation. Adult English certainly does not impose this differentiation. All three children, it will be recalled, came to express non-existence mainly by the use of 'no more', rejection by 'don't', and denial by 'not'. But as Bloom notes, the important point is that the progressive differentiation in the forms by which negation was expressed was directly related to the three semantic categories, and she cited further evidence that the process did not occur the other way round, i.e. that it did not happen that children acquired new forms like 'don't' or 'not' which caused the emergence of new negative categories. The crucial evidence is that when children first began to use a new type of negative reference such as rejection or denial, they did so by using a primitive structure that previously had expressed the earlier-acquired concept, non-existence. For example, non-existence had originally been expressed by 'no more'. But as this category began to develop, it was expressed by other syntactic forms such as 'don't' and 'can't'. When rejection first began to be expressed, the original 'no more' was used. And as rejection developed as a category and began being expressed in several ways, as, for example, by adding 'don't' as an operator, denial emerged using the primitive 'no more'. In other words, all three children used the primitive form 'no more' to express newer functions. The form used for non-existence developed and was expressed through the use of more complex forms. Thus, learning to express new semantic categories of negation did not require the learning of new structures at that time. Furthermore, it was not the case that new linguistic forms were used productively by the children before they understood the cognitive notions these forms expressed. Rather, new and more complex structures for particular categories developed only after these categories had been expressed with simpler, familiar structures. There was strong evidence in Bloom's data, then, that cognitive categories of negation developed before the acquisition of linguistic forms to refer to them. And as we have seen, the emergence of these categories may follow a similar developmental order in children acquiring strikingly different languages.

A few years ago, I made a study of the development of time concepts during the acquisition of language by two of the children in Roger Brown's study (Cromer, 1968). Some of the findings are of interest in that they indicate that the understanding of certain temporal notions precedes the acquisition of linguistic forms proper for their expression. A short review of the findings in four categories which bear on this point follows – the expression of the order of events in time, a category called 'unactuals', another called 'relevance', and finally the expression of timeless events.

The two children studied were Adam and Sarah and their speech was examined from two years three months to five years five months in the case of Sarah, and from two years three months to six years two months for Adam. As the two children had similar mean utterance lengths at similar chronological ages, only the ages and the order of development will interest us here. The speech protocols of the children were made from fortnightly recording sessions in the home, but in order to study the changes, only the protocols from approximately four-month intervals were examined. Each utterance was scored for its intended reference using situational and contextual cues.

One of the scoring categories was 'point in time' with each reference to past, present, or future being noted. Some utterances referred to more than one point in time. At the earliest ages almost all utterances with relations between two points in time preserved the occurring order of events, and it was not until after four years in Adam and four years two months in Sarah that the children began to reverse these relations occasionally. An average of about 8 per cent of relations no longer preserved real order after these ages. Now what is interesting is that the ability to reverse the order of events in time did not arise with new linguistic forms such as the acquisition of particular conjunctions. The kinds of reversals being referred to here are not the type wherein two significant events are reversed in descriptive retelling – an ability which arises even later as we will see in the next section. Rather, these points in time often refer to single events only, as expressed in natural conversation. They are not even noticeable to most observers unless a careful scoring is made. Some examples will make this clear. The following are drawn from the records and illustrate reversals in temporal order:

D'you know the light wents off? (present–past)
I like everything I liked. (present–past)
Look what I found. (immediate future–past)
Wanna see what I coloured? (immediate future–past)

These sentences may seem like any others and the observer feels certain he has heard similar utterances by the child at earlier ages. In fact he *has* heard similar utterances – except that until age four, they have retained temporal order. Compare these with utterances retaining temporal order:

Can I put it on his chest so it be a button? (future–later future)
I hope he won't bother you. (present–future)

And that is the important point. Most of the reversals use linguistic forms which were available to the child at an earlier age.

Related to this ability to reverse temporal relations is the use made of two words, 'before' and 'after'. In order to retain the actual order of events, 'after' must come at the beginning of an utterance while 'before' must be inserted in the middle, as in:

After X, (then) Y
X before Y

To reverse order, however, just the opposite placement of the two terms is necessary, as in:

Y after X
Before Y, X

In the two children whose temporal reference was being charted longitudinally, these two terms were rarely used. Indeed, Sarah never used either of them to relate two points in time in the protocols studied. Adam made his first use of one of the words at four years six months, but in a way which retained the actual order of events. Only after age four years ten months did he make use of a reversed order. These terms are specifically focused on time relations and it is interesting that they should arise rather late in the child's language acquisition. The Clarks (see Clark, 1970; Clark and Clark, 1968) have made careful studies of the use of these terms by young children and have found that three and a half year olds retain the actual order of events in time in their spontaneous speech. They have also found in a memory experiment that children were better able to remember the sense of sentences which retained temporal order. They also noted that in the children's preference for response mode, syntactic considerations played a part and sentences were preferred which had the subordinate clause in second position. Thus, transformational complexity has an influence which must be considered. Nevertheless, in utterances of equal syntactic complexity, children before age four tend to use only those in which the actual order of events in time is maintained.

Statements of a hypothetical nature are based on an ability to move one's viewpoint about in time. A true hypothetical, as defined here, means the predication of a future event on another event which is also in the future – the hypothesized event being slightly later than the event on which it depends. For example, in 'If it rains, I will take my umbrella', the possibility of rain is taken as a future event which, if it occurs, will result in the even later event of taking the umbrella. This is, however, only one type of 'unactual' or 'unactualized' event. There are other types which make a different use of time reference. For example, in counter-factual statements such as 'If you had telephoned, I would have come to your aid', a possibility in past time is noted which did not, in fact, occur. Hypothetical and counter-factual statements therefore require complex cognitive abilities which include the ability to refer to 'possibilities' as well as the ability to change one's vantage-point in a time sequence.

It may be that a primitive type of 'possibility' is to be found in the ability to pretend. In Adam and Sarah, pretending was present in some of the earliest protocols; it was expressed by such utterances as:

Dis could be a . . . his house
Dis could be the mother
Dis'll be the blanket

It was almost a year and a half later that 'possibility' was first expressed, for although there was a single utterance by Adam at three years two months which seemed to indicate 'possibility' ('Maybe its can . . . go dis way'), it was only after four years six months that 'possibility' emerged as a category in regular use, as in:

Someping might come out my pocket
I bet I could play it
Think cows would like this?
We can do all three (where context indicated 'possibility' and not 'ability')

And it was only at this age, four years six months, that hypotheticals began to appear in regular use. Examples include:

If you keep on going, it's gonna get bigger on this side and bigger on that side, right?
What you think would happen if I put a stick?
Don't tear it again or I turn you into a puppet

There are two points of interest here. First, the expression of hypotheticalness does not depend on the acquisition of some new linguistic form. It is expressable, for example, by the use of 'if' in a subordinate clause or by the use of 'or' as a conjunction. Second, the child has had the ability to make statements of the same linguistic type at an earlier age, but he has done so only when they make a different kind of reference. At four years and after, Adam began making use of utterances, the meaning of which can be called 'uncertainty of conditions':

Maybe that's my Daddy
In case you're hungry, I got grain
See if the flowers would like to watch me

In these utterances, the speaker is asking for a determination of facts or conditions, the nature of which is unclear to him. Some linguistic forms were available to the child which could have been used to express hypotheticalness, but they were not used with that meaning until several months later, after age four years six months. Sarah's use of hypotheticals was very limited but the pattern was the same. She evidenced an early use of pretending and a somewhat later acquisition of possibility and hypotheticalness (four years ten months).

Slobin (1966) has made a similar observation on children acquiring Russian as their native language. He points out that, grammatically speaking, the hypothetical is exceedingly simple. Its emergence, however, in Russian-speaking children is quite late. Slobin concludes that it is the semantic and not the grammatical aspect which is difficult for the child.

The third category from which there is some evidence that particular cognitive abilities precede their normal (adult-like) linguistic expression is that of 'relevance'. Use of 'relevance' indicates that the speaker is noting the importance of a referred-to event to the time indicated by his utterance. For example, a statement like 'The lamp fell' tells us nothing about the current state of the lamp; it may still be in the fallen position or it may have been righted some time ago. However, when we say 'The lamp has fallen', the use of the perfect tense would appear to indicate that the lamp is still in a fallen position at the time of the utterance or is in a state effected by the fall. In other words, the state of the lamp or the consequence engendered by its falling is relevant to the utterance we are making. Linguists have often referred to the function of the perfect tense as being one of 'current relevance' of a past event. It is possible to extend the term, however, to include not only the relevance of some event in the past, but also the relevance of future events on current behaviour. We will only consider here the more usual meaning of 'relevance'.

There are two approaches one can take in studying relevance from the past: one can trace the development of the perfect tenses in the children or one can trace the cognitive development of relevance, i.e. the development of the ability to use this type of reference regardless of the linguistic devices used to express it. Looking first at the use of the perfect tense by Adam and Sarah, one immediately found that its use was rare. In Adam's record the first meaningful use of the perfect occurred at four years six months. But Sarah never once used the perfect tense through five years five months in the protocols examined. The reason for the late emergence of the perfect tense is difficult to understand. To illustrate the elements of the perfect tense, let us examine the sentence, 'I have seen it.' The essential features include the use of 'have' as an auxiliary verb with the main verb consisting of the past participle, 'seen'. In many cases the past participle is the same as the past tense of the verb, as with 'tell' becoming 'told' and 'have told'. But there are a number of common verbs which have a distinct past participle, as in 'see', 'saw' and 'have seen'. In linguistic terminology, the formation of the perfect depends on the grammatical feature 'have -en' which requires a rule of affix movement. Now what is interesting in all this is that both Adam and Sarah possessed all of the necessary elements for the production of the perfect tense at a much earlier age. Both were using 'have' as a type of auxiliary ('have to') from two years eleven months. At that time they had a sufficient 'production span capacity' to produce the perfect tense. It is also noteworthy that the 'Be -ing' involving affix movement and other grammatical characteristics like 'have -en' were occurring before the age of three. The children also possessed, at an early age, some specific past participles like 'seen' and 'gone'. Adam and Sarah, then, possessed all the necessary elements and the capacity to produce utterances of a sufficient length to combine them at a very early age. Furthermore, an analysis of the utterances of the parents revealed that they were using the perfect tense (although with a somewhat lower frequency than other grammatical forms). So both Adam and Sarah were being exposed to this grammatical feature. It is thus very difficult to see why the children were not producing the perfect tense at an earlier age – difficult, that is, until the *meaning* of the perfect tense is examined. And when the data are analysed from that point of view, it becomes apparent that the ability to use the perfect tense properly rests on a late-developing ability to consider the relevance of another time to the time of the utterance. Although it is exceedingly difficult to specify the speaker's intention, there are nevertheless situations in which relevance is important. If there is a point in the child's development before which he ignores a relation between a past event and the present, but after which he begins to relate the two, then we may have found the reason for the late emergence of the perfect tense. In Adam, in the language samples between the ages of two years three months and four years, there were no attempts to make such a relation. But at four years there was one utterance which appears to be the first use of the category of relevance. It was at four years six months that Adam first used the perfect tense, but at that time and shortly thereafter he made several utterances which included the notion of relevance, even though in many of these he employed other linguistic forms which were available at a much younger age:

Hey, what else you bring the pyjamas for?
How come you didn't bring your car today?
This one is the mostest tight you ever saw
You finished me lots of rings

The data from Sarah are even more striking for she never used the perfect tense in the speech samples which were analysed. Nevertheless, regular use of the notion of relevance began at age four years six months. Sarah did not use the perfect tense, but instead seems to have developed uses of 'now' and 'yet' to refer to the relation of past time into the present. For example, to an adult question as to the state she was in, Sarah replied, 'Now, hit myself' (= 'I just hit myself' or 'I have just hit myself'). Other utterances at four years six months, like 'You didn't peek yet?' and 'Did ya peek yet?' may not seem strange until the context is noted:

Adult: When are you gonna let us peek?
Sarah: When I'm finished.
Did ya peek yet? (= relevance expressable either by 'Did you peek?' or 'Have you peeked?')

Again, what is interesting is that although Sarah had the components to produce utterances like these at an earlier age, she did not use them to indicate relevance before four years six months. A similar conclusion can be drawn from the early use of past participles in both children. An examination of their use indicates that they were not instances of the perfect tense from which the auxiliary 'have' was merely dropped. Rather, no early uses of the past participle by either child ever referred to relevance. Examples include:

Kitty gone
All done
Light broken

It would appear, then, that the reason why children were not producing the perfect tense at an early age was because they were not making reference to what the perfect tense usually expresses. Once they did begin to communicate this meaning, they did so by using various linguistic forms which had been at their disposal (e.g. using 'now' and 'yet' appended to utterances about the past). And it was only then that they began in addition to acquire the perfect tense.

One final temporal category we will consider is that of 'timeless utterances'. Something rather special is intended by this term. It is not meant to refer to descriptions, definitions, or even to 'states' of persons. While these may often be thought to be timeless, they are, in fact, from a behavioural point of view, usually rooted in the present. Thus, if the child points to a toy and says 'It's red', he is really describing or making reference to something which is phenomenally present. Something very different occurs, however, when the child develops the cognitive ability to take some action or event which normally occurs at some point in time, and lifts it out of any particular situation and so imbues it with a timeless quality. An example of this 'true timelessness' would be Adam's utterance, 'Playing a banjo is good exercise for your thumb.' Although the playing of the banjo could have taken place in the past, or might be occurring at the time of the utterance, or might even take place in the future, the central idea of the statement is specifically concerned with none of these, or rather with all of these. The action of playing a banjo has been removed from a time sequence. This is what is meant when an utterance is classified as 'timeless'.

Timeless references seem to develop slowly out of a type of description which I have designated as 'timeless characterizing descriptions'. Such descriptions go beyond the 'present time' of the utterance in that they describe what something 'does' or what something is 'for' even though the object or event referred to is present when the utterance is made. In the speech samples from both Adam and Sarah the most primitive form of timeless characterizing descriptions is found at three years two months. These include:

Tiny car for what?
Dat push it?
De wheels turn?
A marble bag for what?
What are dose for?

In nearly all instances at three years two months, timeless characterizing descriptions ask a question concerning how something works or what it does. In a sense, none of them really takes an action out of a timed context except in so far as an explanation is asked for. However, at about four years timeless characterizing descriptions have advanced from being used merely to seek explanations to include descriptions of actions:

Dis goes up
Is that how you do it?
It's something that you eat

And it is also at four years in Adam and four years two months in Sarah that true timeless references begin to be used. Some examples of utterances expressing this ability to take something out of a timed context are:

I save dem
I never have no cookies
I keep falling down
I have a good time at school
I always lose things when I move
Paul blames everything on his own self

So far, the development of four types of reference has been traced in the utterances of two children in the Roger Brown study. For all of these, our attention has been focused on the meaning of each utterance taken in its entirety. However, there is another fact which is rather startling. All of the speech protocols were searched for any *words* which had something to do with time. This search revealed that the children began spontaneously to use time words of a particular reference type only when they had begun to make reference to that category in their complete utterances. Thus, the words 'always', 'sometimes' and 'never' were not used by the children until they had begun to express timelessness at ages four years and four years two months. It is rather startling that in the two unrelated children the emergence not only of temporal categories expressed by these words, but the very words used, should parallel one another so closely. Similarly, words related to relevance, in that they look forward or backward in time from the time of the utterance, only appeared once the children were cognitively able to make reference to that category. For example, it was not until Adam was four that he began to use the phrase 'about to'. His first use of the word 'remember' (if one can consider it a type of looking back into the past from the present) also occurred at that time. And it will be recalled that it was at four that Adam had first begun to be able to use the category 'relevance'. More complex words related to that category appeared at even later ages: 'until' (four years ten months), 'yet' (five years two months) and 'just' as in 'You just messed mine' (five years six months). Similarly, Sarah's first use of lexical items bearing on the category of relevance was at four years two months when she began using 'remember' and 'just'. At four years six months she began to use 'yet' in the interesting way discussed earlier.

The emergence of words referring to specific types of time reference only when that reference has begun to be expressed by the child, often in utterances not necessarily using time words at all, was found not only for the categories mentioned here, but for a number of other categories as well, e.g. expressions of duration and speed. Such evidence is damaging for a theory of language acquisition which holds that the child imitates the words he hears around him and thus builds up a series of categories through language. But there is even more direct evidence that cognition precedes language and indeed determines its acquisition. Robbins Burling (1959) studied the acquisition of language by his bilingual son who, for a time, beginning at one year four months, was brought up speaking both English and Garo. Garo is a language of the Tibeto-Burman group spoken in an area of India where Burling lived while making a two-year anthropological study. He noticed that in some cases his son 'simultaneously learned English and Garo words with approximately the same meanings, as though once his understanding reached the point of being able to grasp a concept he was able to use the appropriate words in both languages'. For example, when he suddenly grasped the meaning of colour terms, he was able to use the English and Garo words simultaneously. Similarly, when he began to use words indicating time such as 'last night' and 'yesterday morning', he also began using the corresponding Garo terms. This would appear to be evidence that cognitive categories affect the acquisition of language rather than the other way round.

Returning to the data from Adam and Sarah, we can attempt an overview of the development of the four categories. Below are listed the ages at which each of the categories first emerged in regular use by the two children.

	Adam	Sarah
Reversals	4:0	4:2
Hypotheticals	4:6	4:10
Relevance	4:0	4:6
Timeless utterances	4:0	4:2

It is striking that these features emerge at approximately the same time, and some two years after the language-acquisition process has begun. And this is only a partial list. Several more temporal features not discussed here were also found to emerge sometime after the age of four or four and a half years (Cromer, 1968). It may be that there is some common factor in these time categories – some cognitive ability which becomes active and permits the expression of several new types of temporal reference. What these new types of reference seem to have in common appears to be an ability to free oneself from the immediate situation or from the actual order of events in time. It is as if the child is now able to 'de-centre' his viewpoint as a speaker so as to approach a temporal sequence in other than real sequential order. This would be a basis for the reversals which emerge at this age. The freedom from the actual order of events in time would permit the child to place himself at other perspectives and thus to consider events which are contingent on future possibilities – the definition of hypotheticals. In addition, this ability to consider time from other viewpoints might also constitute the cognitive ability necessary for considering the relevance of other times to the time of the utterance. And this ability to stand outside the actual order of events in time is indeed essential to the very notion of utterances which have been defined as 'timeless'.

But whether the advances at this age are considered together in the framework of a new cognitive ability to de-centre from one's own immediate viewpoint as regards the flow of time, or whether each of the new achievements is seen as being due to specific new cognitive attainments, the evidence is strong that changes in cognition precede the acquisition of new linguistic forms which are normally used by adults to express them. Such a view would go a long way towards explaining some otherwise mysterious phenomena. For example, before certain particular cognitive changes occur, the child is exposed to many types of linguistic behaviour, which include both structures (e.g. the perfect tense) and lexical items (e.g. whole categories of time words) which he does not make a part of his spontaneous speech and which, indeed, he rarely imitates. Furthermore, the structures he does use are limited only to particular types of reference. After particular cognitive changes have occurred, however, the child not only begins to use the forms he has at his disposal to express new ideas and relationships, but he rapidly acquires new forms of expression which he lacked until that time. It may even be that the developing cognitive abilities stimulate the child into an active search for or a heightened awareness of particular forms and structures used by adult speakers to express the newly understood relationships. Language acquisition may not be the passive process of merely imitating the adults in the environment as was once supposed. In his very earliest utterances the infant is imposing his structure on the language he hears. But what about acquisitions at later ages when the basic linguistic structures have been mainly acquired? Do cognitive processes assert an influence even then? It is to some evidence concerning cognitive effects at later ages which we will now turn our attention.

Evidence from later language acquisition

The relevant work on the relation between cognitive structures and language acquisition at later ages comes from the Piagetian school of thought. It will be recalled that the Piagetian view is that language is not the source of the operations of thought but is itself structured by those operations. Hermina Sinclair-de-Zwart (1969) carried out an investigation of the verbal abilities of children at different levels on the standard Piagetian conservation task. Conservation studies require the child to indicate whether an amount of water remains the same when poured into different vessels. Young children (about four or five years) believe that the amount changes with the shape of the container, and that, for example, if water from a standard beaker is poured into a tall narrow container, the latter receptacle will have 'more'. Older children, who have achieved conservation, compensate the dimensions. They say that the amount of water has remained the same and often justify their answer by pointing out that while the level of the water is higher, the new container is also narrower so that what has been gained in height has been lost in width. Piaget claims that this compensation is of central importance for it shows that the child has achieved a stage of operational thinking which is based on certain structural developments which underlie thought processes. Such a view has been challenged, however. Bruner, Olver and Greenfield (1966) have claimed, for example, that young children are perceptually seduced by the height of the liquid. Conservation is achieved, according to this view, through the mediation of the symbolic properties of language, which eventually override the apparent (perceptual) differences in amount. There is here, then, a direct confrontation between those who hold that thought structures language and those who feel that language processes in some cases aid thought.

From a linguistic point of view, there are at least three things to note in the child's speech *vis-à-vis* conservation: (a) the child's use of comparatives as opposed to absolute terminology in describing materials differing in two dimensions, (b) his use of differentiated instead of undifferentiated terms, and (c) the types of sentences he uses to coordinate the two dimensions. Sinclair-de-Zwart directly studied these processes by having the children carry out tasks of the type, 'Find a pencil that is longer but thinner' (comprehension), and having them describe the differences between materials differing in two dimensions, as with two pencils, a short thick one and a long thin one (production). The children, after undertaking the conservation test, were then divided into three groups: those totally lacking conservation, those at an intermediate stage and those who had achieved conservation. Sinclair-de-Zwart reports that all three groups performed about equally well in the comprehension task. But she reports differences between conservers and total non-conservers on the verbal-production task. For convenience I have attempted to arrange the figures she reports into Table 1. These results by themselves do not provide sufficient grounds on which to base a definite judgement as to the relation between language and operational thought. All one has is a correlation between conservation ability and the spontaneous use of complex structures and differentiated terminology. But whether new linguistic structures and terminology *cause* operational thought to come about, or whether the new thought structures make it easier for the child to use more advanced language patterns, cannot be determined on the basis of these figures. For the non-conservers, for example, any percentage which is greater than zero could be interpreted as evidence that some children are acquiring language structures which will later make conservation possible. But these same figures could also be interpreted as evidence that some non-conserving children have the more complex linguistic structures without these giving rise to conservation and operational thinking. It is this latter interpretation that Sinclair-de-Zwart adheres to, and she carried out a second series of experiments to support her view.

Table 1 Sinclair-de-Zwart's results on the language used by conservers and non-conservers

	Non-conservers	Conservers
% using comparatives to describe plasticine (continuous quantity)	10[a]	70
% using comparatives to describe marbles (discontinuous quantity)	20	100
% using differentiated terms for different dimensions	25[b]	100
% using two sentences coordinating two dimensions	10[c]	80

[a] Sinclair-de-Zwart reports that 90 per cent of the non-conserving children used absolute terms, e.g. ' one has a lot and the other has a little '.
[b] 75 per cent used undifferentiated terms giving one word for both dimensions, e.g. using 'small' for both shortness and thinness.
[c] 90 per cent of the non-conserving children described only one dimension or used four separate sentences. Sentences coordinating the two dimensions would be, e.g. 'This is tall but it's thin; this is short but it's wide.'

An attempt was made to teach the non-conservers the more advanced language, i.e. differentiated terminology, comparative terms and coordinated structures to describe differences in two dimensions. Sinclair-de-Zwart found that differentiated terminology (e.g. 'short' instead of 'little' and 'thin' instead of 'little') was easy to teach. Comparative terms like 'more' and 'less' were more difficult to teach to non-conservers, and coordinated sentence structures the most difficult of all. However, even the children who successfully learned these expressions rarely advanced on the conservation test. Only about 10 per cent of these language-taught children acquired conservation. However, many of the children who remained non-conservers began to notice and make reference to the differing dimensions. Sinclair-de-Zwart concluded that verbal training may lead children to pay attention to important features in the conservation task, but such language training does not of itself lead to conservation and operational thinking.

Finally, there are two studies on the relation of productive language ability to another aspect of operational thought, reversibility. Inhelder (1969) reports a study of seriation ability that she and Sinclair undertook. The ability to seriate a number of sticks of increasing size is made possible, like conservation, by the thought structures which are available to the child once he has achieved the stage of operational thinking. It is said that the child is unable to put the sticks into an order of increasing or decreasing size and to insert new sticks into their proper place in the series until he is able to conceptualize a particular stick as being at the same time both longer than some sticks and shorter than others in the series. It was found that verbal descriptions of the materials paralleled the stages on this task. Youngest children used only two descriptive terms, long and short, to describe successive pairs of sticks. Slightly older children used three descriptive terms. But at the stage which precedes operational solution, children were able to use comparatives. They described the sticks once again using only two terms, but one of these was in a comparative form. Thus, they would give as their verbal description statements like 'short, longer, longer, longer . . .'. But what is significant is that when they were asked to describe the series a second time beginning at the other end they were unable to do so. The children seemed unable to describe a stick they had just called 'longer' as being 'shorter'. Thus the lack of reversibility would seem to extend to the verbal descriptions as well.

Somewhat related to this is a study by Ferreiro and Sinclair (1971) on the inability of children who have not yet reached the Piagetian stage of operational thinking to reverse linguistically the order of two events in time. This notion has some striking similarities to the inability to reverse temporal viewpoints at an earlier age which has previously been discussed. Ferreiro and Sinclair presented the child with some actions carried out on dolls in front of him. One of the child's tasks was to describe the actions but he was made to talk about the second action first. For example, in one situation, first a girl doll washed a boy doll and then the boy doll went upstairs. In their inverse-order description, the youngest children (about four and a half years) did one of two things. Some simply repeated their original description which retained temporal order and thereby did not comply with the instruction to begin with the second action: 'She cleaned him and then he went up.' Other children at this age complied with the instructions, but did not supply any temporal indicators, as in 'He went upstairs and she washed him.'

At the next stage, children about five and a half years always complied with the instructions to begin their verbal description with the second event, but they were incapable of using correctly the temporal indicators necessary to describe the actual order. Some found it impossible, saying, 'The boy . . . the boy . . . No. You've got to start with the girl.' Other children attempted various solutions to the problem. Some simply inverted the order in their description: 'The boy went to the top of the stairs and afterwards the girl cleaned him.' Others attempted the curious solution of inverting the *action*: 'He goes downstairs again and the girl washes his arms.' Still others inverted the actors and the events so that the action performed in the second event was attributed to the actor in the first: 'The boy goes and washes her face and then it's her that goes upstairs.' Yet other solutions consisted of attributing a neutral action to the actor in the second event: 'The boy came, she washed his face and then he left.' At this stage, a series of questions about the order of events revealed that the children knew perfectly well which event had occurred first and which had come second. But they were unable to code this reversibility linguistically. Ferreiro and Sinclair conclude that the child at this stage is unable to make a correct inverse description because his 'syntactic transformations are not yet integrated into a system which permits the conservation of the entire semantic content'. This aspect of the linguistic transformational system only becomes possible when the child has attained the stage of operational thinking, for the structures necessary for reversibility are not available until that stage of thought is reached.

Not a great deal of work has been done with older children on the relation between meaning and thought on the one hand and the acquisition of language on the other, partly because it had often been assumed that most aspects of language acquisition were complete well before the age of five years. But with increased attention now being given to structures which are not acquired until ten or eleven years of age in some cases (see, e.g. Chomsky, 1969; Cromer, 1970, 1972; Kessel, 1970), we can look forward perhaps to new experimental studies on this complex topic.

The cognitive hypothesis

Near the beginning of this review, it was noted how psychologists, until recently, for the most part favoured the view that language structured the thought processes. It may be recalled that the Sapir–Whorf hypothesis, in its strong form, claimed that the way we view the world, the way we process and understand reality, is almost totally determined by the language we speak. With increasing research on language acquisition, however, the pendulum has begun to swing in the other direction. We have seen that in his very first words the child is not merely imitating the language he hears about him; he is creating a set of categories to make reference to particular relations. Piagetian theorists have argued that the child begins his language acquisition process only when the cognitive processes of the sensori-motor stage have been completed. At slightly later ages, evidence has been quoted which seems to indicate that each new acquisition is made possible only through particular cognitive advances. We have seen how the earliest operations of verbs code only a specific set of cognitive meanings. We have also seen that the acquisition of prepositions depends on the advancing understanding of spatial relationships. In addition, we have noted the differentiation and addition of different types of negation as the child grows older. We have seen that a number of grammatical relationships are lacking until the child is cognitively able to free his viewpoint from an egocentric point in the flow of time. Evidence has also been reviewed that even more advanced linguistic techniques must await particular cognitive developments such as those formulated in the Piagetian stage of operational thinking. It would appear, then, that a position directly the reverse of that put forward by the Sapir–Whorf hypothesis is indicated, and we can call this the 'cognitive hypothesis'.

To parallel Whorf's wording of the hypothesis of linguistic determinism (see p. 186), the cognitive hypothesis might possibly be phrased like this: we are able to use the linguistic structures that we do largely because through our cognitive abilities we are enabled to do so, not because language itself exists for all merely to imitate. Cognitive processes differ not only at different ages but in how they enable the individual to break down the language that he hears to secure the elements which he can understand and produce.

The evidence adduced so far has been in support of the cognitive hypothesis. But it must also be noted that this is only part of the story. There are linguistic structures, including some which are found at the very earliest ages as well as others which appear later, whose acquisition seems to be little related to the maturing cognitive processes. We will, therefore, turn now to a very brief review of a few ideas and studies which seem to indicate that some aspects of language development operate relatively independently of more general cognitive abilities.

The independent development of language

One of the advocates of the cognitive hypothesis, Sinclair-de-Zwart (1969), made the claim that developing cognitive processes are necessary in order to acquire language. She put forward the view that the reason language acquisition does not begin until about the age of one and a half to two years is due specifically to the need for the processes of sensori-motor intelligence to be complete, and indeed she bases much of her attack on Chomsky's view of innate linguistic mechanisms on this time lag between the first manifestations of practical intelligence during that period and the first verbal productions. There may be other reasons for that time lag, but even if Sinclair-de-Zwart's view is accepted, it is possible to speculate, as mentioned earlier, whether those cognitive processes, even if necessary, are nevertheless sufficient to account for the language-acquisition process. This same question has been posed in a different context.

Roger Brown (1970a) has examined the first 'sentences' of a chimpanzee and compared them to the first utterances in the children he has been studying. The chimpanzee, Washoe, is being raised by Allen and Beatrice Gardner (Gardner and Gardner, 1969) and is being taught the sign language used by the deaf in North America. By three years of age, Washoe has been able to acquire a certain amount of communication ability. Whether that ability constitutes a grammar is still open to doubt. McNeill, in a personal communication, has speculated that Washoe may have a single rule of an evolutionarily primitive grammar: increase the number of signs used in proportion to the subjective importance of the message. In practice, this might mean, for example, that the chimpanzee, wanting the door opened to go outside, might sign 'open'. With a small degree of emphasis, she might sign 'you open'. With greater emphasis she might sign 'hurry open you out go' and so on. In all these, although the signs might have a meaning on a one-to-one basis, there would be no evidence for a real grammar beyond the rule of adding more signs to indicate greater emphasis. The order in which Washoe produced the signs did not itself seem to carry a grammatical meaning. And Roger Brown notes that this is in sharp contrast to the children he was studying. The children indicated various grammatical meanings through the use of definite word orders. In the data, violations of order were exceedingly rare. For Washoe, at three years of age, there was no evidence that order played any part in the communication process, and without this, or without some evidence of differential marking of meaning in some way, one is not yet able to infer that Washoe possesses a grammar.

Now Brown also notes that the kinds of meanings expressed by the children in their first sentences appear to be extensions of sensori-motor intelligence. He reasons that if these meanings truly are extensions of sensori-motor intelligence, then they are probably universal but not innate, as they would be built up through sensori-motor experience. Furthermore, these meanings would not be limited to man but might operate in animals as well. And in view of the fact that at least to age three, the chimpanzee still gives no positive evidence of a grammar in her signing, Brown carefully points out: 'Grammatical relations are defined in purely formal terms, and while they may, in early child speech, be more or less perfectly coordinated with the semantic rules, the two are not the same' (p. 222). In other words, the possession of sensori-motor intelligence would still not explain the *expression* of that intelligence in language. That early grammar expresses the meanings which sensori-motor intelligence makes possible does not in itself solve the mystery of how these meanings are conveyed by a grammar. So Washoe, in spite of possessing sensori-motor intelligence, might never necessarily acquire a grammatical language.

David Premack (1969) has also made an attempt to teach a type of language to a chimpanzee. He used a number of plastic symbols with metal backing which would adhere to a magnetic slate. He was able to teach the chimpanzee to use the plastic pieces as signs for particular objects such as bananas and apples, and as the names of individuals. After this initial step, he then moved on to teach 'sentences' expressing various relations. For example, the chimpanzee, Sarah, was able to carry out instructions coded in the symbols 'Sarah insert banana pail apple dish', and would correctly place the banana in the pail and the apple in the dish after having built up this hierarchical structure over time from the simpler structures, 'Sarah insert banana pail Sarah insert apple dish' and 'Sarah insert banana pail insert apple dish' in which the second uses of 'Sarah' and 'insert' were progressively eliminated. Premack was also able to teach Sarah how to communicate various relationships such as 'same' and 'different', and 'yes' and 'no'. For example, once she had learned to place the symbol for 'same' between two like objects, or between the name of the object and the object itself and to place the symbol for 'not same' between unlike objects, she was able to indicate with symbols for 'yes' and 'no' when these relations were used correctly. If the message placed on the board was (X) (same as) (X) or (X) (not same as) (Y), Sarah would reply with the symbol for 'yes'. And when messages like (X) (not same as) (X) or (X) (same as) (Y) were put up, she would reply 'no'. Premack does not make the claim, however, that the chimpanzee has or can be taught a grammatical system in the same sense as a human being, although he speculates on the possibility of the existence of grammars of varying degrees of weakness in the feeble-minded and in animals (Premack and Schwartz, 1966). He concludes instead that the functions of language are not uniquely human. If by this we can take the meaning that some aspects of the deep structure of human language may be unique but that this is not true of the semantics, then this would appear to be similar to Roger Brown's tentative conclusion that animals may have, for example, sensori-motor intelligence, but lack the uniquely human ability for expressing that intelligence in grammatical structures.

But why might it be important that this distinction be kept clear? Some linguists have already proposed that semantics and deep structure be equated (Fillmore, 1968; McCawley, 1968) or that surface structures be generated directly from a semantic base (Schlesinger, 1971a, 1971b), and in terms of descriptive adequacy it is difficult to choose between these types of grammars and the Chomskyan model with specifically linguistic deep structures (Chomsky, 1965).

One possibility is that a Chomskyan analysis may prove to be the more useful one for studying certain types of language disorders. With this in mind, another interesting study may be usefully cited. Mrs Jenny Hughes, under the direction of Neil O'Connor at the Medical Research Council unit, studied the communication ability of children who were classified as receptive aphasics. These children, though of normal intelligence, as measured on non-verbal tests, seem to be unable to acquire language in spite of intensive efforts to achieve this. Hughes used essentially the same materials with the children as Premack did with Sarah, the chimpanzee. She reports (Hughes, 1972) that the aphasic children rapidly acquired all of the functions taught: names for objects, verbs like 'give' and 'point to', direct and indirect objects, negation, modifiers and questions. That these children were able to acquire these functions rapidly in twice-weekly half-hour sessions in less than ten weeks, shows that their ability to understand and even communicate such functions is not impaired. We do not know why aphasic children are unable to acquire language. Probably there are multiple reasons and these may vary from individual to individual. But is it possible that in some of these children there is some impairment to a specifically linguistic mechanism which Chomsky claims is innate in human individuals? It may, then, be useful not to discard the distinction between semantic meanings and deep structure, for as the few studies of other species and of aphasic children show us, one may have all sorts of cognitive abilities and semantic meanings while lacking the means to communicate these in a truly grammatical language.

There are other reasons why certain properties of language appear to be independent of cognition. During normal language acquisition in unimpaired children, various stages can be observed while the child is acquiring particular linguistic structures, and these stages do not appear to be related to a growth in 'meaning'. Earlier, the work of Lois Bloom (1970) and of McNeill and McNeill (1968) on negation was discussed. Ursula Bellugi (1967) based her doctoral dissertation on the development of negation by the children of the Roger Brown study. In following the means by which negation was expressed, she found a series of structural stages. At first, the child simply attached a negative morpheme such as 'no' or 'not' to the beginning of an utterance, so as to produce sentences like 'no wipe finger' and 'not fit'. In the second stage, the negative appeared in five unrelated grammatical settings, and there were still no transformations. For example, in addition to the 'direct print-out of the base', as in 'no Rusty hat', some negatives were used with demonstrative pronouns (e.g. 'that no fish school'), some had the element 'why not' prefixed to negative sentences (e.g. 'why not cracker can't talk?'), and others made use of 'don't' and 'can't' either in demonstrative sentences (e.g. 'I don't sit on Cromer coffee') or in imperatives (e.g. 'Don't eat daisy'). In the third stage, there were seven types of negative structures. The direct print-out of the base had disappeared. Auxiliary transformations had begun in which the negative was truly attached to the auxiliary verb, and thus sentences like 'Why not cracker can't talk?' disappeared, i.e. 'don't' and 'can't' were treated as transformed from a negative element and an auxiliary instead of being used as vocabulary items with negative meaning.

Bloom (1970) claimed that in her own study, by paying attention to the semantic correlates of the negative sentences, she was able to study the syntax of negation more deeply. Although the negative sentences produced by the children she studied matched the surface features that Bellugi found, Bloom was able to specify some structures as making particular kinds of negative reference. As was noted earlier, rejection came to be mainly signalled by 'don't', and denial by 'not'. Non-existence, the developmentally earliest form, was mainly signalled by 'no' plus an element and by 'can't'. It would appear here, then, that the structure used is determined by meaning. However, Bloom noted that as each new category was acquired, it was expressed by a form which was already being used to convey the earlier meaning. Thus, non-existence, the first concept of negation to be expressed grammatically, became the grammatically most complex form, while reference to rejection and denial were made with simpler forms initially used to indicate non-existence. If to express the meaning of non-existence, the child comes to use more and more complex techniques over time, these new structures cannot be being acquired due to advances in 'meaning'.

It is possible that there are other cognitive constraints than 'meaning'. For example, there may be limitations due to what the child at a particular age can process. Or there may be a limitation on the number of elements he can produce in a single utterance. Bloom

(1970) has made a very convincing case for a cognitive limitation on production. She postulates a 'reduction transformation' in order to account for the differences between the underlying structure necessary for the assumed semantic interpretation and the reduced surface structure which the child actually produced. The evidence which she used to support this position consisted of sequential utterances of the child which exhibited both the expansion of some elements and deletion of others, in conjunction with semantic interpretation. For example, in the child's sequence of utterances,

Raisin there
Buy more grocery store
Raisins
Buy more grocery store
Raisin ə grocery store

it becomes apparent that whenever the subject of the sentence was expressed, either the verb, the object, the adverbial phrase, or more than one of these was omitted. This means that the child has organized the linguistic categories in a hierarchical structure and this accounts for the ability of the child to add categories without increasing sentence length, i.e. by deleting some categories when other categories either occurred or were expanded. Bloom claims that such an interpretation is supported by the semantic interpretation of the situation. For example, take the following set of utterances which one of the children, Kathryn, produced:

Kathryn under bridge
Kathryn ə make ə under ə bridge
Make ə more under bridge
Make ə car under bridge

Only by assuming that the child is employing a reduction transformation can one account for the relationship between 'Kathryn' and 'bridge' in the first utterance of the set, for in the observed situation in which the utterance was produced Kathryn was not under the bridge.

It is also interesting to note that the production limitation is not on sentence length as such. Bloom believes it to be rather a cognitive limitation in handling structured complexity. That is, it appears that the number of syntactic operations within a sentence increases the 'cognitive weight' of the sentence. But what determines which categories are eliminated? Bloom suggests that the cognitive limitation interacts with linguistic constraints in some as yet unspecified manner. She notes, for example, that it was often a more recently acquired form which was most likely to be deleted by the children.

But there are still other linguistic progressions which appear to depend neither on changes in meaning nor on changes in cognitive complexity or the growth of the cognitive capacities of the child. For example, Ursula Bellugi also studied the development of 'self-reference' during the acquisition of pronominalization or the formation of pronouns by the child (Bellugi-Klima, 1969; Bellugi, 1971). She found that there was a progression through several stages. At the earliest stage, the child used his own name in all positions, as the mother did about half the time. During this stage he was making utterances like:

Adam home
Adam go hill
Like Adam book shelf
Pick Adam up

In the second stage, he began to substitute the pronoun 'I' for his name if it occurred in the first position in the sentence, and occasionally produced both together:

I like drink it
I making coffee
I Adam driving
1 Adam do that

And at the same stage he was substituting 'me' for his name if it occurred other than in the first position in the sentence (with the exception of vocatives and greetings). This strategy produced some adult-like sentences:

One for me
Wake me up
Why laughing at me?

But it also produced a regular pattern of errors:

Why me spilled it?
What me doing?

At the third stage, the rules changed and the child now produced 'I' if his name served a nominative function in the sentence, and he produced 'me' if it served an object function in the sentence:

That what I do
Can I put them on when I go outside?
You watch me be busy
You want me help you?

That is, the child's pronouns no longer depended on sentence position but on grammatical function.

There are even further stages in the process having to do with reflexives like 'myself', but this is enough to illustrate the point. A number of things can be noted. First of all, no strict theory of imitation could account for these findings. Instead, the child is clearly developing his grammar in a systematic and regular manner. The set of rules that he has at a particular time produce a regular set of errors when judged against adult grammar (e.g. 'Why me spilled it?', 'What me doing?', etc. at the second stage). It is therefore clear that his grammatical system has characteristics which are not shared by the adult model. The series of stages show that these systems change over time. But most important for our present argument, the developments are not solely based on meaning or reference. Throughout, the meaning has remained the same – reference to self. It is also difficult to see how cognitive constraints could have played a part except in as much as later rules sometimes result in simplification. But while such simplification may reduce cognitive strain, the child must have had the capacity to produce the cognitively more cumbersome utterances at a time just prior to the application of any simplifying rule. Cognitive constraints and their progressive easing would not appear to play a role in the acquisition of this and many other linguistic structures. Especially difficult to explain in terms of either meaning or the progressive easing of cognitive constraints would be the many structures mentioned earlier, which are acquired rather late – sometime between five and twelve years of age (see e.g. Chomsky, 1969).

We have already touched on some of the findings of Roger Brown in an earlier section having to do with cognition preceding language (Brown, 1973). It may be recalled, for example, that he cited evidence that the three earliest operations on verbs encoded the earliest semantic meanings attributed to the child. But Brown was not looking solely for the way semantics affected acquisition. In his study, he subjected the data to three analyses: semantic complexity, grammatical complexity and the frequency of the use of particular forms by the parents of the three children. He specifically looked at the development of fourteen early morphemes in these terms. The morphemes whose grammatical acquisition he followed included the '-ing' of the present progressive, regular ('-ed') and irregular past tense, regular and irregular third person singular, plurals, possessives, the prepositions 'in' and 'on', the articles 'a' and 'the', and the copula and auxiliary 'be'. There was a high degree of correlation between the order of acquisition of these grammatical elements by the three children. Analyses of parental utterances showed that there was a high degree of correlation between the frequency of use of these morphemes among the parents. But there was no meaningful correlation between the order of acquisition by the children and the frequency of use by the parents. It appears that the frequency with which a form is used, though similar in these adults, has little effect on the order of acquisition by the children.

But the order of acquisition across the children was very similar. Brown compared this order both to the degree of semantic complexity (the more complex defined as containing elements of the less complex) and to the order of grammatical complexity (based on the transformational grammar of Jacobs and Rosenbaum, 1968). And his findings indicated that both of these notions about equally well predicted the order of acquisition. There was evidence that transformational complexity was a determinant of the order of acquisition, but the evidence was alternatively interpretable as demonstrating that semantic complexity was a determinant of the order of acquisition. Since both semantic and grammatical complexity seem to be confounded in the acquisition of these fourteen morphemes, it would appear difficult to render a judgement on their differential effects. However, a very ingenious solution has been offered by Dan Slobin (1971a).

After reviewing data to support the argument that there are cognitive prerequisites for the development of grammar, Slobin also notes that at some point formal linguistic complexity also plays a role in acquisition. For example, children learning Finnish lack yes/no questions at an age when children learning other languages have acquired them. The reason these are lacking in the Finnish children appears to be that yes/no questions are a particularly complex form in Finnish. They are not formed by the use of a rising intonation but by adding a question particle to the word and moving that word to the front of the sentence. Similarly, we know that very young children are able to understand and use plural forms. But Slobin reports that in Egyptian Arabic, the complete set of plurals is not acquired until nearly fifteen years of age! Again, it happens that this is an especially complex grammatical form in Arabic. There are many special irregular forms; there are differences depending on whether a counted or collected noun is used; and things numbering three through ten take the plural, while eleven or more take the singular.

Slobin's suggestion as to a way to study the differential grammatical complexities of language is to make use of bilingual children. If the bilingual child acquires new expressions in both languages at the same time, then the formal devices in the two languages are similar in complexity. We have already quoted an example of this by Burling (1959) whose child was brought up speaking both English and Garo. And Slobin quotes some examples from children simultaneously acquiring Russian and Georgian. If the new expressions are acquired at different times, however, then a difference in formal complexity would be suggested. Slobin gives an example of a bilingual child acquiring both Serbo-Croatian and Hungarian. Hungarian has a number of case endings for expressing spatial locations. The child had acquired these in Hungarian but at the same time had practically no locative expressions in Serbo-Croatian. And the locative expressions in Serbo-Croatian appear to be grammatically more complex in that they require both a locative preposition before the noun in addition to case endings attached to the noun.

Aside from the semantic generalities across children learning different languages, it is also possible to judge from the situational context when a child possesses particular meanings even though these are not yet being expressed grammatically. The whole study of intended reference discussed in an earlier section was devoted to showing how cognition preceded language acquisition. What we are emphasizing now is that grammatical structure has its own complexities which often resist acquisition once the child is attempting to express particular meanings. Another example which makes this clear is taken from Bloom's work (1970). She found that one and the same expression could be fulfilling different grammatical functions if meaning was taken into account. For example, the utterance 'Mommy sock' was interpretable as expressing a subject–object relation where the mother was putting the child's sock on the child; but the same utterance, 'Mommy sock' was interpreted as expressing the genitive relation (possession) when the child was picking up a sock belonging to Mommy. The possessive was meaningfully used before the child acquired the 's in order to produce utterances like 'Mommy's sock'.

We can see then, that cognitive development and linguistic development do not necessarily proceed together. The child, once he has the cognitive ability to understand certain relationships, will attempt to express these in language. As Slobin has pointed out, sometimes the linguistic means of expression for the new concept will be easily accessible, as with the Hungarian locative, and sometimes grammatical complexity will make the form inaccessible, as with the Arabic plural. Thus cognition can make certain understandings available, but there may be linguistic constraints.

The cognitive hypothesis: weak form

Earlier, in a discussion of the Sapir–Whorf hypothesis which held that language structured thought, we noted that some theorists had moved away from the extreme position and advocated what was called the 'weak form' of the Sapir–Whorf hypothesis. This weak form held that, while language did not wholly determine thought, it influenced thinking because of the categories made available by the language. Easy codability of a concept by a language made that concept easily available and thus more likely to be used in thinking.

We have seen that there is accumulating evidence instead, that it is cognition which determines language acquisition, but we have also seen that language has its own influences quite apart from meaning. Some linguistic changes, while not being solely determined by meaning, await other types of cognitive change due to their complexity. But there were still other structures whose late acquisition or changes over time seemed neither due to meaning nor to purely cognitive developments which eased particular cognitive constraints.

It would appear, then, that the cognitive hypothesis must also be modified. The 'weak form' of the cognitive hypothesis would hold that we are able to understand and productively to use particular linguistic structures only when our cognitive abilities enable us to do so. Our cognitive abilities at different stages of development make certain meanings *available* for expression. But, in addition, we must also possess certain specifically linguistic capabilities in order to come to express these meanings in language, and these linguistic capabilities may indeed be lacking in other species or in certain pathological conditions. Though language development depends on cognition, language has its own specific sources.

That indeed is really the same as the position put forward in 1934 by the Russian psychologist Vygotsky. In his classic work, *Thought and Language*, Vygotsky held that thought and speech have different genetic roots and that these two processes develop along different lines and independently of each other. The two processes are clearly distinct and can be observed in a pre-linguistic phase in the development of thought and in a pre-intellectual phase in the development of speech. It appears that much of what is being discovered during the current vogue of psycholinguistic research supports Vygotsky's view. Who knows – perhaps both Piaget and Chomsky are right!

References

ADAMS, P. (ed.) (1972), *Language in Thinking*, Penguin.
BELLUGI, U. (1967), 'The acquisition of the system of negation in children's speech', unpublished doctoral dissertation, Harvard University.
BELLUGI, U. (1971), 'Simplification in children's language', in R. Huxley and E. Ingram (eds.), *Language Acquisition: Models and Methods*, Academic Press.
BELLUGI-KLIMA, U. (1969), 'Language acquisition', Paper presented at the Symposium on Cognitive Studies and Artificial Intelligence Research, Wenner-Gren Foundation for Anthropological Research, Chicago, March.

BERNSTEIN, B. (1961), 'Social structure, language and learning', *Educ. Res.*, vol. 3, pp. 163–76.

BEVER, T. G., FODOR, J. A., and WEKSEL, W. (1965a), 'Is linguistics empirical?', *Psychol. Rev.*, vol. 72, pp. 493–500.

BEVER, T. G., FODOR, J. A., and WEKSEL, W. (1965b), 'Theoretical notes on the acquisition of syntax: a critique of "context generalization"', *Psychol. Rev.*, vol. 72, pp. 467–82.

BLOOM, L. (1970), *Language Development: Form and Function in Emerging Grammars*, MIT Press.

BROWN, R. (1956), 'Language and categories', in J. S. Bruner, J. J. Goodnow and G. A. Austin (eds.), *A Study of Thinking*, Wiley.

BROWN, R. (1970a), 'The first sentences of child and chimpanzee', in R. Brown, *Psycholinguistics: Selected Papers by Roger Brown*, Free Press.

BROWN, R. (1970b), *Psycholinguistics: Selected Papers by Roger Brown*, Free Press.

BROWN, R. (1973), *A First Language*, Harvard University Press.

BROWN, R., and BELLUGI, U. (1964), 'Three processes in the child's acquisition of syntax', *Harv. educ. Rev.*, vol. 34, pp. 133–51.

BROWN, R., and FRASER, C. (1964), 'The acquisition of syntax', in U. Bellugi and R. Brown (eds.), 'The acquisition of language', *Mongr. Soc. Res. Child Devel.*, vol. 29, no. 92, pp. 43–79.

BROWN, R., and HANLON, C. (1970), 'Derivational complexity and the order of acquisition in child speech', in J. R. Hayes (ed.), *Cognition and the Development of Language*, Wiley.

BROWN, R., and LENNEBERG, E. H. (1954), 'A study in language and cognition', *J. abnorm. soc. Psychol.*, vol. 49, pp. 454–62.

BROWN, R., and LENNEBERG, E. H. (1958), 'Studies in linguistic relativity', in E. E. Maccoby, T. M. Newcomb and E. L. Hartley (eds.), *Readings in Social Psychology*, 3rd edn, Holt, Rinehart & Winston.

BROWN, R., CAZDEN, C., and BELLUGI-KLIMA, U. (1969), 'The child's grammar from I to III', in J. P. Hill (ed.), *Minnesota Symposia on Child Psychology*, vol. 2, University of Minnesota Press.

BROWN, R., FRASER, C., and BELLUGI, U. (1964), 'Explorations in grammar evaluation', in U. Bellugi and R. Brown (eds.), 'The acquisition of language', *Mongr. Soc. Res. Child Devel.*, vol. 29, no. 92, pp. 79–92.

BRUNER, J. S. (1964), 'The course of cognitive growth', *Amer. Psychol.*, vol. 19, pp. 1–15.

BRUNER, J. S., OLVER, R. R., and GREENFIELD, P. M. (1966), *Studies in Cognitive Growth*, Wiley.

BURLING, R. (1959), 'Language development of a Garo and English speaking child', *Word*, vol. 15, pp. 45–68.

CARROLL, J. B. (ed.) (1956), *Language, Thought and Reality: Selected Writings of Benjamin Lee Whorf*, MIT Press and Wiley.

CHOMSKY, C. (1969), *The Acquisition of Syntax in Children from 5 to 10*, MIT Press.

CHOMSKY, N. (1959), 'A review of *Verbal Behavior*, by B. F. Skinner', *Language*, vol. 35, pp. 26–58.

CHOMSKY, N. (1962), 'Explanatory models in linguistics', in E. Nagel, P. Suppes and A. Tarski (eds.), *Logic, Methodology, and Philosophy of Science*, Stanford University Press.

CHOMSKY, N. (1965), *Aspects of the Theory of Syntax*, MIT Press.

CHOMSKY, N. (1966), *Cartesian Linguistics*, Harper & Row.

CHOMSKY, N. (1968), *Language and Mind*, Harcourt, Brace & World.

CHOMSKY, N., and HALLE, M. (1968), *The Sound Pattern of English*, Harper & Row.

CLARK, E. V. (1970), 'How young children describe events in time', in G. B. Flores d'Arcais and W. J. M. Levelt (eds.), *Advances in Psycholinguistics*, North-Holland Publishing Co.

CLARK, H. H., and CLARK, E. V. (1968), 'Semantic distinctions and memory for complex sentences', *Q. J. exp. Psychol.*, vol. 20, pp. 129–38.

CROMER, R. F. (1968), 'The development of temporal reference during the acquisition of language', unpublished doctoral dissertation, Harvard University.

CROMER, R. F. (1970), ' "Children are nice to understand": surface structure clues for the recovery of deep structure', *Brit. J. Psychol.*, vol. 61, pp. 397–408.

CROMER, R. F. (1972), 'The learning of surface structure clues to deep structure by a puppet show technique', *Q. J. exp. Psychol.*, vol. 24, pp. 66–76.

CROMER, R. F. (1973), 'Conservation by the congenitally blind', *Brit. J. Psychol.*, vol. 64, pp. 241–50.

DAVENPORT, R. K., and ROGERS, C. M. (1970), 'Intermodal equivalence of stimuli in apes', *Science*, vol. 168, pp. 279–80.

DE LAGUNA, G. A. (1927), *Speech: Its Function and Development*, Indiana University Press, 1963.

DODD, B. (1972), 'Effects of social and vocal stimulation on infant babbling', *Devel. Psychol.*, vol. 7, pp. 80–83.

ERVIN-TRIPP, S. (1966), 'Language development', in M. Hoffman and L. Hoffman (eds.), *Review of Child Development Research*, vol. 2, University of Michigan Press.

ERVIN-TRIPP, S. (1971), 'An overview of theories of grammatical development', in D. I. Slobin (ed.), *The Ontogenesis of Grammar: A Theoretical Symposium*, Academic Press.

FAULKNER, W. (1929), *As I Lay Dying*, Penguin, 1970.

FERREIRO, E., and SINCLAIR, H. (1971), 'Temporal relations in language', *Int. J. Psychol.*, vol. 6, pp. 39–47.

FILLMORE, C. J. (1968), 'The case for case', in E. Bach and R. T. Harms (eds.), *Universals in Linguistic Theory*, Holt, Rinehart & Winston.

FLAVELL, J. H. (1963), *The Developmental Psychology of Jean Piaget*, Van Nostrand.

FURTH, H. G. (1966), *Thinking Without Language: Psychological Implications of Deafness*, Free Press.

FURTH, H. G. (1969), *Piaget and Knowledge*, Prentice-Hall.

FURTH, H. G., and YOUNISS, J. (1971), 'Formal operations and language: a comparison of deaf and hearing adolescents', *Int. J. Psychol.*, vol. 6, pp. 49–64.

GARDNER, R. A., and GARDNER, B. T. (1969), 'Teaching sign language to a chimpanzee', *Science*, vol. 165, pp. 664–72.

HATWELL, Y. (1966), *Privation sensorielle et intelligence*, Presses Universitaires de France.

HENLE, P. (ed.) (1958), *Language, Thought, and Culture*, University of Michigan Press.

HERMELIN, B., and O'CONNOR, N. (1964), 'Crossmodal transfer in normal, subnormal, and autistic children', *Neuropsychologia*, vol. 2, pp. 229–35.

HOIJER, H. (ed.) (1954), *Language in Culture*, University of Chicago Press.

HOUSTON, S. H. (1970), 'A reexamination of some assumptions about the language of the disadvantaged child', *Child Devel.*, vol. 41, pp. 947–63.

HUBEL, D. H., and WIESEL, T. N. (1962), 'Receptive fields, binocular interaction, and functional architecture in the cat's visual cortex', *J. Physiol.*, vol. 160, pp. 106–54.

HUGHES, J. (1972), 'Language and communication: acquisition of a non-vocal "language" by previously languageless children', unpublished Bachelor of Technology thesis, Brunel University.

INHELDER, B. (1969), 'Memory and intelligence in the child', in D. Elkind and J. H. Flavell (eds.), *Studies in Cognitive Development*, Oxford University Press.

INHELDER, B., and PIAGET, J. (1955), *The Growth of Logical Thinking from Childhood to Adolescence*, Basic Books, 1958.

INHELDER, B., and PIAGET, J. (1959), *The Early Growth of Logic in the Child*, Harper & Row, 1964.

JACOBS, R. A., and ROSENBAUM, P. S. (1968), *English Transformational Grammar*, Blaisdell.

JAKOBSON, R. (1941), *Child Language Aphasia and Phonological Universals*, Mouton, 1968.

JAKOBSON, R., and HALLE, M. (1956), *Fundamentals of Language*, Mouton.

JAKOBSON, R., FANT, C. G. M., and HALLE, M. (1952), *Preliminaries to Speech Analysis: The Distinctive Features and their Correlates*, MIT Press.

JAMES, W. (1890), *The Principles of Psychology*, vol. 1; authorized, unabridged edn, Dover Publications, 1950.

KAPLAN, E., and KAPLAN, G. (1971), 'The prelinguistic child', in J. Eliot (ed.), *Human Development and Cognitive Processes*, Holt, Rinehart & Winston.

KENDLER, T. S. (1963), 'Development of mediating responses in children', in J. C. Wright and J. Kagan (eds.), 'Basic cognitive processes in children', *Mongr. Soc. Res. Child Devel.*, vol. 28, no. 86.

KESSEL, F. S. (1970), 'The role of syntax in children's comprehension from ages six to twelve', *Mongr. Soc. Res. Child Devel.*, vol. 35, no. 139.

KOEHLER, O. (1972), 'Non-verbal thinking', in H. Friedrich (ed.), *Man and Animal*, Paladin.

LANTZ, D., and STEFFLRE, V. (1964), 'Language and cognition revisited', *J. abnorm. soc. Psychol.*, vol. 69, pp. 472–81.

LENNEBERG, E. H. (1962), 'Understanding language without ability to speak', *J. abnorm. soc. Psychol.*, vol. 65, pp. 419–25.

LENNEBERG, E. H. (1964), 'Speech as a motor skill with special reference to nonaphasic disorders', in U. Bellugi and R. Brown (eds.), 'The acquisition of language', *Mongr. Soc. Res. Child Devel.*, vol. 29, no. 92.

LENNEBERG, E. H., and ROBERTS, J. M. (1956), 'The language of experience', *Indiana University Publications in Anthropology and Linguistics*, no. 13.

LENNEBERG, E. H., REBELSKY, F. G., and NICHOLS, I. A. (1965), 'The vocalizations of infants born to deaf and hearing parents', *Vita Humana (Human Development)*, vol. 8, pp. 23–37.

LIND, J. (ed.) (1965), 'Newborn infant cry', *Acta Paed. Scand.*, suppl. 163.

LURIA, A. R., and YUDOVICH, F. IA. (1956), *Speech and the Development o Mental Processes in the Child*, Penguin, 1971.

LYONS, J. (1966), 'General discussion to David McNeill's paper, "The creation of language" ', in J. Lyons and R. J. Wales (eds.), *Psycholinguistic Papers*, Edinburgh University Press.

LYONS, J. (1970), *Chomsky*, Fontana/Collins.

MCCAWLEY, J. D. (1968), 'The role of semantics in a grammar', in E. Bach and R. T. Harms (eds.), *Universals in Linguistic Theory*, Holt, Rinehart & Winston.

MACNAMARA, J. (1972), 'Cognitive basis of language learning in infants', *Psychol. Rev.*, vol. 79, pp. 1–13.

MCNEILL, D. (1966), 'Developmental psycholinguistics', in F. Smith and G. A. Miller (eds.), *The Genesis of Language*, MIT Press.

MCNEILL, D. (1970a), *The Acquisition of Language*, Harper & Row.

MCNEILL, D. (1970b), 'The development of language', in P. H. Mussen (ed.), *Carmichaels's Manual of Child Psychology*, vol. 1, Wiley.

MCNEILL, D. (1970c), 'Language before symbols: very early child grammar', *Interchange*, vol. 1, pp. 127–33.

MCNEILL, D., and MCNEILL, N. B. (1968), 'What does a child mean when he says "no"?', in E. M. Zale (ed.), *Proceedings of the Conference on Language and Language Behavior*, Appleton-Century-Crofts.

MANDELBAUM, D. G. (ed.) (1949), *Selected Writings of Edward Sapir in Language, Culture, and Personality*, University of California Press.

MANDELBAUM, D. G. (ed.) (1961), *Edward Sapir, Culture, Language, and Personality: Selected Essays*, University of California Press.

MILLER, G. A. (1962), *Psychology: The Science of Mental Life*, Penguin.

MILLER, G. A., and MCNEILL, D. (1969), 'Psycholinguistics', in G. Lindzey and E. Aronson (eds.), *The Handbook of Social Psychology*, vol. 3, 2nd edn, Addison-Wesley.

MOWRER, O. H. (1954), 'The psychologist looks at language', *Amer. Psychol.*, vol. 9, pp. 660–94.

O'CONNOR, N., and HERMELIN, B. (1971), 'Inter- and intra-modal transfer in children with modality specific and general handicaps', *Brit. J. soc. clin. Psychol.*, vol. 10, pp. 346–54.

PARISI, D., and ANTINUCCI, F. (1970), 'Lexical competence', in G. B. Flores d'Arcais and W. J. M. Levelt (eds.), *Advances in Psycholinguistics*, North-Holland Publishing Co.

PIAGET, J. (1970a), *Genetic Epistemology*, Columbia University Press.

PIAGET, J. (1970b), 'Piaget's theory', in P. H. Mussen (ed.), *Carmichael's Manual of Child Psychology*, vol. 1, Wiley.

PIAGET, J., and INHELDER, B. (1948), *The Child's Conception of Space*, Routledge & Kegan Paul, 1956.

PIAGET, J., and INHELDER, B. (1966), *The Psychology of the Child*, Routledge & Kegan Paul, 1969.

PREMACK, D. (1969), 'A functional analysis of language', Invited address before the American Psychological Association, Washington, DC.

PREMACK, D., and SCHWARTZ, A. (1966), 'Preparations for discussing behaviorism with chimpanzee', in F. Smith and G. A. Miller (eds.), *The Genesis of Language*, MIT Press.

REESE, H. W., and LIPSITT, L. P. (1970), *Experimental Child Psychology*, Academic Press.

RICKS, D. M. (1972), 'The beginnings of vocal communication in infants and autistic children', unpublished Doctorate of Medicine thesis, University of London.

SACHS, J. (1971), 'The status of developmental studies of language', in J. Eliot (ed.), *Human Development and Cognitive Processes*, Holt, Rinehart & Winston.

SAPIR, E. (1949), see MANDELBAUM (1949).

SCHLESINGER, I. M. (1971a), 'Learning grammar: from pivot to realization rule', in R. Huxley and E. Ingram (eds.), *Language Acquisition: Models and Methods*, Academic Press.

SCHLESINGER, I. M. (1971b), 'Production of utterances and language acquisition', in D. I. Slobin (ed.), *The Ontogenesis of Grammar: A Theoretical Symposium*, Academic Press.

SINCLAIR, H. (1971), 'Sensorimotor action patterns as a condition for the acquisition of syntax', in R. Huxley and E. Ingram (eds.), *Language Acquisition: Models and Methods*, Academic Press.

SINCLAIR-DE-ZWART, H. (1969), 'Developmental psycholinguistics', in D. Elkind and J. H. Flavell (eds.), *Studies in Cognitive Development*, Oxford University Press.

SKINNER, B. F. (1957), *Verbal Behavior*, Appleton-Century-Crofts.

SLOBIN, D. I. (1966), 'The acquisition of Russian as a native language', in F. Smith and G. A. Miller (eds.), *The Genesis of Language*, MIT Press.

SLOBIN, D. I. (1971a), 'Cognitive prerequisites for the development of grammar', Paper presented at the fifth meeting of the Southeastern Conference on Linguistics, University of Maryland, May.

SLOBIN, D. I. (ed.) (1971b), *The Ontogenesis of Grammar: A Theoretical Symposium*, Academic Press.

SLOBIN, D. I. (1971c), *Psycholinguistics*, Scott, Foresman.

SMITH, N. V. (1971), 'How children learn to speak', *Listener*, 2 December.

SMITH, N. V. (1973), *The Acquisition of Phonology*, Cambridge University Press.

SMITH, S. M., BROWN, H. O., TOMAN, J. E. P., and GOODMAN, L. S. (1947), 'The lack of cerebral effects of d-tubocurarine', *Anesthesiology*, vol. 8, pp. 1–14.

SPIKER, C. C. (1963), 'Verbal factors in the discrimination learning of children', in J. C. Wright and J. Kagan (eds.), 'Basic cognitive processes in children', *Mongr. Soc. Res. Child Devel.*, vol. 28, no. 86.

VETTER, H. J., and HOWELL, R. W. (1971), 'Theories of language acquisition', *J. psycholing. Res.*, vol. 1, pp. 31–64.

VYGOTSKY, L. S. (1934), *Thought and Language*, MIT Press; Wiley, 1962.

WHORF, B. L., see CARROLL (1956).

WHORF, B. L. (1952), *Collected Papers on Metalinguistics*, Department of State, Foreign Service Institute, Washington, DC.

WHORF, B. L. (1958), 'Science and linguistics', in E.E. Maccoby, T.M. Newcomb and E. L. Hartley (eds.), *Readings in Social Psychology*, 3rd edn, Holt, Rinehart & Winston.

WOLFF, P. H. (1969), 'The natural history of crying and other vocalizations in early infancy', in B. M. Foss (ed.), *Determinants of Infant Behaviour*, vol. 4, Methuen.

Acknowledgements

Acknowledgement is due to the following for reproduction of illustrations in this volume.

Chapter 1, Figure 2: Academic Press
Chapter 1, Figure 3: Academic Press
Chapter 1, Figure 4: Academic Press
Chapter 2, Figure 2: *Journal of Experimental Child Psychology*
Chapter 4, Figure 1: R. L. Fantz and *Science*
Chapter 4, Figure 2: R. B. McCall, J. Kagan and Academic Press
Chapter 4, Figure 3: II. S. Ross, H. L. Rheingold, C. O. Eckerman and Academic Press

The quotations on page 185 and page 186: Dover Publications
The quotation on pages 187–8: University of California Press

Index

257

Maternal Deprivation Reassessed

Michael Rutter

'A classic in the field of child care' *New Society*

Twenty years have passed since 'maternal deprivation' was first greeted with a storm of controversy. Some early views have been modified, but the basic proposition – that lack, loss or distortion of child care have a very important effect on psychological development – has received substantial support.

Why and how are children adversely affected? Dr Rutter reviews the qualities of mothering needed for normal development and considers both the short-term and long-term effects of 'maternal deprivation'. He concludes that the term covers a wide range of *different* experiences with quite *different* effects on development.

What is now needed, Dr Rutter argues, is a more precise description of the different aspects of 'bad' care and 'bad' effects. In starting on these tasks and in reappraising briefly and clearly the whole concept of 'maternal deprivation', Dr Rutter has written a book which will be necessary reading for all those concerned with the upbringing, care, teaching or treatment of children.

'The subject matter is of the greatest importance not only for child care but also for adult psychiatry. It will provide an excellent starting point for teaching seminars for a variety of disciplines'
Stephen Wolkind, *British Journal of Psychiatry*

The Social Psychology of Teaching

Editors: A. Morrison and D. McIntyre

Teaching is both familiar and intriguing; yet at the same time hard to analyse, and complex and subtle in its effects upon the taught.

The editors of this central volume of the Penguin Modern Psychology Readings have matched their articles with three criteria: 'that they should present teaching as an applied social psychology; that they should focus upon professional teaching within the settings of school and classroom; and that they should demonstrate empirical procedures and findings of practical interest to practising teachers and a wider audience.'

The editors, Arnold Morrison and Donald McIntyre, are the authors of the widely successful Penguin Modern Psychology texts, *Teachers and Teaching* and *Schools and Socialization*.

Penguin Modern Psychology Readings 'should be of inestimable value to psychology students, to students in other social sciences, and for that matter to the educated general reader' *The Times Educational Supplement*

The Puzzle of Pain

Ronald Melzack

The field of pain research and theory that lay conceptually stagnant for almost a century has suddenly become alive. Psychology, physiology and clinical medicine have all contributed to the new developments, and as a result of recent progress exciting new techniques have been proposed for the treatment of pain.

Professor Melzack examines the various facets of pain from a well-defined theoretical framework. He offers the Melzack–Wall 'gate-control' theory as an up-to-date basis for understanding pain mechanisms and suggesting new forms of treatment. In the first half of his book he describes the psychological, clinical and physiological aspects of pain; in the second he looks at the major theories of pain in terms of their ability to explain pain phenomena and their implications for the control of pain. Written with the clarity and authority one expects from a leading exponent of pain theory, *The Puzzle of Pain* should prove of immense value not only to psychologists, but also to those working or studying in medicine, physiology, anatomy, pharmacology, neurosurgery and related fields.

'This is a very good and useful book which reviews a good deal of the physiological evidence. The writing is clear and straightforward throughout, and altogether this can be recommended very highly as an excellent introduction to the subject of pain' H. J. Eysenck, *New Society*

Dreams and Dreaming

Selected Readings

Editors: S. G. M. Lee and A. R. Mayes

Before the 1950s most investigations of dreams and dreaming were concerned with the content of dreams, in particular with their function and meaning. For those who remained unconvinced by the explanations of psychoanalysis and analytical psychology, the discovery in 1953 of rapid eye movement (REM) sleep seemed to hold out the possibility of a more 'scientific' theory being formulated.

This absorbing collection of papers draws together some of the most influential findings in the field. The first half of the volume includes accounts of some early dream theories, an investigation of the content of children's dreams, and an exposition of the classic theories of Freud and Jung. The second half offers a variety of papers on REM sleep, and the effects of its deprivation, and goes on to look at the question of the dream state in relation to visual perception, motivation, information processing, drugs and biochemical processes.